QUEST FOR VICTORY

QUEST
FOR VICTORY

French Military Strategy 1792-1799

Steven T. Ross

South Brunswick and New York: A. S. Barnes and Company
London: Thomas Yoseloff Ltd

© 1973 by A. S. Barnes and Co., Inc.

A. S. Barnes and Co., Inc.
Cranbury, New Jersey 08512

Thomas Yoseloff Ltd
108 New Bond Street
London W1Y OQX, England

Library of Congress Cataloging in Publication Data

Ross, Steven T.
  Quest for victory.

  Bibliography: p.
  1. France—History, Military—1789–1815.   I. Title.
DC151.R67   1973   944.04   79–146774
ISBN 0–498–07499–4

Printed in the United States of America

Contents

5

Maps

Introduction

During the eighteenth century, rulers and statesmen frequently embarked on bold diplomatic and strategic ventures. France and her allies tried to dismember the Hapsburg domains in the 1740s. Austria in league with Russia and France attempted to destroy Prussia's status as a great power during the Seven Years' War. England and France battled constantly for colonial supremacy. Austria sought to annex Bavaria; Russia and Austria planned to drive the Turks from the Continent and then divide the conquered lands between themselves, and the three eastern courts partitioned and finally destroyed Poland.

In addition to wars of conquest, monarchs in their perpetual search for power did not hesitate to intervene in the internal affairs of other states. Both Spain and France supported the efforts of Stuart pretenders to recapture the English Crown. The French and Spanish Bourbons also assisted American rebels in their struggle with Great Britain. Prussia aided Belgian revolutionaries against the Hapsburg emperor, and Russia sided with a faction of Polish magnates who opposed their king and his reform-minded followers.

The quest for power was relentless. No belief in the virtues of order and moderation restrained ambitious statesmen. No principles of law, religion, or morality held aggressive rulers in check. Great powers regarded weaker states as legitimate prey and were equally content to turn on each other if a favorable opportunity arose. There was no lack of greed or dearth of ambition within the ranks of old-regime politicians and diplomats, and only mutual suspicion and rivalry held back the most aggressive. Since each power looked upon the others as actual or potential rivals, no state was willing to allow another to increase its strength. Consequently, if a ruler sought new conquests, others would either demand a share of the spoils or fight to prevent his foe from amassing new provinces or colonies.

The general equality of armed might prevailing among the great powers made it even more difficult for a state, acting alone, to make extensive conquests. The major continental powers— France, Austria, Prussia, and Russia—possessed armies number- ing anywhere from 130,000 to 200,000. Officers usually came from the aristocracy, while the rank and file were beggars, vagabonds, and the unemployed. Governments occasionally conscripted peas- ants but generally preferred to recruit their long-term mercenary soldiers from the economically nonproductive elements of society. Great Britain based her strength on an excellent navy sup- plemented by a small standing army that could be strengthened by hiring regiments from German princes. Mutual animosity and military parity made it impossible for a single power to impose its will on the others, and consequently most aggressive enterprises fell short of complete success.

In the Austrian Succession War, England supported Austria against France, and the Hapsburg state emerged intact save for the loss of Silesia, which though serious was far from crippling. Later England aided Prussia, and the Hohenzollern monarchy preserved its great power status and territorial integrity. En- gland defeated France at sea and in colonial warfare but in 1763 accepted a compromise peace that left France with some of her most valuable possessions. Prussia stymied Austrian efforts to take Bavaria and played a leading role in checking the Austro- Russian assault upon the Ottoman Empire. Poland disappeared from the map only because the eastern courts found mutually acceptable formulas for dismemberment.

The advent of revolution in France did not change the nature and objectives of diplomacy. Security and expansion remained the goals of politicians and statesmen, including those of revo- lutionary France. French leaders in the 1790s employed diplo- macy, armed force, and subversion in a manner similar to that of their old-regime counterparts. The French did, however, de- vise new military techniques that gave them hitherto unimagined power, enabling them to become the single strongest continental state.

France went to war in 1792 because politicians thought they could use foreign conflict as a means of gaining domestic power. At first the nation was not prepared for hostilities, but the pressure of battle finally compelled the state's leaders to take drastic steps to enable the new regime to survive. They established a centralized government able to control the activities of local officials and citizens, created a mass conscript army, found men to lead it, and devised new tactics and new combat formations to enable it to fight effectively. The revolutionary government also took control of the nation's economic life in order to arm its soldiers and finance its war effort. By raising an army of unparalleled size and strength, French leaders forged an instrument of national policy so strong that it became possible for them to attempt to impose their will upon all of their enemies.

Devising strategy for the employment of their new forces, however, produced problems rarely encountered by the nonrevolutionary states of Europe. Civil-military relations, which had not been a serious issue during the old regime, became critically important in republican France, because ambitious generals often tried to impose their own plans on the civilian authorities. Popular opinion also became an important factor in French strategic decision making. Old regime monarchs had been able to send their armies to war and conclude treaties without reference to popular desires. In England parliamentary opinion did on occasion have an impact on foreign policy, but parliamentary opinion was by no means identical with popular opinion because it involved a rather limited elite. In republican France, however, governments did have to consider public reaction in planning military operations or face the prospect of insurrection or drastic loss of support in elections. Throughout the revolutionary era, French leadership had to produce military plans that not only brought battlefield triumphs but also fulfilled diplomatic objectives, kept generals obedient to the political authorities, and met with public approval.

Republican France was not completely successful in its quest for victory, but it did attain a striking number of diplomatic and strategic triumphs. The First French Republic produced more conquests that any previous regime and laid the foundations for Napoleon Bonaparte's attempts to dominate the entire Continent.

QUEST FOR VICTORY

1
War and Politics
1789-1792

When France took up arms against Austria and Prussia in the spring of 1792, the nation was not prepared to fight a major war. French leaders, struggling for power at home, failed to devise an effective diplomatic and military strategy. Moreover, the state's armed forces were weak and disorganized. Consequently, Austro-Prussian armies hurled the French forces back from their frontiers and began to march on Paris, threatening the very existence of the Revolution and the nation.

Ironically, it was the French who were most anxious for war. Almost from the beginning of the Revolution influential political factions sought to propel the nation into war, intending to use the hostilities to gain domestic political power. The count of Artois, the king's brother and leader of the aristocratic emigrants who had been leaving the country since July, 1789, established a counter-revolutionary central committee at Turin. From his headquarters he attempted to incite insurrections against the National Assembly and issued constant appeals to the European powers, urging an armed crusade against the Revolution.[1]

Louis XVI, Marie Antoinette, and the court also opposed the changes wrought by the revolutionaries. Louis was unwilling to work with the aristocrats, who had in the past effectively opposed royal authority, so he devised a counterrevolutionary policy of his own. As early as November, 1789, he secretly informed Charles IV, the Bourbon ruler of Spain, of his repudiation of the National Constituent Assembly's reforms. In 1790 he sent a secret denunciation of the Revolution to Joseph II, emperor of Germany, ruler of the Hapsburg patrimony, and Marie Antoinette's brother, and at the year's end he commissioned a secret agent to solicit foreign intervention against the Assembly.[2] Louis then began preparations to escape from Paris. He intended to join royalist army regiments on the eastern frontier while foreign powers conducted threatening demonstrations. Louis would then "negotiate" with the powers, "save" France from invasion, and insist upon a full restoration of royal authority as the price of continued protection.[3]

Most deputies in the National Assembly, on the other hand, wanted to avoid foreign entanglements. Peace was essential in order to complete their reforms and stabilize the new regime. The deputies also realized that war would strengthen the king's authority because he was still commander in chief of the nation's armed forces. Moreover, members of the Assembly were aware that a foreign war would in all probability spark internal rebellions. Finally, the delegates knew that the army was not ready to fight. Most army officers were of noble extraction, and after 1789, they had joined their fellow aristocrats in opposition to the Revolution and were leaving the country in ever-increasing numbers. Among the officers who remained at their posts were many who disliked the Revolution. The loss of officers not only decimated the army's command structure but also led to a decline of morale and discipline in the enlisted ranks. Nor could the patriots rely upon the mercenary regiments or the National Guard troops, who though loyal to the Revolution lacked the training necessary to fight a major war.[4] Thus pro-Revolutionary factions believed that war would produce not only military catastrophe but also a successful counterrevolution.

The Assembly, therefore, sought diligently to avoid hostilities. In the spring of 1790 England and Spain clashed over control of the Nootka Sound on the Pacific coast of North America. Spain seized several British ships in the Sound, and the English began to mobilize their fleet. War appeared imminent, and Spain appealed to France for armed assistance under the terms of an earlier alliance treaty. The Assembly, however, refused to risk war and took steps to limit the monarch's authority in foreign affairs by subjecting his right to declare war to prior legislative approval. The Assembly then issued a proclamation declaring that France would never undertake an aggressive war. Finally, the legislators established a Diplomatic Committee to supervise the foreign minister and the king and to stop them from initiating any bellicose diplomatic activities.[5]

The Assembly offered further proof of its pacific intentions by refusing to support revolutions in Liège and Belgium and by dealing tactfully with German clerics and princes who owned estates in Alsace. The Assembly also moved cautiously when deciding the fate of Avignon. The legislators applied their laws abolishing feudalism and nationalizing church lands to foreign enclaves in Alsace but offered the German owners cash compensation.[6] Revolt and rebellion in Avignon, a papal domain located within France, led to French occupation in 1791. Most of Avignon's people wished to join France, but the Assembly delayed annexation until several months after Pope Pius VI condemned the Revolution.[7]

Fortunately for France, the great powers, despite their growing hostility toward the Revolution, were too involved elsewhere to intervene immediately. In 1789 Austria and Russia were at war with the Ottoman Empire in a grandiose effort to partition the Turkish state. Prussia and England opposed Austrian and Russian expansion and encouraged Sweden to attack Russia. Prussia, meanwhile, supported aristocratic and clerical rebels resisting Joseph II's reform efforts in Belgium and Hungary, as well as Polish reformers trying to create a more effective regime. Berlin intended to use Poland as a counterweight to Vienna and St. Petersburg. Finally, Frederick William II, the Hohenzollern monarch, signed a treaty with the sultan, calling for the liberation of all Turkish territory, and mobilized a large army in Silesia.[8]

War again appeared imminent, but England refused to support Prussia. William Pitt had no intention of fighting for Hohenzollern aggrandizement. He wanted only to restore the *status quo* in Eastern Europe. The Nootka Sound dispute made him even more anxious to maintain peace on the Continent. Pursuing this goal, he offered his good offices as mediator between Prussia and Austria, and Leopold II, who had succeeded his brother Joseph in February, 1790, accepted the British offer in April, hoping to extricate himself from a difficult diplomatic situation while gaining time to restore order within his domains. In July Prussian and Austrian diplomats met in the small Silesian town of Reichenbach. Prussia demanded territorial compensations, but England refused to support Hohenzollern pretentions, and Berlin and Vienna agreed to accept the prewar *status quo*. In September Leopold concluded an armistice with the sultan. Catherine of Russia continued to attack the Turks, and Pitt began to contemplate armed intervention against Russia. Frederick William, still seeking new provinces, joined the British in sending an ultimatum to the czarina in March, 1791, demanding that she abandon her war against the Ottoman Empire; Catherine ignored the threat. Parliamentary opposition to military adventurism forced Pitt to abandon his warlike stance, and Catherine was able to conclude her campaign successfully.[9]

The eastern crisis made it impossible for the powers to contemplate intervention in French affairs, but as the war threat in the Balkans subsided, rulers were able to turn their attentions to the Revolution in the west. In 1790 Frederick William had suggested to Leopold joint action to restore Louis XVI to power. The Hohenzollern monarch expected to obtain some German territory as compensation for his efforts in behalf of the Bourbons, and suggested that the Hapsburgs take some French provinces as indemnities. Leopold had ignored this proposal, but having settled his diplomatic problems and restored order within his kingdom, he was by the spring of 1791 prepared to consider intervention in France. Unlike the Prussians, the Hapsburg ruler was not interested merely in acquiring new territory. Rather, he wanted to create a new diplomatic axis capable of assuring Austria's security. Leopold had lost the czarina's friendship when he concluded his armistice with the Turks, and he wanted to replace the Russian alliance with a Prussian connection. The Hapsburg monarch wanted the Austro-Prussian alliance to guarantee Poland's security and independence and to intervene in France to restore a large measure of Louis XVI's authority. Leopold thus sought to prevent any power from gaining control of Poland.

He also intended to use Prussia as a check to Russia in the east while employing France, which was still tied to Austria by treaty and marriage connections, as a counterweight to Prussia in the west.[10]

In June, 1791, Leopold met with a Prussian agent and concluded a preliminary treaty calling for mutual aid against internal rebellions, preservation of Polish freedom, and joint efforts to form a European concert to regulate French affairs. He also arranged to meet Frederick William at the Saxon town of Pillnitz in August. At this juncture he was anxious to conclude a final treaty with Prussia, having just learned that Louis and his queen were about to flee Paris and embark on a counterrevolutionary coup. Leopold wanted to be ready to mount a multipower military demonstration to terrorize the Assembly into restoring the Bourbon monarchy's power.[11]

Louis's coup, however, collapsed before Leopold and Frederick William ever met. On June 20 the royal family fled Paris, but government officials quickly caught their ruler at Varennes and brought Louis and his family back to Paris under guard. News of the sovereign's flight and subsequent arrest provoked a major outburst of antimonarchical sentiment in Paris. The Assembly, wishing to avoid antagonizing foreign powers and to stem a rising tide of domestic radicalism, decided to retain Louis as king despite his proven hostility to the Revolution. The government suppressed antiroyalist agitation but could not completely silence demands for a second revolution.

The Varennes incident also forced Leopold to alter his policy. It was no longer a question of restoring Louis's authority; rather the emperor now had to find a quick and effective method of helping the Bourbon king retain his tottering throne. He therefore decided to threaten military intervention, hoping to frighten the French into maintaining the monarchy. On July 6 he publicly appealed to the powers requesting common action to save the French throne. He then signed the preliminary agreement with Prussia, and set off for Pillnitz.[12]

At Pillnitz Leopold pursued a cautious policy designed to help Louis and to avoid a war that would give Frederick William an excuse to demand compensations. Therefore, he sought a formula that was strong enough to bolster French moderates and silence radicals yet sufficiently flexible to avoid drifting into war. On August 27, 1791, the Austrian and Prussian rulers issued their declaration. It stated that all rulers were concerned for Louis's safety and asked the other powers to join them in devising a plan to restore the French king's power. Then and in that case, the declaration concluded, Leopold and Frederick would take steps to implement the common policy.[13] Though seemingly belligerent, Leopold realized that the call for a multipower congress rendered the declaration harmless. He knew that the powers would never agree on a single course of action, and, consequently, the threat of military intervention in France was only a diplomatic ruse.

Initially, the declaration helped produce the desired effect; the Assembly restored Louis. In September the king received the new constitution, accepting, at least momentarily, a new role as constitutional sovereign, hoping to increase the crown's popularity before attempting to alter the new regime. On November 12, 1791, Count Kaunitz, the Austrian foreign minister, issued a circular letter to his ambassadors, informing them that the French had become moderate and Louis was secure.[14]

Despite the apparent success of the Pillnitz Declaration, the danger of war was by no means over. Many Frenchmen missed the point of the Austro-Prussian pronouncement and regarded the statement as a warlike threat. Moreover, émigré threats of invasion bolstered a growing war psychosis in France. Finally, several political factions joined their voices to those groups who already believed that war was the best avenue to power at home. The Austrians persisted in their belief that threats would continue to produce a moderate reaction in France, but by the winter of 1791 their policy served mainly to strengthen the prowar cliques.

When the newly elected Legislative Assembly first met in October, 1791, 130 deputies registered as members of the Jacobin Club. The Jacobins wanted to liberalize the constitution and grant political rights to the lower classes, and many of them wanted to go to war against the Hapsburgs. Jacques Pierre Brissot, a lawyer, journalist, and deputy from Paris, was the leading advocate of war. He and his allies felt that war would be profitable for those businessmen who supported his clique. Brissot also believed that if he could convince the Assembly to adopt his policy the king would have to place him and his followers in control of the government. Moreover, war would enable the Brissotins to strike out at the enemies of the Revolution, including the king, who, the Brissotins suspected, was fundamentally opposed to the new regime. Finally, Brissot believed that a successful war would gain continued popular support for his faction.[15] For the Brissotins, then, war was a means to destroy counterrevolutionary elements and gain political control of the nation.

Two influential military men, the marquis de Lafayette and the count of Narbonne, also favored a foreign war. Both were former nobles who had supported the Revolution in its early stage, but who had come to believe that the reformers had gone too far. They wanted to wage a quick, victorious war in the Rhineland, win popular prestige at home, and then turn their armies against domestic radicals. After restoring a large measure of royal authority, the two generals expected to become the real leaders of the nation. With influential connections among the 264 moderate Feuillant deputies, Lafayette and Narbonne were willing to join the Brissotins in a tactical alliance to lead France into war. Among the 345 independent deputies many feared foreign invasion and questioned the king's loyalty to the constitution. Consequently, they became willing to support politicians who called for harsh measures against the state's enemies.[16]

The prowar factions took their first step to promote hostilities by convincing the Assembly on November 29 to pass a resolution calling upon Louis to order the elector of Trier to dissolve the armed emigrant bands assembling in his domains. The bellicose politicians assumed that the elector would appeal to the emperor, and war would follow.[17]

To everybody's surprise Louis responded quickly and favorably. On December 9 he appointed Narbonne to the war ministry, and on December 14 he informed the Assembly that he had sent an ultimatum to Trier ordering the elector to disband the *émigré* bands in a month's time or face the prospect of war. Louis, of course, did not want a victorious conflict. The growth of radical sentiment at home had convinced him that his policy of ruling as a constitutional monarch until public opinion shifted in his favor was doomed to failure. He therefore concluded that the only way for him to regain power was by means of a French defeat. He wanted an armed congress to crush the nation's armies and invade the country, thus forcing the populace to turn to the crown to save them from total defeat. Louis would then negotiate with the powers and demand a restoration of royal authority as the price of his mediation. To compel the powers to act Louis approved the ultimatum and at the same time secretly informed the Hapsburg emperor that he wanted the elector to reject the French note.[18]

Meanwhile, in the Assembly the prowar factions began to prepare for war. Despite the opposition of Maximilien Robespierre in the Jacobin Club and of a few moderate deputies, the Assembly passed legislation calling for the mobilization of three field armies and the expansion of the military establishment by 169 battalions, a total of 101,000 men, drawn from volunteers serving in local National Guard units.[19]

Persisting in the belief that harsh language would strengthen French moderates and subdue radicals, Leopold replied to the French king's ultimatum on December 21. He informed Paris that the elector would disband the emigrant groups, but that henceforth the Austrian army would protect the German princes against French aggression.[20]

Leopold's note, however, strengthened the prowar cliques in the Assembly, and the deputies responded by granting increased funds for military preparations. The deputies also instructed the foreign minister, Antoine Delessart, to send special envoys to Prussia and England. At Berlin the envoy was to offer supreme command of the French armies to the duke of Brunswick, one of Europe's most renowned soldiers who also looked favorably upon the Revolution. The delegate was also to convince Frederick William to remain neutral if France went to war with Austria. The London mission was to propose an Anglo-French concert to regulate European affairs and thereby neutralize England. On January 14, 1792, a prowar deputy proposed that the government call upon the Hapsburg ruler to state whether or not he intended to abide by the Franco-Austrian alliance of 1756 and renounce all plans to form a concert against France. An unsatisfactory answer or no reply at all by March 1 would constitute for the Assembly a declaration of war.[21]

Leopold responded to these threats with threats of his own. On

January 17 he ordered the mobilization of forty thousand men and pressed Berlin to conclude a definite alliance treaty. Frederick William II signed a treaty with Leopold II on February 2. The two courts agreed to promote a European concert to reorder French affairs, and on February 14 Leopold told Paris that French radicals posed a threat to European tranquility and that Austria and Prussia intended to protect the Continent from subversion and restore Louis XVI to his rightful position as the true ruler of France.[22]

Once again, however, Leopold failed to intimidate the Assembly. By January 25 the deputies had already adopted the bellicose proposal of January 14 and after the receipt of the latest Austrian note demanded immediate military action. Narbonne assured the Assembly that the armies were fully prepared for war and went on to demand that Louis purge moderates from his cabinet and declare war.[23]

Louis, however, responded by removing Narbonne from office. His action did not mean a change of policy. Louis still wanted a war, but he hoped to delay hostilities until Austria and Prussia were ready. The Brissotins, seeking immediate action, lashed back by accusing the foreign minister of participating in a counterrevolutionary plot and opened impeachment proceedings against him. Other moderate ministers hastened to resign to avoid a similar fate. Louis then capitulated to the left in order to retain his throne until the powers could come to his rescue. He therefore appointed Charles François Dumouriez as foreign minister.[24]

An ambitious soldier and diplomat, Dumouriez also wanted war. Like Lafayette and Narbonne he intended to use a victorious army to restore royal power and enhance his own influence. His policy differed from that of the other generals in several respects. First, Dumouriez intended that he, rather than Lafayette or Narbonne, should dominate the government after a military coup against the Assembly. Secondly, he wanted to invade Belgium rather than the Rhineland. Finally, Dumouriez was an ally of the Brissotins, whereas Lafayette and Narbonne worked primarily with the Feuillant faction. Soon after his appointment, he solidified his tactical alliance with Brissot's clique by securing the finance and interior ministries for members of the Brissotin faction.[25]

The accession of Dumouriez and the Brissotins marked the triumph of those who sought war against Austria. Events outside France also hastened the beginning of war. Leopold died on March 1, 1792. His heir, Francis II, was twenty-four, inexperienced in foreign affairs, hostile to France, and quite willing to transform his father's threats into deeds. He informed Frederick William of his willingness to send fifty thousand men against France and on March 18 directed Kaunitz to reply to the French note of January 25. The Austrians bluntly told the French that they would not give up plans to form a concert to intervene in France.[26] Francis then turned his attention to settling the issue of compensations for himself and Frederick William. The Hohenzollern ruler had already agreed to cooperate with Catherine of Russia in regulating Polish affairs, and Frederick William decided to insist on compensation for the costs of a French campaign at Polish expense. Francis agreed to abandon his father's policy of preserving an independent Poland and on March 21 gave preliminary consent to a Russo-Prussian partition. In return he proclaimed his interest in reviving the old scheme of exchanging Austrian Belgium for Bavaria.[27] Although the powers did not sign a formal treaty on the question of future indemnities, they had, at least for the moment, arrived at a mutually acceptable solution of a potentially devisive issue and could devote their efforts to preparing their French invasion. At this point war was inevitable, and additional communications between Paris and Vienna were simply formalities to set the stage for the outbreak of hostilities.

On March 27 Dumouriez demanded a reply to earlier notes calling for a clarification of Austria's intentions. Kaunitz responded by informing Paris that his note of March 18 was his final answer. Early in April Francis and Frederick William agreed to appoint the duke of Brunswick to command the main allied army, and Dumouriez informed his fellow ministers that Francis had definitely broken the 1756 alliance and was intent on war. France, he declared, had no choice but to fight, and he asked the ministers to recommend that the king call upon the Assembly to declare war. On April 20, 1792, Louis appeared before the Legislative Assembly and appealed for the declaration. That evening the deputies voted overwhelmingly for war.[28]

The declaration called for war against the king of Bohemia and Hungary, an attempt to confine hostilities to a clash between France and the Hapsburg monarchy while the princes of the Holy Roman Empire remained neutral. This effort failed; Prussia mobilized, and Frederick William agreed to send an army in July to join Austria's invasion of France.

In seeking war French leaders had regarded hostilities primarily as a means of attaining political influence at home. Strategic and diplomatic considerations played a secondary role. Consequently, French diplomatic preparations were minimal and strategic planning inadequate. Although they had to fight two major powers, French leaders failed to obtain a single ally. Furthermore, the French neglected to establish diplomatic objectives. Some military and political leaders had called for an invasion of Belgium; others wanted to march into the Rhineland; but there was virtually no discussion of the ultimate disposition of these regions. Lacking a diplomatic design, the French government could not create a coherent military strategy. Strategy is a means of fulfilling diplomatic goals, but in 1792 the French had neither a viable diplomatic scheme nor an effective plan of military operations.

To compound French problems the nation's armed forces were in such disarray that it was doubtful if the army could carry out its minimal task of defending the state from invasion.

On paper the French army looked powerful. It was composed of 150,000 regulars and the 101,000 volunteers of 1791. For combat the government had divided its troops into three field armies. The largest force, the army of the North, contained about 34,000 active troops plus 25,500 men in garrisons. Led by Marshal Rochambeau, a veteran of the Seven Years' War and the American revolutionary campaigns, the army of the North faced the Belgian frontier. To its right stood the 20,000 man army of the Center under Lafayette's command. The Center covered the eastern portion of the Belgian frontier and Lorraine. Marshal Luckner, a German professional who joined the French army in 1763, directed the army of the Rhine, which guarded Alsace with 43,000 men. Troops not serving with the active armies remained in depots to complete their training and to serve as replacements.[29]

The troop strength figures were, however, misleading, for instead of over 250,000 men under arms the generals had but 94,700 soldiers ready for action.[30] Nor were most of the troopers fully prepared for combat. The volunteers lacked the training and experience necessary to sustain themselves in the formal linear style of fighting common to all armies of their day. In 1792 the officer corps was about 50 percent under strength because of continued emigration. There were not enough leaders to train the volunteers, and even the regular regiments were short of commanders and continued to suffer from lowered morale and efficiency.[31] Thus despite the belief in the invincibility of their arms, French leaders deployed an army that was singularly unprepared to fulfill its assigned tasks.

Aware of the army's weakness, Rochambeau opposed any offensive operations even after the declaration of war, but Luckner and Lafayette wanted to march into Germany, and Dumouriez still wished to invade Belgium. With the backing of the Brissotins Dumouriez succeeded in convincing the government to adopt his strategy. Rochambeau soon received orders to march on Mons and Brussels while Lafayette's army took Namur and Liège.[32]

The ensuing offensive was a fiasco. Although the Austrians had but thirty thousand troops in Belgium, the French army, which should have been able to take its objectives with relative ease, collapsed. On April 28, twenty-three hundred French soldiers advanced on Tournai and fifteen thousand advanced toward Mons. Upon sighting an Austrian patrol the first force panicked. By April 29 it had fled back across the frontier after killing one of its generals who had sought to stem the flight. The larger force, after a brief clash with Austrian cavalry pickets, also retreated in haste. On April 30, Rochambeau reluctantly sent a third force into Belgium. It advanced to Furnes, turned about, and marched back to its camp.[33]

Rochambeau then resigned in disgust, and Luckner took command of the army of the North. On May 19 he met with Lafayette to draw up new plans. Rochambeau also attended the meeting as an advisor, and although he counseled against further attacks, Luckner and Lafayette ignored his advice and prepared another advance on Belgium. On June 9, twenty thousand men moved on Courtrai and took the town ten days later. A small counterattack, however, unnerved Luckner, who ordered a retreat, and by the end of the month the army was back in France.[34]

Early in July Lafayette prevailed upon Luckner to exchange commands. Contemplating a coup against the Assembly even without a preliminary victory, the marquis wanted to command the army of the North because it was closer to Paris than the Center army. He was, however, worried that the soldiers in the North would not follow him because they had never served under his command. He therefore suggested that the troops as well as the commanders exchange places, and Luckner, never known for his political acumen, agreed.[35] Thus, at precisely the moment when the generals should have been devoting all of their energies to improving the combat capabilities of their soldiers and preparing to counter the forthcoming allied offensive, they were busily engaged in a politically motivated and strategically useless countermarch.

In Paris the government not only failed to control the field commanders but also proved unable to bolster the army's fighting strength. On July 11 the Assembly declared the nation to be in danger and the following day declared that 50,000 new volunteers should serve as replacements for the active armies and 33,600 other enlistees should form forty-two new battalions.[36] The new troops, however, had even less training than the volunteers of 1791, and consequently would not be able to perform any useful military function for many months. The failure to increase the size and effectiveness of the armies thus left the French nation in a poor position to counter an Austro-Prussian attack.

Fortunately for France her enemies failed to act quickly. The fate of Poland forced Vienna and Berlin to concentrate on eastern European affairs to the detriment of their efforts in the west. In July, during their discussions concerning future compensations, the czarina suddenly invaded Poland. Allied with reactionary Polish magnates Catherine undertook to destroy the Polish constitution of 1791, which had the potential of restoring Poland's political vitality. Catherine's move upset Austrian and Prussian calculations, and both powers soon entered into separate, secret talks with the Russians.[37] The mutual suspicion created by these negotiations caused Francis and Frederick William to retain the bulk of their armies at home rather than employ them in a swift western campaign. Consequently, only 42,000 Prussians out of a total of 170,000 and 70,000 Austrians out of the 180,000-man Hapsburg army prepared to attack France. With the addition of Hessian and French *émigré* contingents the allied forces in the west numbered only 122,000, and the necessity of providing garrison and depot units lowered the active allied force to 97,000.[38]

The duke of Brunswick led the main invasion force, consisting of 42,000 Prussians, 30,000 Austrians, 5,500 Hessians, and 4,500 French emigrants. Bearing the formidable reputation earned under Frederick the Great, the Prussian troops encumbered themselves with a huge, slow-moving supply train and obsolete artillery. Moreover, many Prussian officers were quite elderly, and the army as a whole had not experienced serious combat since the 1760s. Like their Prussian counterparts, the Austrian soldiers followed the cautious methodical, tactical system common to old regime armies. The elderly duke of Brunswick, in full accord with this style of fighting, preferred clever marches and sieges to decisive battlefield encounters.[39] Thus, excessive military caution compounded the delays caused by diplomatic intrigue, and by August 10 the allied army had yet to cross the French frontier.

Allied inactivity led, at least indirectly, to the failure of one of their major objectives—the salvation of Louis XVI. In June Louis had attempted to hold the radicals in check until foreign help arrived by dismissing his Brissotin ministers and Dumouriez. The Brissotins retaliated by appealing to the Parisian people, but having mobilized the *sans-culottes* found it impossible to restrain them. Continued inflation, the appearance of the Brunswick manifesto threatening Paris with destruction if any harm came to the royal family, and Lafayette's public denunciations of the radicals served only to rouse the Parisians to new heights of fury. The monarch reappointed a Brissotin ministry. The Brissotins, having regained power, sought to fend off a new revolution and tried to calm the *sans-culottes;* but it was too late. Revolutionaries seized the city hall, and on August 10, 1792, a force of Parisians and provincial volunteers, on their way to the front, stormed the Tuileries. Louis fled to the Assembly, but the revolutionaries forced the deputies to suspend the monarch and call for elections for a National Convention to decide the king's fate and write a new democratic constitution. A Provisional Executive Council from the defunct Assembly was, under the watchful eye of the Paris Commune, to govern the nation until the National Convention assembled.[40]

Lafayette then sought to rally his army against the new revolution, but his soldiers refused to follow him. On August 19, he fled to the Austrian lines where Hapsburg officials promptly threw him in prison. On the same day Brunswick's army finally entered France. Allied delays had thus enabled the revolutionaries to destroy the monarchy and rid themselves of at least one disloyal general. The new French regime was, however, no better prepared to defend the nation than the old. Unless it took drastic and effective war measures, the Prussian and Austrian invaders, despite their diplomatic rivalries and strategic inertia, would defeat and destroy the divided unorganized French state.

On August 24, Brunswick's army forced the demoralized garrison of Longway to capitulate. Dumouriez, who had gone to the front after his dismissal from office, replaced Lafayette as commander of the army of the North. He chose to ignore this threat, persisting in his plan to invade Belgium. At Sedan on August 29, he held a council of war with his subordinate commanders and persuaded them to approve his strategy.[41] Dumouriez argued that an offensive into Belgium would compel the Austrian contingent in Brunswick's force to move into the Low Countries and that this loss would compel the duke to halt his advance. Dumouriez also realized that he could win greater public prestige by launching a spectacular attack than by waging a defensive campaign. Furthermore, the general had his own political ambitions that would be best served by a Belgian invasion. His original plan to use his army to restore the crown's authority was no longer feasible, but the idea of creating an independent Belgium with himself as ruler was appealing. Obviously to fulfill this particular objective Dumouriez had to conquer the Austrian Netherlands.

Although authorities in Paris were not aware of Dumouriez's political ambitions, they nevertheless opposed his strategy on military grounds. They felt that Brunswick's army posed an immediate danger to French security, a danger that had to be eliminated before French armies mounted any offensives. The war minister, therefore, advised Dumouriez to concentrate his forces in the Argonne Forest, the last natural barrier between the Allied army and Paris. Dumouriez, however, rejected this advice[42] and continued preparing to attack north into Belgium, thereby allowing Brunswick to advance virtually unopposed to the walls of Verdun. The duke invested the city on August 29. Although Verdun was one of the nation's strongest fortresses, the garrison lacked munitions, supplies, and determination, and the civilian inhabitants were reluctant to sustain the rigors of a protracted siege. The city capitulated on September 2. Brunswick had thus captured one of France's major defensive bastions, broken the line of the Meuse, and separated the army of the North from the army of the Center. This triumph also forced Dumouriez to abandon his preparations for an offensive. Instead, he led a nineteen thousand-man detachment from the northern army to the Argonne in a desperate attempt to hold back the allies.[43]

The manifest inability of French arms to halt the Austro-Prussian army compelled the government to make one of the most important strategic decisions of the whole revolutionary era. Most members of the Provisional Executive Council concluded that their troops could not possibly stop the inexorable allied advance on Paris. They therefore advocated that the government evacuate the capital and move south behind the Loire River. By giving up Paris and all of northern France without a serious fight the Council hoped to gain the time necessary to reform and revitalize the field armies and then launch counterattacks.

Georges Jacques Danton, the minister of justice, vehemently opposed this plan. A figure with a checkered past that included shady financial dealings and political intrigue with the court, émigrés, and the duke of Orleans, Danton was, nevertheless, a brilliant orator with a talent for swift, bold decisions.[44] His close connections and popularity with the sans-culottes made him an imposing figure in the Provisional Government. He believed that Paris was the heart of the Revolution and the national defense effort and that its loss would spell catastrophe and collapse for France. He therefore insisted that the Fench continue to resist in the eastern departments and defend Paris at all costs. By reasoned argument and implied threat of new popular uprisings, Danton won over the Council to his policy of defending Paris to the last man. On September 2, the very day that Verdun fell to the Prussians, he appeared before the Legislative Assembly and delivered an impassioned oration calling upon the deputies to mobilize the nation for a gigantic effort at self-salvation. Concluding with the stirring words,

> The warning bell when it sounds is not an alarm signal; it sounds the charge against our country's enemies. To defeat them, gentlemen, we need boldness, more boldness, always boldness and France is saved,[45]

he convinced the Assembly to stand and fight. The deputies had already placed the Parisian National Guard on a war footing and had begun the construction of an armed camp outside of the city. After the speech, they voted an additional four million francs to arm newly recruited volunteers and appointed a twelve-man committee to assist the Council in implementing defense measures.[46] Soon thirty-two thousand men reached Chalons where Luckner took command. These reserves were, however, unfit for combat, and the Austrians and Prussians continued to inch forward. Thus the new defense measures were not immediately effective, but Danton had, nevertheless, accomplished his major objective—the French government was going to fight in front of Paris.

In the battle zone Dumouriez tried to hold the passes in the Argonne, but he was too late. Before his troops could firmly entrench themselves, Brunswick's Austrian detachments broke through at LaCroix au Bois on September 12, and then drove off a hastily mounted counterattack. Dumouriez in turn abandoned the entire Argonne barrier and marched his force south to the small village of St. Menehould. There he issued an appeal to François Kellermann, who had replaced Luckner in command of the army of the Center, to join him. Luckner sent a similar appeal, and Kellermann, moving swiftly, led his force of thirty-six thousand men and fifty-eight field guns to link up with his brother general. By September 19, Kellermann's troops had reached Dumouriez's force, known as the army of the Ardennes, and took up positions on its left flank around the hamlet of Valmy.[47]

Save for the volunteers at Chalons there was on September 19

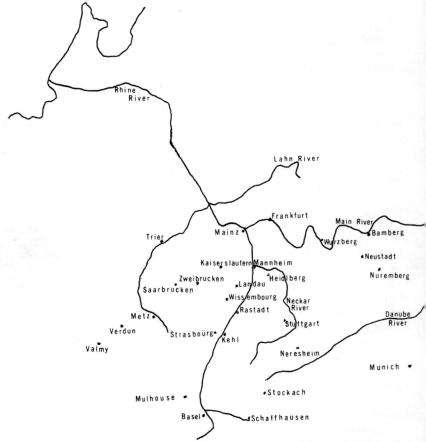

no organized French army between Brunswick and Paris, because Kellermann and Dumouriez had stationed themselves *south* of the Allied force. The duke, however, feared that if he marched directly on the city, the Center and Ardennes armies would attack his flank and rear echelons. He therefore ordered his regiments to wheel south and destroy the last organized French units before advancing on Paris.[48]

On the morning of September 20, 1792, as the National Convention held its first meeting, Brunswick's Prussian advanced guards probed through a thick fog seeking out the French main line of resistance. Kellermann's artillery opened fire and drove them back, and the duke brought forward his main force—thirty-four thousand men.[49]

After a short artillery barrage, Brunswick sent his infantry forward. Had they reached the French positions they would probably have defeated their untried foes, but the duke failed to take into account the effectiveness of French field guns. Prior to the Revolution, the artillery had become the most modern and efficient in Europe. Furthermore, the artillery corps, in contrast to other service arms, contained a high percentage of officers of middle class extraction. These bourgeois officers remained loyal to the Revolution and stayed at their posts with the result that emigration did not hurt the artillery corps as much as the infantry and cavalry. In 1792 the French artillery was still highly efficient. It was the most effective service in the nation's armed forces and proved its worth at Valmy.[50]

French field guns unleashed a withering fire against the Prussians, who wavered and then fell back.[51] The Prussians in turn laid down a barrage of their own. One shell struck a French munitions cart near one of Kellermann's main batteries, causing a tremendous explosion. As smoke and debris rose above the battlefield the French foot soldiers began to panic. Officers managed to restore order in the ranks, and Kellermann rushed a reserve battery forward to replace the guns destroyed by the explosion. Meanwhile, the duke, seeking to profit from the momentary confusion in the French lines, sent in a second assault, but the French were ready. The Prussian infantry advanced for about eight hundred yards under heavy cannon fire, halted, held their ground for a few moments, and finally retreated. Brunswick never ordered a third attack.[52] Ten days later the Allied army began to retreat back to Germany.

Only some fifty thousand French and thirty-four thousand Prussians fought at Valmy, and only three hundred French and two hundred Prussians fell during the battle. Valmy was in reality little more than a cannonade, and the opposing infantry formations never fired a shot. Still Valmy ranks as one of the most important clashes in the history of modern warfare. It justified Danton's decision to defend Paris and halted the first effort of the European powers to crush the Revolution. Two days after the battle, the new National Convention proclaimed that France would henceforth be a Republic.

Valmy insured the infant Republic's immediate survival, but the new regime had to solve enormous problems. Political rivalries continued to plague the Convention and the country; war continued, and the armies still lacked training and discipline. In the midst of these problems the government had yet to devise a strategy that would bring victory to French arms.

NOTES

1. For an excellent study of the counterrevolution see Jacques Godechot, *La Contre-révolution doctrine et action 1789–1804.*

2. Godechot, *La Contre-révolution,* describes court policy. See also Feuillet de Conches, *Louis XVI, Marie Antoinette et Madame Elizabeth lettres et documents inédits,* 1: 390–91.

3. Godechot, *La Contre-révolution,* pp. 168–70, discusses the reaction of the emigrants and foreign rulers to Louis's attempt at counterrevolution.

4. Louis Hartmann, *Les officiers de l'armée royale et la Révolution,* describes the impact of the Revolution on the army.

5. See Albert Sorel, *L'Europe et la Révolution française,* vol. 1; and J. Holland Rose, *William Pitt and the Great War,* for descriptions of the Nootka Sound affair.

6. See Pierre Muret, "L'affaire des princes possessionnes d'Alsace et les origines du conflict entre la Révolution et l'Europe," *Revue d'histoire moderne,* vol. 1.

7. See Albert Mathiez, *Rome et la constituante.*

8. See Albert Sorel, *La question d'Orient au XVIIIe siècle;* Adolf Beer, *Die orientalische Politik Oesterreichs seit 1774;* and J. H. Clapham, *The Causes of the War of 1792,* pp. 8–14.

9. Georges Lefebvre, *La Révolution française,* pp. 212–13; and Clapham, *Causes of the War,* pp. 59–68.

10. See Kurt Heidrich, *Preussen im Kampfe gegen die französiche Revolu-*

tion bis zur zweiten Teilung Polens; and Sorel, *L'Europe et la Révolution française,* vol. 1, for a discussion of Austrian and Prussian policy.

11. Conches, *Louis XVI, Marie Antoinette et Madame Elizabeth,* 1: 465–74; and Leopold Neumann, *Recueil des traités et conventions conclus par l'Autriche avec les puissances étrangères depuis 1763 jusqu'à nos jours,* 1: 452–53.

12. Neumann, *Recueil des traités,* 1: 453.

13. Ibid., pp. 467–69.

14. Conches, *Louis XVI, Marie Antoinette et Madame Elizabeth,* 4: 99, 212–14, 230–31. Marie Antoinette did not accept the Constitution, and on October 19 and November 2 she wrote secretly to Leopold asking for armed intervention. Leopold, however, chose to ignore her pleas; see also A. R. von Vivenot, ed. *Quellen zur Geschichte der Deutschen Kaiserpolitik Oesterreichs,* 1: 270–71.

15. See H. A. Goetz-Bernstein, *La diplomatie de la Gironde Jacques-Pierre Brissot.*

16. Clapham, *Causes of the War,* pp. 108, 118–20; and Émile Dard, *Le Comte de Narbonne.*

17. Conches, *Louis XVI, Marie Antoinette et Madame Elizabeth,* pp. 271–76.

18. See Jules Flammermont, *Négociations secrètes de Louis XVI et du Baron Breteuil décembre 1791–juillet 1792.*

19. *Réimpression de l' Ancien Moniteur,* 9: 637.

20. *Archives des Affaires Étrangères, Correspondance poltique,* no. 363 (hereafter, AAE) .

21. Georges Lefebvre, *La Révolution française,* p. 234; and AAE, no. 363.

22. AAE, no. 363; and Neumann, *Recueil des traités,* 1: 470–75.

23. AAE, no. 363; and *Rapport fait par le ministre de la Guerre L. de Narbonne à l'Assemble-Notionale le 11 janvier 1792* (Paris: 1792) .

24. Clapham, *Causes of the War,* p. 177.

25. See Arthur Chuquet, *Dumouriez;* and Goetz-Bernstein, *La diplomatie de la Gironde.*

26. AAE, no. 363; and André Fugier, *Histoire des relations internationales,* vol. 4, *La Révolution française et l'Empire napoléonien,* p. 42.

27. See R. H. Lord, *The Second Partition of Poland,* for a discussion of the events leading to the partition.

28. AAE, no. 363; and *Réimpression de l'Ancien Moniteur,* vol. 12, nos. 112, 113.

29. Ministère de la Guerre État-Major de l'Armée Archives historiques, Ordres de bataille des armées en campagne 1792–1815, carton X^{P3} (hereafter, Min. de la Guerre, AH) .

30. Ibid.

31. See Spencer Wilkinson, *The French Army before Napoleon;* and Matti Lauerma, *L'Artillerie de campagne française pendant les guerres de la Révolution,* for studies of the condition of the various branches of the French army.

32. Chuquet, *Dumouriez,* pp. 79–81.

33. Min. de la Guerre, AH, carton XP3.

34. Ibid.

35. R. W. Phipps, *The Armies of the First French Republic,* 1: 68–70, 90–93; see also 2: 5.

36. *Réimpression de l'Ancien Moniteur,* 13: 107–8, 138.

37. For studies of the Second Partition see Lord, *Second Partition of Poland;* Vivenot, *Quellen zur Geschichte,* vol. 3; and Fedor Martens, *Recueil des traités et conventions conclus par la Russie avec les puissances étrangères,* vol. 2.

38. Archives nationales, AF II, carton 281 (hereafter, AN). This carton contains an official French account of the 1792 campaign.

39. For an excellent study of the state of the allied armies see Arthur Chuquet, *La première invasion prussienne (11 août–2 septembre 1792).*

40. See Albert Mathiez, *Le dix août.*

41. AN, AF II, carton 281.

42. Ibid.

43. Ibid.

44. See Georges Lefebvre, "Sur Danton," *Études sur la Révolution française.*

45. *Réimpression de l'Ancien Moniteur,* 13: 601.

46. Ibid., pp. 602–3, 635.

47. AN, AF II, carton 281.

48. Ibid.

49. Ibid.; see also Arthur Chuquet, *Valmy.*

50. For studies of the French artillery see Ernest Picard, *L'Artillerie française au XVIIIᵉ siècle;* Jacques Boudon, "Le service de l'artillerie du XVIᵉ siècle à nos jours," *Revue d'Artillerie,* vol. 98; Jacques Allix, *Système d'artillerie de campagne;* and Jean Colin, *L' éducation militaire de Napoléon.*

51. Chuquet, *Valmy,* pp. 208–9.

52. Ibid., p. 214; and AN, AF II, carton 281.

2

From
Triumph to Disaster

After Valmy, Austro-Prussian relations continued to deteriorate, and the French attacked successfully on several fronts. Other powers, however, entered the war against the Republic and forced France back on the defensive. Defeat on the frontiers plus counter-revolution and dissension within republican ranks confronted the nation's leaders with a situation far more series than the crisis of 1792. By the summer of 1793 France was on the brink of total collapse.

As the Prussian army withdrew from Valmy Frederick William opened negotiations with Dumouriez. After consultations with Paris, the general entered the discussions, hoping to disengage the Prussians from their Austrian alliance. Frederick William, however, had no serious intention of deserting Francis and initiated the talks to delay the French from pursuing his army. The Hohenzollern monarch also wanted to use the negotiations as a threat to compel Austria to grant immediate concessions in eastern Europe.[1]

Early in October Austrian and Prussian diplomats met at Merle in Luxembourg to iron out details of each power's postwar compensations. The Austrians assumed that neither they nor the Prussians would take any territory until after they had defeated France. The Prussians, however, refused to wait and demanded immediate compensation at Polish expense. Furthermore, they threatened to withdraw their army from the west if Francis rejected their demands. The concurrent talks with the French added credibility to Frederick William's position.[2]

The Hapsburg Emperor reluctantly agreed to allow Prussia to take indemnities from Poland immediately, and on January 23, 1793, two days after Louis XVI's execution, Frederick William signed a partition agreement with Catherine. In the second partition Russia took the Polish Ukraine and White Russia, and Prussia obtained Danzig, Posen, Kalisz, and Torun.[3] Thus as the French people destroyed the Bourbon monarchy, a king and an empress virtually obliterated Polish independence. Upon learning the details of the treaty, Francis was amazed and infuriated. He dismissed Kaunitz and in his place appointed Baron Johan Amadeus Thugut. A clever, secretive, devious diplomat totally devoted to Hapsburg interests, Thugut immediately sought to restore the balance of power vis-à-vis Prussia. He began to contemplate taking territory from Poland, Venice, or France.[4] Thugut saw Prussia, not revolutionary France, as Austria's chief rival. Consequently, at precisely the moment that the Republic took the offensive, the Allies were more divided than ever.

The first French offensive was an immediate success. At the end of September General Adam Philippe Custine led seventeen thousand men into the Rhineland. Designed as a large raid to prevent the Allies from reinforcing their forces in Belgium, Custine's march carried all before it. The Austrian and Prussian troops withdrew to the east bank of the Rhine, and the local rulers simply fled. The Rhennish people refused to fight for their princes, and many welcomed the French as liberators. Worms surrendered on October 4, Mainz on October 21, and by the end of the month Custine occupied the entire Rhineland south of the Moselle and crossed the river to take Frankfurt.[5] On the Sardinian frontier republican forces quickly overran Nice and Savoy. Once again the inhabitants refused to fight to preserve the old order and many hailed the French arrival.[6]

These offensives were, however, diversionary efforts, because Dumouriez and his Brissotin allies, who dominated the Convention, decided to renew the plan of striking at Belgium. At the end of October forty thousand men, their morale vastly improved as a result of Valmy, entered Belgium and marched on Mons. The Austrians, fourteen thousand strong, moved into defensive positions in front of the city, where on November 6 the French attacked. Dumouriez launched his main assault against Austrian units around the small village of Jemappes. Covered by a hundred field guns, the infantry rushed forward in dense columns. Time and again well-aimed Austrian volleys tore into the columns, inflicting huge losses. Fierce cavalry counterstrokes added to the carnage, but after each repulse the French reformed and renewed their advance. Finally, the weight of numbers brought victory to French arms. Republican troops broke through the Austrian lines, threatened the exposed flanks, and forced the Hapsburg generals to withdraw to avoid annihilation. The Austrians fell back behind the Meuse, leaving all of central Belgium exposed and defenseless.[7]

Dumouriez then ordered an immediate advance. By November 14 the tricolor flew in Brussels, and by the end of the month republican troops held Louvain, Liège, and Antwerp. Their sudden triumphs, however, created new problems for the Republic's leaders; they had to decide quickly upon a means of governing their conquests and arranging the political future of their acquisitions.

Since officials of the deposed regimes had either fled or refused cooperation, the French of necessity had to work with individuals well disposed toward revolutionary ideas. In fact the French had been working with foreign revolutionaries months before the fall of Belgium. Just before the outbreak of war, Brissot assured the French public that victory was certain because people everywhere would rise against their masters and aid French armies. After April, 1792, the French created a series of foreign legions: Belgian, Swiss, German, Savoyard, and Dutch. These units consisted of refugees who, with French help, intended to revolutionize their homelands.[8]

There were indeed many people who hoped for French liberation, but despite their gestures toward internationalizing the France's leaders did not really intend to create an international Revolution the French never lost sight of their own interests.

movement. Rather, they wanted to employ foreign radicals exclusively against the Republic's enemies. Paris never planned to unleash revolution against neutrals or to inflame the entire Continent. The French did not employ the volunteer units against neutral states; they only used them against hostile powers and even went so far as to name the Dutch recruits the Free Foreign Legion to avoid offending the stadtholder, who was still neutral.[9] Nevertheless, early contact with foreign democrats plus the necessity to find local support in occupied lands led the French to work with Belgian and German revolutionaries.

In accordance with the policy of employing foreign democrats in French interests, the National Convention issued the First Propaganda Decree on November 19, 1792. The document promised aid and friendship to all people wishing to attain liberty. Sounding like a call to international revolt, the decree in reality had a specific and limited intent. The Convention had previously received pleas from foreign radicals for protection against counterrevolutionary reprisals, and the declaration was in effect a promise of French support to the Belgian and Rhennish democrats. The Convention thus assured foreign radicals that i' was safe to cooperate with French civil and military authorities. The foreign minister then informed Great Britain and the Swiss Confederation that the proclamation did not apply to neutrals, a clear indication of the limited scope of the decree.[10] The decree also contained an implied warning to neutral states that France would export social upheaval if they entered the war. Finally, the Propaganda Decree reassured the French people that they were not alone and that millions in other lands were awaiting a chance to aid the Republic.

Meanwhile, Dumouriez's political maneuverings in Belgium forced the Convention to give greater precision to its occupation policies. Still attempting to create an independent Belgian state with himself as leader, Dumouriez proposed to the Convention that the Belgians elect their own government. Paris agreed, because although the French government remained ignorant of their general's ambitions, they felt that a friendly regime in Belgium would make occupation easier and perhaps even frighten the Hapsburgs into seeking peace. With French approval Belgian democratic clubs proceeded to elect delegates to work with the Republic's army.[11]

Dumouriez, however, discovered that the Belgian democrats had no intention of picking him as their ruler and that the local radicals did not in fact enjoy wide popular support. To win over the Belgians Dumouriez turned to more conservative social elements. He ordered his subordinates to cease requisitioning supplies and instead buy them from local contractors. Lacking the cash to pay the businessmen, he tried to raise a loan from the clergy and in return promised to preserve their estates and the traditional privilege of collecting manorial dues and tithes. Finally, he asked Paris to authorize an invasion of the United Provinces in order that he might later evacuate them in return for Dutch recognition of his control of Belgium.[12]

His schemes, however, failed to produce the anticipated results. The Convention, wishing to avoid adding another foe to the allied ranks, forbade him to invade the Dutch Republic; the Belgian populace did not rally to his private cause; the clergy failed to produce funds sufficient to supply his army; and the soldiers, unpaid, ill fed, and clothed in tatters, deserted in droves. Furthermore, the Convention became suspicious of his ultimate plans and objectives.[13]

On December 14, 1792, the Convention issued a Second Propaganda Decree. Designed to prevent ambitious generals from introducing policies contrary to the government's intentions, the new document set forth an explicit course of action for officers in occupied territories. The generals were to abolish tithes, feudal dues, and all other remnants of aristocratic privilege. Then they were to convoke primary assemblies that would in turn organize provisional governments to work with the French, and confiscate property belonging to ruling princes, nobles, and churchmen. Finally, the military authorities were to issue *assignats* to pay for supplies and employ the confiscated property as security for the paper money.[14]

By establishing a general occupation policy, the Convention sought to clarify civilian-military relations and establish its supremacy over the generals. The government also tried to force the nation's enemies to bear the costs of the war and at the same time lighten the tasks of occupation by appealing to pro-French groups.[15]

Among the Belgians, however, reaction to the decree was largely unfavorable. The inhabitants hesitated to accept French paper, and elections for a Belgian Convention produced a majority that called for the restoration of the old social and political order. Local democrats thereupon concluded that it was impossible to create an independent republic and that their only safety from counterrevolutionary retribution lay in union with France. After the Belgian elections, the French drew a similar conclusion. Paris realized that annexation of Belgium would strengthen the Hapsburg's resolve to pursue the war and alarm neutrals. On the other hand, annexation would reassure pro-French groups, close avenues of political adventure to ambitious generals, and strengthen the nation's strategic position. Consequently, Danton and Lazare Carnot told the Convention in February, 1793, that France had a natural and historical right to the frontiers of the Rhine, Alps, and Pyrenees. Since the Convention had already annexed Nice and Savoy to protect local republicans, to deny the region's resources to the enemy, and to bolster the national boundaries, it had little difficulty in following the same policy in the Low Countries. In March primary assemblies met throughout Belgium, and under the supervision of French military authorities requested annexation. Paris responded favorably to the petitions, and province by province incorporated Belgium into the Republic. The Convention followed the same policy in the Rhineland, and after a Rhennish convention asked to join the Republic, the deputies approved annexation.[16]

The French had thus moved from a policy of creating republican regimes in conquered lands to direct incorporation. Ideological and diplomatic considerations played a secondary role in French policy formation. The Convention was not trying to inflame Europe with revolutionary fervor, nor did the deputies consider at length the diplomatic impact of the annexations. The Convention's primary concerns were to enhance French strategic security, finance the war at enemy expense, provide protection for those foreign radicals who assisted the Republic's war effort, and limit the influence of the military. By the beginning of 1793 annexation of Belgium and the Rhineland appeared to be the most effective means of accomplishing these objectives.

The expansion of France was, however, short lived. New powers entered the war, the military balance shifted against the Republic, growing internal strife further hampered the regime, and the French once again had to wage desperate defensive battles for survival.

England was the first major power to join Austria and Prussia. Pitt had long opposed the principles of the Revolution but had remained neutral during the opening phase of the war. French policy in Belgium, however, alarmed him, for he, like other English statesmen before and after him, felt that control of Belgium by a major power with significant naval capacity posed a serious threat to British security. Thus as French occupation policy transformed itself from temporary to permanent possession Pitt became progressively more hostile.

Another French move—the opening of the Scheldt River—further angered the English. The 1648 Treaty of Westphalia had closed the Scheldt to navigation in order to destroy the commercial position of Antwerp and increase Dutch trade. In the winter of 1792 the French had no desire to anger either Great Britain or the United Provinces but believed that an effort to win the support of the Belgian business and commercial class was worth the risk of antagonizing the maritime powers.[17] In response to the opening of the river, William V, the stadtholder of the United Provinces, appealed to Britain for assistance in case of further hostile French action. Pitt promised assistance, and on November 29 William Grenville, the secretary of state for foreign affairs, informed the French government that England's continued neutrality depended upon the withdrawal of the First Propaganda Decree and the reclosing of the Scheldt. Pitt called out the militia on December 2, and on December 20 obtained parliamentary approval for the addition of twenty thousand sailors to the fleet. The Cabinet then halted grain and raw material shipments to France.[18]

Paris assured London that the opening of the Scheldt was not designed as a hostile act and that the Propaganda Decree did not commit France to assist any and all seditious elements, especially in areas where the Republic had no vital interests. The French also pointed out that England had assisted Dutch rebels against Spain, and that by helping Belgian and Rhennish radicals against the Hapsburgs France was only following a traditional method of war and diplomacy. These efforts, however, produced no results, and in mid-January the French envoy reported that the British were continuing and even hastening the warlike preparations.[19]

On January 24, Pitt ordered the Republic's envoy out of England, thereby rendering further negotiations impossible. At this point the French realized that they had but two choices: fight England and Holland or abandon Belgium. War with the maritime powers was dangerous. Both states had large fleets that could virtually destroy French seaborne trade, and the two powers were wealthy and willing to use their financial strength to subsidize the Republic's foes. On the other hand, surrendering Belgium was equally risky. Foreign radicals would lose faith in French promises, the government's prestige and the nation's morale would suffer, and Austria and Prussia would score a significant strategic victory without having to fire a shot. The Convention, therefore, decided that the danger of adding new powers to the enemy ranks was less than the perils involved in giving up Belgium without a fight. Concluding that their determination to retain Belgium made war inevitable, the French decided to strike first. On January 21, 1793, Paris instructed Dumouriez to invade the United Provinces and on February 1 declared war on Great Britain.[20]

Other states quickly joined the antirepublican Coalition. Spain had rejected all French diplomatic initiatives after Louis XVI's execution and prepared for war in hopes of gaining support for claims to several Italian principalities. Assuming again that hostilities were inevitable, the Convention declared war on Spain on March 7. Other powers, anxious for spoils, hastened to enter the powerful Coalition. The Papal States, Naples, Tuscany, Parma, Modena, Sardinia, and Portugal, soon joined the allies. George III of England brought his Hanovarian patrimony into the conflict, and in April the Imperial Diet of Germany declared war on France.

Great Britain with her enormous financial resources became

the driving force behind the First Coalition. Pitt concluded treaties with the other major powers—Austria, Prussia, and Spain —calling for diplomatic and military coordination. The British also provided financial support for several of the secondary allied states. Although conflicting war aims and mutual suspicion plagued the Coalition, the Allies, nevertheless, possessed formidable strength. Some 54,800 Austrians, 11,400 Prussians, and 4,200 imperial troops backed by 38,000 English, Dutch, and Hanoverian soldiers faced 100,000 Frenchmen in Belgium. Between the Meuse and Moselle 33,400 Austrians supported the Coalition's forces in Belgium and protected the right flank of the Allied armies on the Rhine. Along the Rhine 56,600 Prussians, 24,000 Austrians, and 32,000 imperial soldiers faced 100,000 republicans. Over 40,000 Spanish troops prepared to cross the Pyrenees, while 30,000 Sardinians plus small detachments from other Italian states watched the line of the Alps held by 40,000 French. The allies thus deployed 330,000 well-trained men against 270,000 French troops.[21]

Despite their numerical inferiority the French decided to strike first and gain the advantage of surprise. Dumouriez intended to lead eighteen thousand men into the United Provinces while his second in command, the Venezuelan Miranda, covered his right by striking at Maestricht, an important Dutch fortress covering the Lower Rhine. Dumouriez also retained a forty thousand-man reserve force to check any Allied counterthrust. The French advanced on February 17, making fair progress against the ill-prepared Dutch. By the beginning of March Dumouriez had captured Breda, but the Austrians had also attacked and struck a telling blow against Miranda.[22]

The Prince of Coburg, the veteran Austrian commander, attacked Miranda with forty-five infantry battalions and fifty-six cavalry squadrons on March 1. He achieved complete surprise, and using his cavalry with deadly effect drove the French all the way back to Aix-la-Chapelle. He continued his attack on March 2, inflicting over six thousand casualties on the French, and throwing them back over the Meuse. Miranda tried to rally his forces at Liège, but Coburg moved forward on March 4, and Miranda, to escape encirclement, retreated toward Louvain. To stem the Austrian drive and protect Brussels, Paris ordered

Dumouriez to abandon his offensive and return to Belgium.
Dumouriez then ordered his troops to march to Antwerp and
in mid-March personally joined Miranda.[23]

In a desperate effort to halt Coburg, Dumouriez with forty-
five thousand men attacked thirty-nine thousand Austrians around
Neerwinden on March 18. The French tried but failed to capture
the town while Coburg threw large cavalry assaults against their
left and center. By nightfall the Austrians had lost two thousand
men, but Dumouriez suffered some four thousand casualties and
had to pull back to Louvain. On March 22, Coburg marched
on Louvain. The French lines held, but renewed attacks on
March 23 pierced Dumouriez's position. He had to evacuate
Louvain and retreat toward Brussels.[24]

His military setbacks coupled with the Convention's decision
to annex Belgium convinced Dumouriez that he could never
fulfill his political ambitions as a servant of the Republic. He
therefore decided to betray his country and, perhaps, win the
backing of the Coalition. He then proceeded to conclude an
armistice with the Austrians. He undertook to evacuate Belgium,
lead his army to Paris, overthrow the Convention, and restore
the monarchy. The Austrians promised not to attack during the
French withdrawal and if necessary assist Dumouriez's coup. The
Convention, already suspicious of the general, grew alarmed at
the speed of his subsequent retreat and his failure to fight
rear-guard actions. The war minister and three commissioners
went to the front to investigate and were prepared to remove
Dumouriez if they suspected treason. The general, however,
struck first. He arrested the officials, turned them over to the
Austrians, and called his troops to turn against the Republic.
The soldiers, however, refused, and on April 5, Dumouriez and a
small band of adherents fled to the Austrian camp.[25] Despite the
coup's failure Dumouriez's defection dealt a severe blow to the
Republic. It shook the nation's morale, led to the evacuation of
valuable military positions in Belgium, and contributed to the
further demoralization of the army.

As the Austrians pushed into Belgium the Prussians renewed
offensive operations on the Rhine. Brunswick's forces retook
Frankfurt in December, and by the spring of 1793 the duke
with eighty thousand men was ready to strike into the Rhine-

land against forty-five thousand Frenchmen. On March 17 the Prussians crossed the river north of Mainz. The French counter-attacked but failed to dislodge their enemies. The Prussians then reinforced their bridgehead and on March 27 and 28 attacked and defeated the army of the Moselle. Custine withdrew into Mainz, but fearing entrapment, he left a twenty-seven thousand-man garrison in the city and led the rest of his army south toward Worms. After detaching a siege force to take Mainz, Brunswick continued his advance while an Austrian contingent crossed the Rhine near Spire. Since there was little to stop the Austrians from moving north on Worms, Custine had no choice but to resume his retreat. By the end of the month his army was back in Landau trying to guard the northern approaches to Alsace.[26]

While their armies advanced, the Coalition members prepared to divide the anticipated spoils. Meeting at Antwerp on April 8, representatives of the major powers immediately rejected Coburg's policy of trying to undermine France's resistance by promising to refrain from taking any French territory. The British laid claim to several of France's colonies, and Austria again put forth the Belgian-Bavarian exchange plan. The English opposed this scheme, for they wanted Belgium to remain in Austrian hands, since the Hapsburgs guaranteed Belgium's security, yet posed no naval problems for England. They suggested that Austria keep Belgium and add to it several French cities. In order to retain British friendship to offset the Prusso-Russian entente Thugut agreed to abandon the exchange, keep Belgium, and expand the Belgian border south to the Somme River. Thugut also reserved the right to seize additional French provinces.[27]

Austro-Prussian relations remained strained as Francis refused to recognize the Second Polish Partition, and Frederick William refused to employ his army with full vigor. Despite the growing rift between Berlin and Vienna the Allied cause still looked promising. The French were demoralized and disorganized, and the Coalition's armies were ready to strike on all fronts.

In the spring of 1793 the front stretching from the Channel to the Meuse River was the strategic center of gravity. Both the Coalition and the Republic concentrated their largest armies in

Belgium and northern France. If the Allies could defeat the French field armies and capture the fortified cities along the Franco-Belgian frontier, Paris would lie helpless before them. The fall of Paris would in all probability result in the collapse of the Republic. To survive the French had to stave off the Allied offensive and protect the nation from invasion.

Fully aware of the necessity of defending their northern frontier, the Convention ordered its generals to attack and disrupt the Allied preparations. An May 1, the army of the North fell upon Allied units moving to blackade Condé. Hastily mounted, the assault was a failure. Several French columns advanced without coordination, and Coburg's troops defeated each force separately. Paris ordered new attacks, and the army of the North advanced again on May 8. Again several columns moved independently, and the Austrians mauled each one severely. The republicans then abandoned offensive operations, left a garrison in Condé to delay the Allies, and went over to the defensive.[28]

Coburg then decided to take Valenciennes. His first move was to dislodge the French from their entrenched camp at Famars to prevent them from launching spoiling attacks against his siege works around Valenciennes. He attacked on May 23 and drove the French from Famars. At this juncture, the prince had three alternatives: invest Valenciennes, pursue the retreating army of the North, or screen the French fortresses and move directly on Paris with all his available troops. A cautious, traditional warrior, Coburg ignored the more daring approaches and on May 30 began his attack on Valenciennes.[29]

A polyglot army of 30,000 men, including Austrian, English, and Hanovarian units supported by 287 cannon and 93 mortars, completed the first line of siege trenches by the night of June 13–14. By July 7 the Allied army had finished its final line of assault parallels while other Allied units reduced Condé. Coburg launched his final attack on Valenciennes on July 25. His troops broke into the city after bitter fighting, and three days later the garrison capitulated.[30]

In the Rhineland the Prussians began their siege of Mainz in April. The French undertook an active defence launching numerous sorties. They failed, however, to disrupt the construction of assault trenches and breaching batteries. Counterattacks

from Alsace also failed to raise the siege. By mid-July the
Prussians were assailing the city's outer defense ring and subjecting the garrison and inhabitants to constant bombardment.
Running short of food and munitions, the French defenders,
reduced to eighteen thousand men, capitulated on July 22. On
the same day the French launched another expedition from
Alsace. They were too late to rescue the Mainz garrison and
upon learning of the city's surrender withdrew to their lines.[31]

Along the Alps two French armies with a combined strength
of some fifty thousand men tried and failed to push the Sardinians back over the mountains. A series of murderous encounters achieved nothing, and by the end of June the French,
crippled by severe losses, adopted a defensive posture. In the
south, where twenty-five thousand French faced forty thousand
Spanish troops, the situation was equally depressing. In mid-
April the Spanish began to cross the eastern Pyrenees and
advanced on Perpignan. In May the Spanish scattered a French
force south of the city, and only the caution of Madrid's generals
prevented them from taking the city, which was in no condition
to offer a sustained defense. The following month the French
managed to check the Spanish advance, but Spanish troops
remained on the Republic's soil and prepared to resume their
offensive. In the western Pyrenees Spanish regiments forced their
way into France and threatened Bayonne.[32]

During the summer the French position continued to deteriorate. On the critical northern front Coburg continued to conquer the French frontier fortresses. After Valenciennes, the
Austrians struck at the French army entrenched near Cambrai.
Paris had meanwhile altered the command structure of the army
of the North in a desperate effort to find a general who could
end the constant retreats. Dampierre had replaced Dumouriez
only to die while trying to save Valenciennes. Custine then took
command but failed to stop the Allies, and Paris put General
Kilmaine in his place. The new commander was no more successful than his predecessors. He believed that his men were too
demoralized to fight for Cambrai. On August 8, after placing
a small garrison in the city, he pulled the army of the North
back to Arras.[33]

A hard-hitting pursuit of the battered French army might

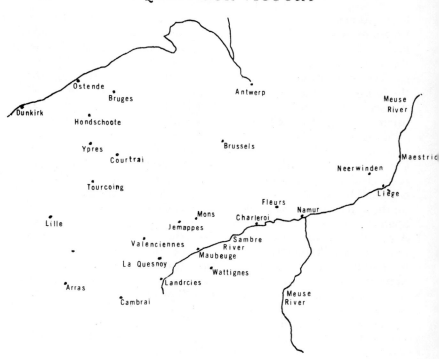

CAMPAIGNS IN BELGIUM AND NORTHERN FRANCE 1792-94

well have opened the routes to Paris. Coburg, however, refused
to abandon his cautious and so far successful strategy. Instead
of concentrating all of his resources for a single massive blow,
the prince allowed the duke of York to lead thirty-seven
thousand men to attack Dunkirk. About fifteen thousand Dutch
troops stationed around Menin watched the French garrison at
Lille. Coburg led forty-five thousand Austrians against Le Quesnoy and left sixty-six thousand in reserve posts across Belgium
and the French northern departments.[34] Coburg's actions may
well have spared the Republic from immediate catastrophe, but

continued Allied victories, even if limited in scope, could well produce the same result over a slightly longer time span. By midsummer the republicans were still unable to undertake effective counterattacks and their situation was desperate.

Nor did the strategic picture improve in other battle zones. Along the German frontier the French held defensive positions stretching from the Saar to the northern Vosges. The Allies launched no major assaults, but the French, weakened by their earlier defeats, were unable to profit from the Coalition's inactivity. Rather than risk new defeats, the Republican generals contented themselves with trying to strengthen their defensive bastions.[35] The Sardinians invaded Savoy in August. Realizing that a Sardinian breakthrough would threaten the Rhone Valley and allow the Coalition to assist counterrevolutionary elements around Lyons, the French mounted savage counterthrusts. They managed to hold the Sardinians to limited gains but failed to push them back across the Alps. In the south the Spanish continued to move on Perpignan. The French retained a tenuous hold on the city, but their position worsened daily. Around Bayonne the republicans attacked fruitlessly, and the Spanish continued to inch forward.[36]

Counterrevolutionary rebellions created additional problems for the Convention. The Vendée, a wild desolate region in western France south of the Loire, had long been a center of counterrevolution. As early as 1791 noblemen in the western departments had created a secret insurrectionary organization. The government infiltrated and destroyed the conspiratorial group in January, 1793, but many individuals avoided arrest and continued their search for an opportunity to strike at the Parisian regime.[37] Most clerics in the Vendée espoused the counterrevolutionary cause and doubtless preached hatred of the Republic to their peasant congregations. The peasantry held long-standing grievances with the middle class of the numerous small towns scattered throughout the Vendée. Prior to 1788 the Vendean bourgeoisie had collected manorial rents from the peasants and dominated the area's manufacturing and commerce. Middle class elements supported the Revolution and gained control of local government. The peasants reacted by rejecting the new regime.[38] In 1790 there had been sporadic outbursts of violence against government officials, and in the winter of 1793 the Convention took a step that mobilized all of the counterrevolutionary elements into a single massive force.

On February 24, the government, trying to reinforce the battered field armies, issued a decree calling for a levy of three hundred thousand men. News of the conscription law reached the western departments by March 10, and on the following day, bands of peasants protesting against the law, which would take them away from their farms and families, began to assault republican officials. By March 13 the entire region save for the larger towns and cities was in the hands of the rebels, who chose leaders like Cathelineau and Stofflet from among their own ranks to lead them in a fight to protect their way of life against the Convention and its local supporters. The nobles then joined the rebellion. Because many of them had military training they soon took control of the peasant irregulars and transformed the revolt into a royalist movement.[39]

By March 20 aristocratic leaders, including the marquises de Bonchamp and d'Elbée, ex-officers, Charette, a former naval lieutenant, and La Rochejacquelein had created a Catholic and Royal Army of thirty thousand men. Essentially a guerrilla force, the Vendeans were well prepared to dominate their home provinces and fend off government expeditionary forces. The Catholic and Royal Army thus compelled Paris to divert thousands of men, needed desperately at the front, to contain the counterrevolution.

Miscalculating the extent of the uprising, the government first pushed small detachments into insurgent territory. The rebels ambushed and overwhelmed each in turn. Early in April the government sent twenty thousand men, most of them National Guardsmen, into the Vendée. Divided into three columns, the republicans entered rebel territory from the north, east, and south. The Vendeans concentrated their troops and fell upon the northern column. Between April 19 and 22, they pushed it back to the Loire and then crossed the river and seized a bridgehead on the north bank. The other columns hastily withdrew. In May the Catholic and Royal Army reduced isolated republican strongholds within the Vendée and defeated another republican force near the coast, taking three thousand prisoners and forty cannon. The Vendeans then proceeded to create a civil administration and a military staff that could by the summer mobilize over sixty thousand men.[40] Of these some eighty-five hundred formed a permanent cadre while the others returned home after each action to await a muster call transmitted from parish to parish by the ringing of church bells.

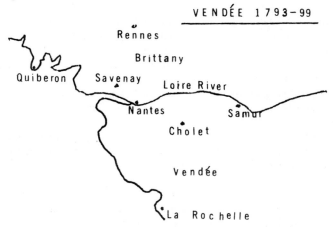

VENDÉE 1793-99

In June, the republicans planned another offensive, but the rebels struck first. Some forty thousand Vendéans stormed Samur on June 9 taking thousands of prisoners. The Vendéans then marched on Nantes, garrisoned by the army of Brest, twelve thousand strong. The republicans in bitter hand-to-hand combat fended off the rebel assault and resumed the offensive. The Vendéans, though unable to carry the war into republican territory, were past masters at defending their own terrain. They ambushed and destroyed the invading columns in the hedgerows of the central Vendée. In the following weeks the republicans managed to fend off rebel attempts to seize a port and enter into direct contact with the Coalition, but the government had no success in stamping out the insurrection in the central Vendée.[41]

Royalist bands, Chouans, also operated in Brittany and Normandy. They never formed a broadly based movement, but operated instead in small units. Consequently, the Chouans were less dangerous to the Republic than the Vendéans, but they did, nevertheless, compel Paris to divert additional forces from the conventional battlefields to the brutal, thankless tasks of counter-insurgency.[42]

A third wave of rebellions created still more problems for the beleaguered Parisian regime. In the Convention Brissot and his clique struggled for power with Robespierre and his Jacobin allies. Robespierre struck a tacit alliance with the Parisian *sans-culottes* by adopting many of their programs, including execution of the deposed monarch, price controls, vigorous efforts to crush counterrevolution, and more energetic conduct of the war. The Brissotins relied upon their numerical strength in the Convention, where they outnumbered the Robespierrists, and upon their support in the provinces, but they failed to control the Parisians. Consequently, on May 31 and again on June 2, thousands of armed *sans-culottes* marched upon the Convention demanding the arrest of leading Brissotins. The Convention capitulated and ordered the Brissotins incarcerated, but many of the proscribed deputies escaped Paris and fled to the provinces, where they rallied their home districts against the capital.

By the second week in June several departments in Normandy and Brittany had joined the Brissotin-inspired federalist rebellion. Local authorities in Bordeaux, Toulouse, Nîmes, Lyons, and Marseilles also took up arms against Paris. In July Toulon joined the federalist ranks. Local royalists, mainly officers of the Mediterranean fleet, joined forces with the republican opponents of the Convention, took charge of the city's defense, and soon gained control of Toulon's civil administration. They transformed the federalist uprising into a royalist movement and called upon the Coalition for assistance. In August London sent a fleet under Admiral Hood's command to Toulon. Hood put fifteen hundred men ashore to bolster the city's defenses. Later another one thousand English, three thousand Sardinian, and fourteen thousand Spanish and Neapolitan soldiers arrived to support the six thousand-man royalist contingent. The British admiral then issued a proclamation stating that the Allies would hold the city until the count of Provence, Louis XVI's brother and claimant to the French throne as Louis XVIII, reestablished the monarchy in France.[43] The Allies had thus captured one of the Republic's most important naval bases along with a large portion of the

French fleet and had established a bridgehead in southern France. Royalists, meanwhile, gained control of Lyons and Corsica. By midsummer over half of the departments were in open rebellion against Paris.

After Valmy, the French in a surge of self-confidence had hurled themselves forward and scored some striking victories. The government, however, had not given detailed consideration to the diplomatic consequences of their military triumphs. Nor had Paris established its supremacy over the generals. Furthermore, the government lost sight of the fact that its soldiers were still poorly equipped and trained and unable to stand the rigors of a long campaign. In conquered lands the problems of retaining local support and restraining the military led to the propaganda decrees and then to annexation again without serious contemplation of the diplomatic repercussions.

The entry of new powers into the war found the French unprepared, and they lost their initial conquests. After a series of major defeats, the republicans abandoned further offensive operations and assumed a defensive stance. The disorganization of the field forces led to more defeats, and counterrevolution added to the government's strategic dilemma. By the summer of 1793 France was on the verge of catastrophe.

Most of Europe was at war with the Republic. Everywhere the Coalition's armies moved forward. On the critical northern front the Allies, despite internal divisions and overcautious strategy, won battle after battle. Counterrevolution raged in the provinces. Political rivalries continued to plague the Convention. Unless the Convention could quickly reinvigorate the war effort and devise a strategy to cope with civil war and foreign invasion, the Revolution and the Republic were doomed.

NOTES

Chapter 2

1. For an excellent description of the French and Prussian negotiations see S. S. Biro, *The German Policy of Revolutionary France*, vol. 1.

2. André Fugier, *Histoire des relations internationales*, vol. 4, *La Révolution française et L'Empire napoléonien*, p. 58.

3. Fedor Martens, ed., *Recueil des traités et conventions conclus par la Russie avec les puissances étrangères*, 4: 228–35.

4. Fugier, *Histoire des relations internationales*, p. 59.

5. Ministère de la Guerre État-Major de l'Armée Archives historiques (hereafter, Min. de la Guerre, AH), Armée du Rhin journal général des opérations 28 septembre 1792 jusqu'au 8 janvier 1794, Mémoires historiques, no. 322.

6. Jacques Godechot, *La Grande Nation*, 1: 77–79.

7. See Arthur Chuquet, *Jemappes et la conquête de la Belgique (1792–1793)*.

8. R. R. Palmer, *The Age of the Democratic Revolution*, 2: 52–54; and Albert Mathiez, *La Révolution et les étrangères*, pp. 65–68.

9. Palmer, *Democratic Revolution*, p. 57.

10. Ibid., p. 59; *Réimpression de l'Ancien Moniteur*, 14: 516–17; and Archives Nationales, AF II, carton 57 (hereafter, AN).

11. AN, DP II, cartons 4, 5. These dossiers contain reports from government agents in Belgium pointing out the advantages of creating a provisional government in the Austrian Netherlands.

12. AN, DP II, carton 5.

13. See Suzanne Tassier, *Histoire de la Belgique sous l'occupation française en 1792 et 1793*.

14. *Réimpression de l'Ancien Moniteur*, 14: 703–55.

15. Ibid., pp. 758–60.

16. AN, AF II, carton 3; see also Philippe Sagnac, *Le Rhin français pendant la Révolution et l'Empire*.

17. *Réimpression de l'Ancien Moniteur*, 14: 535.

18. On British policy see A. W. Ward and G. P. Gooch, *The Cambridge History of British Foreign Policy 1783–1919*, vol. 1; and J. Holland Rose, *William Pitt and the Great War*.

19. Archives des affaires étrangères, Correspondance politique, no. 586 (hereafter, AAE).

20. AN, AF II, carton 3.

21. Min. de la Guerre, AH, Ordres de bataille des armées en campagne, 1792–1815, carton XD3.

22. Min. de la Guerre, AH, Armées de la République situations générales 1792–1800, carton B1245.

23. Ibid.

24. Ibid.; see also R. W. Phipps, *The Armies of the First French Republic*, vol. 1, for a description of the French defeats in Belgium.

25. AN, AF II, carton 69.

26. See Phipps, *Armies of the First French Republic,* vol. 2.

27. S. S. Biro, *The German Policy of Revolutionary France,* 1: 9–11, 113–19, 145–48, 177–81.

28. Min. de la Guerre, AH, cartons Xᴰ3, B¹245.

29. For accounts of the summer campaign see Émile Bourdeau, *Campagnes modernes,* vol. 1; and J. W. Fortescue, *A History of the British Army,* vol. 4, pt. 1.

30. Arthur Aspinall, ed., *The Later Correspondence of George III,* 2: 53–54, 65–66. This volume includes the duke of York's account of the siege and capitulation of Valenciennes. The duke commanded English troops in the Low Countries.

31. See Émile Bourdeau, *Campagnes modernes,* vol. 1; and Phipps, *Armies of the First French Republic,* vol. 2.

32. Min. de la Guerre, AH, carton B¹245.

33. Ibid.

34. Ibid.

35. Ibid.

36. Ibid.

37. Arthur Goodwin, "Counter-Revolution in Brittany: The Royalist Conspiracy of the Marquis de la Rouerie 1791–1793," *Bulletin of the John Rylands Library* vol. 39 (1957) .

38. See Charles Tilly, "Some Problems in the History of the Vendée," *American Historical Review* vol. 67 (October, 1961) ; and Jacques Godechot, *La Contre-Révolution doctrine et action 1789–1804,* chap. 11.

39. AN, AF II, carton 9; and Peter Paret, *Internal War and Pacification, The Vendée 1789–1796.*

40. Paret, *Internal War;* see also Emile Gabroy, *La Révolution et la Vendée,* vol. 1; and J. M. Savary, *Guerres des Vendéens et des Chouans contre la République française,* vol. 1.

41. See Paret, *Internal War;* and Godechot, *La Contre-Révolution.*

42. Savary, *Guerres,* vol. 1.

43. On the Federalist revolts see R. M. Brace, *Bordeaux and the Gironde 1789–1794;* and Min. de la Guerre, AH, Précis historique sur le siège de Toulan en 1793, no. 400.

3
Turn of the Tide

Late in the summer of 1793 republican leaders began to deal successfully with the problems of internal anarchy, foreign invasion, and civil strife. The Allies, still mutually suspicious, failed to effectively coordinate their diplomacy and strategy, while the French developed governmental machinery designed to mobilize the nation's resources. In the fall the republicans launched vigorous counterattacks, halted the Coalition's armies, and crushed the internal counterrevolutions. In the spring of 1794 the French unleashed major offensive operations. The armies of the First Republic drove foreign soldiers from French soil and then carried the war back into their enemies' domains.

In 1793 France had to create a regime able to control its subordinate officials and citizens if the Republic were to survive, but as the nation's armies retreated on all fronts the incumbent government appeared singularly unsuited to the tasks involved in rallying the nation for massive resistance. Factional disputes split the Convention; ministers of the Provisional Executive Council frequently opposed the policies set by the elected deputies; the Parisian populace with its own set of economic and political goals watched the Convention suspiciously, and local authorities often refused to take orders from Paris.[1]

In response to the growing chaos the Convention on January 1, 1793, created a Committee of General Defense to improve the government's efficiency. This large unwieldy body of eighteen and later twenty-five members had little real power.[2] In the spring, military reverses and Dumouriez's treason forced the Convention to create a more authoritative supervisory body. On April 6, 1793, the deputies established a Committee of Public Safety and authorized it to observe and accelerate the actions of the Executive Council. The Committee could also suspend ministerial decrees and issue emergency decrees of its own.[3]

Dominated by Danton the new Committee failed to stop the Allies or repress internal insurrections. Furthermore, Danton's attempt to negotiate with the Coalition at a time when France had little to offer in return for peace made many deputies suspicious of his motives. Some even came to suspect him of royalist sympathies. On July 10 the Convention removed him from the Committee and began to appoint the men who were to guide the nation's destiny for the next critical eleven months.[4]

With Maximilien Robespierre as their dominating figure the men who served on the reconstituted Committee represented a cross section of the politically active French public. The twelve members included five lawyers, two army officers, two authors, an ex-noble, an actor, and a former Protestant pastor. Before 1789 all of them had been successful in their chosen careers and in 1793 were hard working, reasonably honest, patriotic, and determined to lead the Republic to victory. Of course they did not agree on all issues. Some, for example, supported the demands of the *sans-culottes* for price controls and direct popular democracy; others opposed popular revolutionism; a third group favored a measure of popular democracy but were determined to create a stable government that would control and regulate the activities of all Frenchmen. Temperaments clashed, and personal antagonisms often divided the twelve members. Still, they realized that the Nation faced catastrophe, and they had to establish a working relationship if France were to survive. They managed to submerge their differences for the moment and set to work to transform the Committee into an autonomous organization, capable of controlling the Convention, the ministers, the armies, and the populace.[5]

On October 10, 1793, the Convention, realizing the need for an effective centralized directing body, placed the Committee in charge of the nation's war effort. Declaring that the French government was revolutionary for the duration of hostilities, the decree delayed indefinitely the implementation of the constitution written in June. The Committee received the authority to nominate generals and regulate the activities of ministers and local government.[6]

Agreeing to extend further the Committee's power, the Convention on December 4, 1793, declared that the twelve members were to supervise the activities of all public functionaries. The law ordered ministers to report on their activities directly to the Committee every ten days. The decree forbade local authorities to alter or interpret decrees emanating from Paris, reduced the power of departmental officials, and replaced locally elected officials in the districts and communes with national agents, who were responsible to the Committee. Finally, the decree empowered the twelve to conduct the nation's diplomatic activity.[7] Known as the Constitution of the Terror, the December 4 law coordinated all previous emergency decrees and defined the nature of the revolutionary regime: the Convention, acting through the Committee of Public Safety, was the sole center of authority; local officials and all other governmental departments and agencies were subordinate to the central government. The Committee thus functioned like a modern war cabinet.

The final step in the evolution of the Committee came on April 1, 1794, when the Convention abolished the council of ministers and replaced it with a dozen commissions that reported directly to the Committee of Public Safety.[8] The October 10, December 4, and April 1 decrees, coupled with purges of opponents in the Convention, enabled the Committee to act effectively as the Republic's single policy-making organ.

To increase their authority in the departments and organize the war effort the twelve made vigorous use of representatives on mission. The system was already in use: the Convention in February had sent two deputies to each department to hasten the levy; deputies on mission had helped organize frontier defenses in April; and in the same month representatives went to the field armies to supervise the generals' conduct, improve troop morale, and hasten the incorporation of volunteers into existing battalions. The deputies had extensive powers. They could spend public funds, requisition supplies, and arrest civil and military officials.[9] The Committee transformed the occasional employment of representatives into a permanent aspect of the revolutionary government.

On May 7 the Committee declared that the deputies on mission were to secure men and material for the armies, keep Paris informed on local conditions, and take an active role in planning and executing military operations. In August the Committee sent a new wave of representatives to the departments and the armies.[10]

The representatives on mission were an important link between Paris and the countryside. They also played a critical role in securing military obedience to the civilian authorities. Members of the Committee went on missions, thereby enhancing the prestige of the other deputies and emphasizing the importance of the entire system of roving agents. Working with the Committee of General Security, a political police, the revolutionary tribunal, and local revolutionary societies, the special delegates enabled the Committee of Public Safety to exercise effective control throughout the nation.

The Committee also enlarged and reorganized the armies. To obtain more men and to satisfy Parisian popular leaders, who were calling for a mass mobilization against the Republic's enemies, Robespierre and his colleagues introduced a general conscription act. On August 23, 1793, the Convention passed the famous *levée en masse* decree, which stated that "henceforth until the enemies have been driven from the Republic's territory, the French people are in permanent requisition for military service."[11] The *levée* directed single men from eighteen to twenty-five years of age to join the army, married men to work in arms factories, women to serve in hospitals, and old men to act as propagandists.[12] The conscription law combined the *sans-culotte's* demand for a popular war with the requisites of military efficiency, and placed the entire nation on a wartime footing.

Under Carnot's general supervision thousands of men joined the colors. The armies had 361,000 men under arms in February and 670,900 by January 20, 1794.[13] By April there were 842,300 troops; in May 869,000; in June 893,000; and in August 1,075,-000.[14] By the fall of 1794, the field armies had a grand total of 1,108,300 men, of whom 850,770 were immediately available for combat.[15] The measure of the Committee's accomplishment may be seen by the fact that Louis XIV built the largest French army prior to 1794 and fielded about three hundred thousand men. France had a population of about eighteen million, meaning that there was one soldier for every sixty inhabitants, a ratio that declined during succeeding reigns. The Committee, governing twenty-four million people, placed one man under arms for every twenty-four citizens, or better than double the old regime mobilization rate. This ratio is even more impressive considering the fact that the Republic employed no mercenaries, who composed over twenty percent of the royal army.

The Committee also organized its enlarged army into effective tactical formations. By a decree of February 21, 1793, the Convention abolished all distinctions between the regular troops, volunteers, and conscripts. The government then reorganized the infantry into demibrigades consisting of one regular and two volunteer battalions. The regulars were to instill discipline in the new recruits, who were by their *élan* to encourage the regulars. The decree established the number of demibrigades at 196, but the requirements of the current campaigns forced the government to delay the execution of the law until the following year.[16] Individual commanders introduced the new system in their armies in 1793, and on January 8, 1794, the government ordered all of the field armies to use demibrigades.[17]

Army commanders also began to group several demibrigades plus cavalry and artillery units into combat divisions. A division contained from two to four demibrigades and mustered anywhere from seven thousand to thirteen thousand men. Artillery and cavalry components also varied depending upon the availability of equipment and the nature of a specific assignment. The division could march and fight either as a single unit or as part of a larger force, thereby giving commanders greater flexibility in planning and executing military operations.[18]

French battlefield tactics also improved. By mid-1793 generals had abandoned the traditional linear formations. The army used a drill book written in 1791. The regulations reflected many of the ideas of J. A. H. Guibert, an old regime reformer who advocated a flexible tactical system combining fire and shock action. The manual sought to train troops to shift quickly from line to column and column to line and left it to commanders to employ the particular configuration of line and column according to local circumstances. By combining the best elements of tactical reforms introduced by the monarchy with the insights of battle experience, field officers devised tactics designed to minimize the lack of training and emphasize the soldiers' *élan* and numerical strength.[19]

Because their men lacked training in linear tactics, republican officers first emphasized shock action. They sought to carry enemy positions with battalion assault columns but soon discovered that, although the columns attained occasional successes, they usually took heavy losses. Well-drilled infantry, backed by large cavalry reserves, frequently halted and then scattered the assault formations. In the course of campaigning, however, French soldiers learned to advance on their own and snipe at the enemy formations. Officers, grasping the value of this technique began to protect the rushing columns with a thick screen of light infantry. Entire companies and even full battalions would deploy as light infantrymen. These skirmishers would cover the columns and direct constant fire into the enemy ranks.[20] Once the light infantry weakened or disorganized a segment of the enemy's lines, battalion columns, forty men wide and twelve ranks deep, would rush forward. Depending upon tactical circumstances the columns would either charge and attempt to shatter their opponent's line, deploy as light infantry and reinforce the skirmishers, move into a rough linear formation and carry on a fire fight, or form a square to fend off cavalry.[21] With the ability to fight as a light infantryman or as part of an assault unit, the French soldier became a formidable warrior. Although the cavalry arm never became very strong, the Republic's field artillery maintained high standards and gave the infantry constant effective support. Tactical formations allowing flexibility on both the personal and unit level increased the striking power of the citizen soldier to a point where he could face the professional armies of old-regime Europe on more than equal terms.

Finally, the Committee developed a cadre of leaders loyal to the Republic and able to effectively employ the new formations. The representatives on mission removed inefficient and disloyal officers and frequently executed them. Individuals of proven loyalty and talent received immediate promotion. Of course not all who lost their commands and lives were guilty as charged, nor were the battlefield promotions uniformly successful. But given the tense and trying circumstances in 1793 and 1794, the Committee and its delegates ultimately managed to find an able group of military leaders.

In contrast to old regime armies where most officers were of aristocratic descent, the republicans drew most of their officers from the middle class. Nobles who remained loyal to the Revolution, though treated with suspicion, also attained high rank. Few peasants became generals, but they did enter the lower ranks of the officer corps in large numbers. Many new officers had previous experience as enlisted men, noncommissioned officers, or junior officers in the Bourbon army; some had served in the National Guard, and others obtained their experience as ordinary soldiers in the revolutionary army. By the fall of 1793 the Committee had created a group of generals who were to carve a permanent niche for themselves in the annals of warfare. Louis C. A. Desaix, Jean Baptiste Jourdan, Jean Charles Pichegru, Jean Bernadotte, Pierre Augereau, Nicholas Oudinot, Louis Lazare Hoche, Louis Nicolas Davout, Jean Victor Moreau, André Masséna, and Guillaume Brune form but part of the list of famous leaders who were generals by 1793.[22]

Republican generals were young—their average age was thirty-three. Most of them lacked strategic ability because they had little formal training. On the other hand, they were excellent tacticians—aggressive, brave, willing to learn on the battlefield, and determined to win.

While expanding and reorganizing their military forces, the Committee also began to mobilize the nation's economy. Their objective was twofold: to equip the fighting forces and to pacify the Parisian *sans-culottes,* who were vociferous in their demands for price controls. Control of prices was the first step in economic mobilization. The *assignat* by 1793 had lost over half its face value, and controls would check inflation, enhance the government's purchasing power, and satisfy the lower classes.

The government instituted its policy of economic regulation in May with the passage of a law establishing maximum grain prices. In July the Convention issued a decree proscribing the death penalty for those withholding goods from the market in order to drive up prices. In August the Convention forbade exports of capital and items of prime necessity without special permits, created public granaries, and placed price controls on fuel, salt, and tobacco.[23] To limit inflation further, the government demonetized all *assignats* bearing the royal seal and converted the state debt into permanent bonds. Creditors received a fixed annuity but could not redeem the bonds. In early September the Convention instituted a forced loan and on September 29 established a general maximum, setting prices and wages throughout the country.[24]

In addition to controlling prices and wages, the Committee also took a direct role in war production. Government workshops established in Paris began to turn out muskets and by 1794 produced 750 weapons per day, almost as many as the combined production of the rest of Europe.[25] Privately owned forges, foundries, and powder mills received government contracts and worked to full capacity. The Convention granted to the Committee thirty million livres for the establishment of new weapons plants and one hundred million francs to buy arms from existing workshops. Representatives on mission helped businessmen expand their factories, requisitioned convents, churches, and other national buildings, and transformed them into power mills and gun-making shops, and even seized church bells, metal church roofs, and metallic objects in *émigré* homes for use in foundries.[26] The Committee drafted workers for service in weapons plants and requisitioned privately owned weapons, horses, shoes, and clothing. Even scientists served by training workers, seeking more efficient production techniques (the government published the results of successful experiments and distributed the information to producers), and creating new weapons.[27]

Most war production remained in private hands, but the Committee subjected it to government control. Entrepreneurs became, in effect, a class of government contractors. The Committee decided what items to produce and dictated their quantity, quality, and price. Although some inefficiency and corruption existed, the government generally succeeded in organizing the French economy for the fight for national survival.

The Committee also reorganized and clarified the Republic's foreign policy. It abandoned all efforts to work with foreign radicals. The twelve members noted that earlier efforts to secure assistance from foreign revolutionaries had produced little for France and had involved the Republic in useless and at times dangerous complications. Consequently, in April the Convention renounced all efforts to intervene in the internal affairs of other states and in June ordered its representatives abroad to avoid participation in local politics.[28] On September 15 the Committee directed its generals to observe the traditional rules of war in occupied regions. It ordered commanders to disarm the inhabitants, take hostages, and levy contributions. The government then established commissions to seize movable wealth and modern machinery and send it back to France.[29] The French retained the notion of forcing the privileged to disgorge their wealth for the Republic's benefit. They did so not so much from ideological predilection, but simply because it was easier to take from the rich than from the poor. In case of dire need the French were quite willing to compel the lower classes to contribute. By late 1793 the Republic abandoned attempts to employ foreign democrats in French interests and pursued their goals with the ordinary weapons of diplomacy and war.

To strengthen French public morale and diplomatic security the Committee ended all efforts to negotiate publicly with members of the Coalition. The twelve realized that open diplomacy would strengthen Danton and others who sought a quick peace. The Committee also believed that since France was on the defensive, the Republic's diplomats had little to offer the Coalition in return for an end to hostilities. Public negotiations would therefore serve only to emphasize the nation's plight, undermine morale at home, and hinder secret diplomatic maneuvers abroad.[30]

In defining the Republic's future diplomatic policy Robespierre and his colleagues assumed that England and Austria were France's most determined and dangerous enemies. Short of military defeat followed by an imposed peace, the Hapsburgs would never give up Belgium or abandon their plans to wrest territory from the Republic. Nor would England, unless defeated in battle, sacrifice either the Low Countries or colonial conquests. The Committee therefore concluded that it had to concentrate its major military effort against these two powers. Aware of rivalries within the Coalition, Robespierre decided to try to detach Prussia from the Allied ranks. He wished to conclude a separate peace with the

Hohenzollern monarch, who would then turn his energies toward eastern expansion, a policy that might compel the Hapsburgs to detach forces from the west in order to counter Prussian expansion. He also wanted to embroil the Turks in war with Austria and Russia, persuade the minor states in Germany and Italy to leave the war, and convince Sweden, Poland, and the Ottoman Empire to form a League of Armed Neutrality to counter the British control of the high seas.[31] The Committee thus sought to divide the Allies and concentrate French military might against the nation's major foes.

France, in the summer of 1793, resembled a besieged fortress with its garrison, reduced to squabbling factions, trying to withstand the assaults of many hostile armies. Still other groups within sought to open the gates to the enemies without. One group of defenders seized power and by force and persuasion welded the others into a united army. The new leaders treated those who disagreed with them as traitors. Dissidents, whether their motives were pure or sullied, theatened the garrison's unity, and the leaders, therefore, struck them down. The defenders then rushed forth to protect their fortress and prepared to launch a vast sortie of their own.

Divisions within the ranks of the attackers helped the French. Angered and humiliated by their setback in Poland, the Austrians were determined to offset Prussian gains by taking territory in the west. To pacify the British Thugut agreed to retain Belgium and add to it French Flanders as far south as the Somme River. He then drew secret plans to seize Alsace and Lorraine and exchange these provinces for Bavaria. Thugut also sought a rapprochement with Czarina Catherine in order to split the Russo-Prussian alliance. Vienna, therefore, recognized the Second Partition Treaty insofar as it applied to Russia and began exploratory talks for a renewal of the Austro-Russian alliance.[32] To gain new lands Thugut was willing to mislead his allies as to Austria's political objectives and to work actively against the interests of a member of the Coalition. For Austria the war against the Republic was less important than the effort to even the score with Prussia.

Like their Austrian rivals, the Prussians were concerned primarily with their own ambitions, and Frederick William II re-

garded his participation in the war against France more as a
bargaining instrument to force concessions from Vienna than as
a fight against French aggression and revolutionary subversion.
Growing Polish resistance to foreign domination led the Hohenzollern monarch to pursue a cautious western policy. Berlin announced that with the reconquest of Belgium Prussia's obligations
under the 1792 treaty were at an end and that Prussian troops
would enter no further campaigns unless Frederick William received a subsidy. The king then left the Rhine, where he had
been leading a portion of his army, and returned to Berlin, where
he was closer to developments in Poland. Moreover, he instructed
his generals in the west to avoid major battles with the French.[33]

Even the British, leaders and paymasters of the Coalition,
failed to devise an effective strategy. Pitt was torn between the
alternatives of trying to crush the Republic in land campaigns
or using England's naval superiority to blockade the Republic's
coasts and capture French colonies. The Cabinet was similarly
divided: Lord Grenville, the foreign secretary, favored a continental policy, while Henry Dundas, the secretary of state for
war, advocated an imperial strategy.[34] Pitt never fully committed
himself to either policy, and British strategy failed to produce
conclusive results either in Europe or overseas.

British forces in Flanders and Toulon were insufficient to play
a crucial role in defeating France, and the limited military contribution in Europe weakened England's influence within the
Coalition. Overseas, Pitt found in the French West Indies an
irresistible temptation and soon committed his state's resources in
an expensive campaign to conquer Saint-Domingue, the richest
colony in the French empire. Revolution came to Saint-Domingue
(Haiti) in 1789 as the planter aristocracy and lower class whites
struggled for power. Additional complications arose when the free
mulattoes tried and failed to gain equality. The planters used
armed Negro slaves to crush a mulatto uprising and then turned
and reenslaved the Negroes. In the summer of 1791 the slaves
launched a major insurrection. Hundreds of whites fled to the
British West Indies where their accounts of the servile rebellion
alarmed local officials. To prevent slave insurrections in British
colonies Pitt increased the colonial garrison to nineteen battalions.
The coming of war with France coupled with appeals from the

French plantation owners for aid convinced Pitt to expand his military commitment in the Caribbean.[35]

In April, 1793, the British occupied Tobago, and in September a small force landed in Saint-Domingue. In November seven thousand additional troops sailed from England with orders to take all French possessions in the West Indies. The slaves in Haiti had meanwhile found a leader who was a match for any European general. A former house slave, Toussaint L'Ouverture, had joined the 1791 revolt and at first cooperated with the Spanish who owned half of Saint-Domingue. He even became an officer in the Spanish army but concluded that the Spanish were no better than the French and that England and Spain, if victorious, would reimpose slavery. At this juncture the Convention abolished slavery in all French colonies, and Toussaint switched sides. He had no intention of fighting to support the Republic's strategy, because his interest was essentially to win freedom for himself and his followers. He nevertheless performed a great service for France by tying down thousands of British soldiers away from the decisive European battlefields.[36] Thus by sending troops to the West Indies Pitt gave the Republic an additional advantage in the fall campaigns.

On the French frontiers the Coalition matched its strategic dispersal of effort with a similar tactical disarray. The duke of York led his British, Hanovarian, and Hessian regiments toward Dunkirk. After throwing back a French sortie from Lille, he captured the outposts around the port and at the beginning of September began his siege. Some twenty-one thousand troops attacked the city while sixteen thousand men guarded the siege force's flanks and rear. Coburg, meanwhile, moved on Quesnoy. On September 12 he checked a French column attempting to relieve the city and then resumed construction of his assault works. In the Rhineland the Austrians tried to invade Alsace, but the French defenses held. The Prussians refused to cooperate with their ally, thus relieving pressure on a vital front. Taking advantage of the failure of Allied coordination, the Committee of Public Safety rushed twelve thousand reinforcements to Flanders and ordered General Jean Houchard to lead a fifty thousand-man relief force to Dunkirk. Carnot ordered Houchard to attack immediately whether or not the army was fully prepared. He and his colleagues realized that French strategic security required a victory in Flanders. The Committee was also aware that the Parisian *sans-culottes,* who had already lashed out against the Crown and the Brissotins because they failed to produce military victories, wanted and expected a triumphant fall campaign.[37] Thus an immediate victory was not only a strategic necessity but also the key to political survival.

A loyal but not very talented officer, Houchard abandoned a plan to capture Furnes and encircle the Allied army in favor of a direct thrust at Dunkirk. On September 6 his columns attacked Hanovarian posts covering the siege works, but despite murderous combat they failed to penetrate the duke's lines. In conjunction with a sortie by the Dunkirk garrison, Houchard attacked again on September 8. Covered by light infantry, the columns advanced against the Allied posts around the village of Hondschoete. While the troops from Dunkirk prevented the duke of York from reinforcing his covering force, Houchard's men broke through the Hanovarians and stormed into Hondschoete. That evening the duke, having lost three thousand men, abandoned the siege and withdrew to Furnes and Ypres. Houchard followed, saw that he could not dislodge the Allies from Ypres, and decided to attack the Dutch forces around Menin. In conjunction with the Lille garrison he assaulted and took Menin on September 13.[38] The French then moved on Courtrai, but Coburg, who had just taken Quesnoy, rushed reinforcements to Flanders. On September 15 an Austrian cavalry attack crushed the French left wing and forced the French to fall back to Menin. The duke of York then sent a column from Ypres to Menin, and its arrival forced Houchard to continue his retreat all the way back to Lille. The Committee then removed Houchard from command. Assuming that his failure to destroy the duke's army and hold Menin were conscious acts of treason, the government tried and executed him.[39] The Battle of Hondschoete, despite its limited results and the subsequent failure around Menin, was, nevertheless, a turning point in the war. The committee had halted an Allied offensive, gained time to build up its armies, and demonstrated to the public its ability to win.

In October the French switched their main efforts to the Sambre River area where Coburg was attacking Maubeuge, an important fortress useful as an advance base for a march on Paris. The Committee attached enormous importance to Maubeuge's salvation. The fortress was critical to the defense of north-central France, and failure to relieve it might anger the *sans-culottes* and lead to another popular insurrection. Carnot personally went to the front to assist General Jourdan, a battalion commander who had become a general and replaced Houchard in command of the army of the North.

While Carnot requisitioned supplies, Jourdan gathered forty-four thousand men and advanced on Wattignes, a fortified village in the Austrian siege lines.[40] On October 15 Jourdan attacked, but Coburg's cavalry cut through the French skirmishers and slashed into the assault columns. The republicans retreated with severe losses, but Jourdan reorganized his men and attacked again on October 16. Despite the facts that the seventeen thousand-man garrison in Maubeuge remained passive and the army's attacks were poorly coordinated due to the inexperience of many of the commanders, one of the columns battled its way into Wattignes and, supported by a twelve-gun artillery battery, repulsed Austrian counterattacks. Shaken by the violence of the French attacks that cost the army of the North some three thousand men, Coburg decided to retreat even though the Austro-Dutch forces were still largely intact. On October 17 he gave up the siege and withdrew into Belgium.[41]

Although the army of the North did not gain a complete tactical victory at Wattignes, the battle was strategically decisive. The French blunted a second Allied offensive and gained security from invasion for the rest of the year. The battle boosted civilian morale and gave the Committee additional time to complete the nation's military and economic mobilization.

On other fronts the French were equally successful in halting the Coalition's offensives. In the Rhineland the French tried and failed to cross the Rhine around Strasbourg on September 12. Two days later the army of the Rhine drove a small Austrian force out of the Vosges, but on September 18 French attacks failed to make any progress. The Prussians then attacked the Moselle army at the end of the month. They pushed the French out of the Saar and began to move on Weissemburg. On October 13 the Austrians joined the Prussian drive on Weissemburg. The combined assault forced the French to evacuate their positions and pull back to defensive positions around Strasbourg. After Wattignes, Carnot rushed reinforcements to generals Hoche and Pichegru, commanders of the French armies in the east. Hoche with the thirty-five thousand-man Moselle army moved forward in an attempt to raise the Prussian blockade of Landau, but on November 17 Brunswick drove off the attack. The Prussians then pulled back to stronger positions around Kaiserslautern. Hoche followed, attacked on November 28, but failed to dislodge his enemies. Hoche attacked again on November 29 and 30, but on each occasion the Prussians repulsed his troops, inflicting heavy losses.[42] The Rhine army, meanwhile, attacked the Austrians, but Pichegru, too, failed to dislodge the Hapsburg troops. The Committee then sent additional troops to Hoche and ordered him to leave a covering force facing the Prussians and link up with Pichegru. The combined force would then attack the Austrians and retake Weissemburg. In mid-December the French began their offensive. In a series of sharp clashes they forced the Austrians to retreat and on December 26 forced them from their fortifications around the city.[43] French troops also held back the Sardinians in Savoy, and along the Pyrenees constant counterattacks managed to halt the Spanish advance on Perpignan.[44] Thus by the end of 1793 the French had halted the Allied offensives on all fronts.

Meanwhile, in the interior, republican forces defeated the counterrevolution. The federalist's revolts collapsed quickly. Many departments voluntarily restored the Convention's authority, and others capitulated after sporadic resistance. By early autumn only the Vendée, Lyons, and Toulon continued to defy the Republic.

Fighting in the Vendée was exceedingly bitter, because both sides commonly shot prisoners and executed civilian opponents. Republicans drowned priests in the Loire, and royalists buried alive wounded prisoners. The tide turned in the Republic's favor when the Mainz garrison returned to France on parole. Since, according to the parole terms, the troops from Mainz could not fight against the Allies for a year, the Committee sent them to the Vendée. In mid-September the Mainz army and the army of Brest began to advance into the center of the rebel-held region. Royalist commanders quickly mobilized the peasant soldiers and ambushed the republican columns as they moved south from Nantes. By

September 22 the royalists had inflicted over two thousand casualties on the Convention's troops and halted their advance. The Republicans then reorganized their forces, combining the Mainz army and units operating around La Rochelle into an army of the West with thirty-two thousand men. In October the new formation advanced into the Vendée from coastal positions while other detachments entered the region from the south and east.[45]

Moving carefully, searching forests and ravines for ambushes, the Republican forces by mid-October reached the central Vendée and hemmed the royalists in near Cholet. On October 16, while fighting raged at Wattignes, the royalists, thirty-five thousand strong, tried to storm Cholet and break out of the republican trap. The army of the West massacred the Vendeans as they rushed toward the village. Thousands of royalists perished, and the peasant guerrillas, their forces shattered, tried to flee the Vendée. About sixty-five thousand soldiers and civilians crossed the Loire into Brittany on October 18. The Bretons, however, failed to join the Vendeans in large numbers, leaving the rebels but one viable alternative—capture a port and obtain arms and supplies from the British fleet. On November 13 the Vendeans tried to take the port of Granville, but the garrison repulsed them. In despair the royalists fled back toward the Vendée. The republicans pursued them and sent other detachments to block the passages over the Loire. The army of the West caught and defeated the royalists near LeMans and on December 23 annihilated the remnants of the Catholic and Royal Army near Savenay.[46] Some rebels escaped from the slaughter and returned to their homes, where they resorted to small-scale guerrilla warfare. The republicans had, however, destroyed the main counterrevolutionary forces and uprooted the royalist civilian organization. The Vendeans could still harass republican forces, but they no longer posed a serious military threat to Paris.

In the Rhone Valley the Convention's forces, forty thousand strong, invested Lyons on September 17. After a lengthy bombardment by a hundred guns, the city fell on October 9. Republican authorities then undertook a purge of royalists and Brissotins, slaughtering their foes with cannon fire in wholesale lots. The Committee then sent reinforcements to General Dugommier who, with the assistance of his artillery commander, Major Napoleon

Bonaparte, was organizing the siege of Toulon. By December 18 thirty thousand French troops had seized positions from which Bonaparte's artillery could bombard the harbor. The Allied position became untenable, and in the evening the British blew up the arsenal, burned twenty-one French warships, and evacuated the port. On the morning of December 19 French troops reentered Toulon.[47] With Toulon's recapture the Republic had crushed its domestic enemies and freed thousands of men for service against the Coalition's armies.

As the Committee prepared for the 1794 campaign, deepening rivalries continued to plague the Coalition. Poland's dismemberment remained as the major irritant within Allied ranks, and Austro-Prussian rivalry in the east hampered the Coalition's ability to combat France.

To many Poles the Second Partition and the continued presence of Russian troops in what remained of their state was a constant affront to their pride. Magnates, petty nobles, and members of the middle class began to form resistance organizations, and local cells established communications among themselves. They also contacted patriots who had left the country after the Second Partition. One prominent refugee, Thaddeus Kosciusko, went to Paris in search of French aid but aside from expressions of sympathy obtained nothing. The resistance groups, however, continued to prepare a rebellion and chose Kosciusko as their commander in chief.[48]

In Warsaw the Russian garrison commander gained fragmentary information concerning Polish plans. He began to jail suspects and disbanded several suspect Polish regiments. The Poles then decided to strike before the Russians completely disrupted their organization, and in March, 1794, a Polish regiment near Krakow launched the rebellion. Kosciusko returned on March 24 and issued a call for a general insurrection. On April 4, with a force of regulars and peasants armed with scythes he defeated a small Russian detachment, and word of his victory convinced thousands to join the uprising. Warsaw drove out the Russian garrison on April 16, the Russians pulled back into the Ukraine to await reinforcements, and Vilna's inhabitants joined the rebellion.

The eastern courts responded with massive force. Seeking to

avoid subversion in his newly won Polish provinces and intent on grabbing additional territory, Frederick William sent fifty thousand troops to take Warsaw. Catherine also amassed a large invasion force. While their enemies prepared to strike them down, the Poles failed to establish internal unity. One group of rebels, led by the king and conservative magnates, wanted only to shake off foreign domination. Otherwise they intended to preserve the social and political *status quo*. A second faction of gentry, officers, bureaucrats, and professional men sought both national freedom and social reform. Some of them even advocated the emancipation of the serfs. Kosciusko attempted a compromise that would satisfy both groups. He advocated granting the serfs personal freedom but retaining the manorial system and personal labor obligations for peasants who remained on noble-owned land. The plan, however, served only to alarm the conservatives and disappoint the reformers and peasantry.[49] Consequently, the Poles lacked cohesion at the very moment when their survival as a nation was at stake.

The Prussians, meanwhile, took Krakow and then marched on Warsaw. By July 2 the Prussians and a Russian corps were ready to storm the city, but Catherine, intending to capture Warsaw herself, refused to assist the Prussian attack. Polish insurgents then captured a Prussian supply and artillery convoy, and Frederick William had to withdraw. With the Prussians out of the way Catherine ordered her armies to advance. On October 10 the Russians defeated the main Polish army and captured Kosciusko. On November 4 the Russians entered the outskirts of Warsaw, slaughtered the defenders, and forced the city to surrender two days later.[50]

Even before Poland's final defeat, Catherine had decided upon the total extinction of Polish independence. The czarina, however, wanted to deny Prussia a major share of the spoils. She decided to arrange the final partition with Austria in order to limit Prussian expansion and perhaps convince Vienna to revive the scheme to dismember the Ottoman Empire. Anxious to check Berlin and gain compensations to offset the results of the Second Partition, Vienna eagerly responded to St. Petersburg's overtures. The Prussians insisted upon retaining Krakow and all Polish territory up to the Vistula. The Russians rejected these demands, and the Austrians sent over twenty thousand troops to Galicia to lend credibility to their own claims to Krakow and other provinces in southwestern Poland. Talks and threats continued for the remainder of the year, but on January 3, 1795, Austria and Russia signed the Third Partition treaty. The two powers divided most of Poland between themselves, leaving a small portion to Prussia. The treaty also included an Austro-Russian alliance against Prussia in case Berlin attempted to alter the settlement by force. The Prussians refused to accept the treaty leaving the issue to fester for more than a year.[51]

Austro-Prussian rivalry in the east had an important impact on the western battlefields. The two courts kept over seventy thousand troops, vitally necessary in Belgium and the Rhineland, in the east. Moreover, Austrian dealings with Russia so angered the Prussians that Frederick William refused all but minimal military cooperation in the west and began to contemplate a separate peace with the Republic. Thus the Coalition had to meet French offensives with its own forces deeply divided.

In drawing plans for the spring campaign the Committee of Public Safety decided to make their greatest strategic efforts in Belgium and rejected plans, presented by field commanders and deputies, that called for offensives into Germany and Italy. The Committee had already concluded that Austria and England were the Republic's most implacable enemies and would make peace only after suffering decisive military reverses. Since the British and Austrians had their main field armies in the Low Countries, the French decided to seek a decision there. The Committee was also aware of the growing rift between Prussia and Austria and began to hope that Prussia would soon desert the Coalition. By striking into Belgium and limiting their blows in the Rhineland the French sought to encourage the peace party in Berlin. Military factors also influenced the republican strategy. The largest Allied armies served in the Low Countries, and, if successful, they could advance across the northern French plain and threaten Paris. On the other hand if the French triumphed in Belgium, they could with relative ease defeat their enemies on other fronts.[52] The Committee thus devised a strategy that, if successful, would fulfill the nation's diplomatic and strategic requirements.

In February, 1794, Carnot completed the plan of organizing

the Republic's soldiers into demibrigades consisting of one regular and two volunteer-conscript battalions. He reinforced the armies in northern France and told the generals to concentrate their forthcoming attacks against a few carefully selected Allied positions. The object was not so such to seize important points, but rather to force the Coalition's field armies to come to their defense and fight on terms and terrain chosen by the French.[53]

The Allied line, consisting of a series of closely linked fortified posts, ran from Ypres through Denain and Valenciennes and from there to the Meuse. The line then followed the Meuse to Namur and ran from there to Trier. More than 150,000 English, Dutch, Austrian, and imperial troops held the posts and served in the mobile field forces. Carnot decided to attack the Allies in Flanders and on the Meuse while standing on the defensive in the center. He therefore directed 75,000 men, the left wing of Pichegru's army of the North, to advance on Ypres and Ghent and after taking these towns wheel east and march on Brussels. Part of the army of the North, 30,000 men, was to hold the central portion of the French line. On the right 64,800 men drawn from the armies of the North, Ardennes, and Moselle, the latter under Jourdan's command, were to march on Charleroi and Namur. The Committee told its generals to avoid slowing their advance by getting involved in sieges, to mask enemy garrisons with small detachments, to seek decisive battlefield encounters, and to pursue and destroy any defeated field army.[54]

The Allies, despite divisions within their ranks, also organized a spring offensive. Vienna convinced Sardinia to attack along the Alps by promising Turin territorial compensation at French expense. In return the Austrians claimed Milan. The British meanwhile agreed to pay Frederick William a subsidy in exchange for the participation of sixty-two thousand Prussian troops in the spring battles. Berlin, however, refused to cooperate closely with London and Vienna, and Frederick William rejected all plans to employ Prussian regiments in Belgium. Without these reinforcements Coburg had little choice but to resume his earlier strategy of attacking fortresses in northern France in order to exhaust the republicans and open a path to Paris.[55]

Coburg intended to take Le Cateau and Landrecies and then attack Cambrai, the last important bastion between his army and

Paris. He began his advance on April 17, and on April 21 defeated a French force marching to relieve Landrecies. On April 26 he defeated a second rescue force, inflicting four thousand casualties on the French, and surrounded the city. Three days later the French opened their offensive. Some twenty-five thousand troops pushed aside an Austrian covering force, took Courtrai, and pushed forward and surrounded Menin. On April 30 the allied garrison fought its way out of the city but not without severe casualties. On the same day the Austrians took Landrecies.[56] The initial battles thus ended in a draw. Coburg succeeded in the center while the French triumphed in Flanders. Neither side, however, had managed to seize the strategic initiative. Consequently, the antagonists resumed their attacks with renewed ferocity.

In the first weeks of May the Allies tried to recapture Menin and Courtrai. On May 10 Austrian cavalry shattered several demi-brigades near Menin, but Pichegru brought fresh troops forward and halted the Allies the next day. Alarmed by the deteriorating situation in Flanders, Coburg decided upon a major counter-thrust in that region. He gathered a force of about sixty thousand men and ordered it to shatter the French left and force the defeated remnants of the army of the North back against the North Sea.[57]

On May 17 the Austrians, organized into six columns, advanced against French units holding Tourconing. The columns, however, failed to coordinate their advance, and the French escaped from Tourconing with few casualties. The republicans then halted several isolated columns and prepared a counterattack. On the morning of May 18, sixty thousand French troops moved on Tourconing while flanking units pinned down Allied forces outside of the town. The French stormed into the town, inflicted heavy casualties on the defenders and compelled a second Allied force to flee hastily to avoid encirclement. Coburg then ordered his entire force to retire to Tournai.[58] Pichegru followed and on May 22 attempted to storm the city. He inflicted four thousand casualties on Coburg's army but lost sixty-five hundred men and failed to capture Tournai.[59] He had, nevertheless, scored a major victory. He gained the initiative in Flanders and forced Coburg to shift reserves from the Sambre-Meuse area at precisely the moment when the French were ready to unleash the second part of their offensive. The strategic balance had thus shifted, for the French were attacking from the Channel to the Meuse while the Allies could do little more than try to fend off the republican offensives.

Under the watchful prodding of Saint-Just, one of Robespierre's most trusted colleagues, French troops first crossed the Sambre River on May 11. Sharp Austrian attacks two days later forced the French to abandon their bridgehead. The day's fighting cost the Austrians twenty-eight hundred men, and the French lost four thousand.[60] Urged on by Saint-Just, the army of the North's right wing and the Ardennes army crossed the river again on May 20, but the Austrians launched another counterattack and drove the French back. The republicans suffered an additional four thousand casualties.[61] Renewed attacks on May 26 withered away under devastating Austrian artillery barrages. Another assault on May 29 carried the French to the walls of Charleroi, but on June 3 thirty-five thousand Dutch and Austrian troops forced the republicans to retreat.[62]

Despite their defeats in the Sambre-Meuse area the French still retained the strategic initiative and quickly switched their efforts back to the Flanders front. Learning that Coburg had sent a large portion of his reserves to the Sambre, Pichegru on June 1 advanced and invested Ypres. On June 10 and June 13 his troops repulsed Allied relief expeditions, and the Ypres garrison capitulated on June 17.[63]

Carnot, meanwhile, organized a new offensive on the Sambre. He placed Jourdan in command of the right wing of the army of the North, the Ardennes army, and the army of the Moselle. He then reinforced this new force, later known as the army of the Sambre-Meuse, to a strength of ninety-three thousand men, and ordered Jourdan to advance and seek a decisive encounter with Coburg's field army.[64]

On June 12 Jourdan crossed the river and advanced on Charleroi. Driven back with a loss of three thousand men on June 16, he renewed his assault two days later and finally secured a permanent foothold on the Austrian side. The Sambre-Meuse army then invested Charleroi in order to draw Coburg into a major battle. The prince rose to the bait and raced to Charleroi's relief, but he was too late. On June 25 the twenty-eight hundred-man garrison surrendered to the French.[65]

On June 26, 1794, Coburg led his seventy thousand-man force against Jourdan's army in an attempt to recapture Charleroi and drive the French back across the Sambre. The republicans took up positions in a rough semicircle in front of Charleroi. Their flanks rested on the river and their battle line passed in front of Fleurs, a small village from which the ensuing battle derived its name. The Austrians came forward in five large columns, and fighting raged throughout the day. Coburg pushed hard against the French center. His men broke through, but Jourdan's artillery held back the Austrians while the general gathered reinforcements. Fresh demibrigades plus six cavalry squadrons advanced and regained the lost ground.[66]

The Austrians also penetrated the French right, driving a division back across the river. The commander of the division next to the defeated formation's left sent three infantry battalions, twelve guns, and a cavalry regiment to cover his exposed flank. Midst burning wheat fields and flaming villages the French in savage hand-to-hand fighting slowed the Austrian advance. Jourdan rushed reinforcements to the threatened segment of his line and, after more bitter fighting, stopped the Austrians.[67] By nightfall Jourdan had lost seven thousand men, but he had held his ground, retained control of Charleroi, defeated Coburg, and inflicted about ten thousand casualties on the enemy.[68]

After the defeat of their field army, the Allies could no longer hold Belgium. All along the front French armies surged forward their numbers and speed, making it virtually impossible for the Coalition's forces to regroup and form a new front. The Allies could do little more than conduct a series of rearguard actions. Pichegru's command took Bruges on June 29, Ostend on July 1, and Mons on July 2, and entered Brussels on July 9, where it linked up with the Sambre-Meuse army. Jourdan's men also took Namur, which fell on July 16.[69]

In Paris the Committee devised an occupation policy designed to strengthen the state's strategic frontiers and reduce the possibility of future invasions. The Committee ordered its generals to disarm all Belgian civilians regardless of their political convictions and levy contributions upon the rich. The Committee also informed the military that the Republic intended to annex strategic portions of Belgium, and Carnot advocated incorporating Belgian territory along a line running from Antwerp to Namur. The Committee also planned to annex the rest of Belgium at a later date or transform it into a satellite republic closely tied to France.[70]

Meanwhile, the French armies continued to advance. Pichegru raced north for the Dutch frontier while Jourdan turned east and followed the Austrians toward Germany. Even the political crisis in Paris, which led to Ropespierre's death and the virtual destruction of the Committee of Public Safety, did not halt the French armies. On July 27, the day Robespierre fell from power, Pichegru's men entered Antwerp, and Jourdan's army took Liège.[71] In August the French recaptured the fortresses taken by Coburg in 1793 and 1794, while Pichegru prepared to invade the United Provinces and Jourdan advanced to the Rhine.[72]

The French were equally successful on other fronts. Counting on the fact that Austro-Prussian rivalry would prevent the Allies from embarking on a major campaign in the Rhineland, the Committee ordered the Rhine and Moselle armies to stand on the defensive from April to July. Their prediction was correct: Frederick William refused requests to send reinforcements to Belgium and confined his activities to guarding the Rhineland. The Prussians did advance around Kaiserslautern, and the Austrians launched a few probing attacks in the Rhine Valley. The French pulled back a few of their more exposed divisions, but throughout the spring and early summer, no major campaign harassed the Republic's eastern frontiers.[73]

After victory in Belgium, the Committee reinforced the Rhine and Moselle armies to a combined strength of seventy-five thousand men. A general offensive in early July failed, but the Committee sent additional reinforcements and called for renewed efforts. With ninety thousand men the republicans on July 12 and 13 destroyed three battalions of Prussian grenadiers and forced the rest of Frederick William's army back toward the Rhine. The Prussian retreat uncovered the Austrian flank, and Hapsburg troops had to join the withdrawal. Unwilling to fight what he now regarded as Vienna's war, Frederick William refused further combat and ordered his army to evacuate the Rhineland. French troops entered Kaiserslautern on July 17 and Trier on August 9.[74] In mid-September the Prussians and Austrians in a rare moment of cooperation advanced suddenly from Mainz toward Kaiserslautern. They took the town after mauling several French divisions, but the Prussians again withdrew from the Rhineland, leaving the Austrians to defend Mainz.[75]

In the south the armies of Italy and the Alps held off Sardinian attacks and even managed to seize several important passes connecting France and Italy. Along the Pyrenees the republicans obtained reinforcements and with fifty-five thousand men drove the Spanish from French territory, invaded Catalonia, and took San Sebastian. Only at sea did the Allies obtain even modest victories. The British after leaving Toulon invaded and occupied Corsica. On the high seas the French organized a grain convoy in American ports of over a hundred ships. The Brest fleet then put to sea to escort the convoy to safety, and the British fleet set out to capture or destroy the grain vessels. The British intercepted the French battle fleet at the end of May. Recognizing England's naval superiority, the republican admiral sought only to draw the British away from the convoy. He accomplished his task in a running battle lasting from May 28 to June 1, and although the French battle fleet suffered heavy losses, the convoy with twenty-four million pounds of flour reached port safely. In the Caribbean the English took the Windward Isles but failed to conquer Saint-Domingue and Guadeloupe.[26] Limited triumphs at sea were, however, not sufficient to offset the Coalition's defeats in Europe.

The Committee of Public Safety had effectively organized France for war and, taking advantage of rifts within the Coalition, had devised a strategy that brought victory to French arms. The Republic's citizen soldiers using flexible, effective tactics executed successfully the government's plans.[77]

NOTES

Chapter 3

1. See R. R. Palmer, *Twelve Who Ruled,* for an excellent description of the problems facing the leaders of France in 1793.

2. Jacques Godechot, *Les institutions de la France sous la Révolution et l'Empire,* p. 260.

3. Ibid., pp. 260–61.

4. Georges Lefebvre, *La Révolution française*, pp. 346–47.

5. Palmer, *Twelve Who Ruled*, supplies biographical data on all of the members of the Committee. There are numerous biographical works on the individual members, including J. M. Thompson, *Robespierre;* Albert Mathiez, *Études Robespierristes*, 2 vols. (Paris: 1917–18) ; E. N. Curtis, *Saint Just Colleague of Robespierre* (New York: 1935) ; Leo Gershoy, *Bertrand Barere A Reluctant Terrorist;* and Marcel Reinhard, *Le Grand Carnot.*

6. The text of this and other decrees may be found in F. V. A. Aulard, ed., *Recueil des actes du Comité de Salut Public avec la correspondance officielle des représentants en mission*, vol. 7 (which covers the period September 22–October 24, 1793) ; see also J. H. Stewart, *A Documentary Survey of the French Revolution*, pp. 479–81.

7. Aulard, *Recueil des actes*, vol. 9; and Stewart, *Documentary Survey*, pp. 481–92.

8. Godechot, *Institutions*, p. 264.

9. Henri Wallon, *Les représentants du peuple en mission et la justice révolutionaire dans les départments*, vol. 1; and Aulard, *Recueil des actes*, vols. 1, 3.

10. Aulard, *Recueil des actes*, vols. 3, 6.

11. Stewart, *Documentary Survey*, p. 472. The full text of the decree is to be found in Stewart's book, pp. 472–74, and in Aulard, *Recueil des actes*, vol. 6.

12. Stewart, *Documentary Survey*, pp. 472–74.

13. Ministère de la Guerre État-Major de l'Armée Archives historiques, Situations générales, 1791–1802, carton B1244 (hereafter, Min. de la Guerre, AH) .

14. Ibid.

15. Archives nationales, AF II, carton 212, dossier 1808, recapitulation générale des armées de terre (hereafter, AN) .

16. Min. de la Guerre, AH, Organization générale de l'armée 1793, carton X84.

17. Ibid.

18. Steven T. Ross, "The Development of the Combat Division in Eighteenth Century French Armies," *French Historical Studies*, vol. 4, no. 1 (1965) .

19. On the evolution of French infantry tactics see Robert Quimby, *The Background of Napoleonic Warfare;* Spencer Wilkinson, *The French Army before Napoleon;* Peter Paret, *Yorck and the Era of Prussian Reform 1807–1815;* and Jean Colin, *La tactique et la discipline dans les armées de la Révolution.*

20. Paret, *Yorck*, points out that old regime armies also employed light infantry, but only for specialized and limited missions. The French used skirmishers as an integral part of their tactical system. See Jourdan to Gen-

eral Duquesnoy, October 14, 1793, in Min. de la Guerre, AH, Armée du Nord et des Ardennes Correspondance, October 1–19, 1793, carton B120. In his message, Jourdan told his subordinate that the untrained volunteers were well suited to function as light infantry and that the army should employ large numbers of skirmishers.

21. Paret, *Yorck,* pp. 66–67. See also Pierre Caron, *La défense nationale de 1792 à 1795.*

22. For biographies of the French generals see Georges Six, *Dictionnaire biographique des généraux et admiraux français de le Révolution et de l'Empire.* For a discussion of the social origins of revolutionary generals and of methods of promotion see Georges Six, *Les généraux de la Révolution et de l'Empire.* Between 1804 and 1815 Napoleon appointed twenty-six marshals. Twenty-four of them had become generals prior to 1800. Seventeen were generals by 1794.

23. For general studies of French economic life during the Revolution see S. E. Harris, *The Assignats;* R. G. Hawtrey, *Currency and Credit;* F. L. Nussbaum, *Commercial Policy in the French Revolution* (New York: 1923) ; and R. B. Rose, "The French Revolution and the Grain Supply," *Bulletin of the John Rylands Library* vol. 39 (1956) . On the development of economic controls see Stewart, *Documentary Survey,* pp. 441–45, 469–72; and AN, AF II, carton 77, dossier 571, which contains lists of import and export permits.

24. See Palmer, *Twelve Who Ruled,* chap. 10, for a description of the French war economy. Stewart, *Documentary Survey,* pp. 492–501, contains the texts of the forced loan and the General Maximum law.

25. See Camille Richard, *Le Comité de salut public et les fabrications de guerre.*

26. AN, AF II, carton 27, dossier 217 contains orders for the establishment of new plants, contracts for weapons, and requisitions. AN, AF II, carton 214A, dossier 1835, also contains contracts and plans for industrial expansion to produce more rifles.

27. See AN, AF II, carton 214B, dossier 1839. This dossier contains requisitions of manpower and material for work in war industries and orders to scientists to find and publish the most modern production techniques.

28. Archives des affaires étrangères, *Mémoires et documents,* vol. 652 (hereafter, AAE) .

29. Min. de la Guerre, AH, Armées du Nord et des Ardennes, Correspondance 16–30, September, 1793, carton B119, contains the order for conduct in conquered regions. It is dated September 18, 1793.

30. AAE, Mémoires et documents, vol. 321, contains an order, dated April 21, from the Committee to the commander of the army of the North telling him to cease peace talks because their continuation would undermine both morale and secret diplomacy.

31. A report from the foreign minister to the Committee of July 1, 1793,

set forth the divisions within the Coalition. It appears in AAE, Mémoires et documents, vol. 321. The Committee's foreign policy was set forth later in the year in a position paper found in AAE, Correspondance politique, vol. 651.

32. A. R. von Vivenot, *Quellen zur Geschichte der Deutschen Kaiserpolitik Oesterreichs*, 4: 220, 355–58. See also Albert Sorel, *L'Europe et la Révolution française*, 3: 490.

33. See S. S. Biro, *The German Policy of Revolutionary France*, vol. 1; and Philippe Sagnac, *Le Rhin français pendant la Révolution et l'Empire*. For more general studies see Hajo Holborn, *A History of Modern Germany 1648–1840*.

34. For studies of British foreign policy see E. D. Adams, *The Influence of Grenville on Pitt's Foreign Policy 1787–1798;* Cyril Matheson, *The Life of Henry Dundas First Viscount Melville, 1742–1811;* J. Holland Rose, *William Pitt and the Great War;* and A. W. Ward and G. P. Gooch, *The Cambridge History of British Foreign Policy 1783–1919*, vol. 1.

35. The following works supply the background for the history of Haiti: Jules Deschamps, *Les colonies pendant la Révolution;* T. L. Stoddard, *The French Revolution in San Domingo,* is useful despite its racist bias; C. L. R. James, *The Black Jacobins,* presents a Marxist view of the revolution in Haiti.

36. For the course of the war and revolution in Haiti see Ralph Korngold, *Citizen Toussaint;* and Charles Moran, *Black Triumvirate*.

37. Min. de la Guerre, AH, Registre de l'État-Major général 18 août 1793 continuée jusqu'au 1 octobre suivant, carton B118.

38. See Houchard's report to the war minister in Min. de la Guerre, AH, Armées du Nord et des Ardennes, Correspondance 1–15 septembre 1793, carton B118.

39. For the order removing Houchard from command see Min. de la Guerre, AH, carton B119. The French removed many officers from command, including Jourdan, Hoche, and Bonaparte. Some, like Custine, perished. In dangerous circustances, governments often react strongly to any apparent threat to their security. For example, during the American Civil War a Congressional committee hunted for disloyal officers and even sent special agents to watch field commanders.

40. Min. de la Guerre, AH, carton B120; and Min. de la Guerre, A.H., Mémoires militaires du Maréchal Jourdan, campagne de 1793, Mémoires historiques, no. 608, (hereafter, MH) .

41. See Jourdan's report to the Convention and his report to the war minister in Min. de la Guerre, AH, carton B120.

42. Min. de la Guerre, AH, Armée du Rhin journal général des operations, 28 septembre 1792 jusqu'au 8 janvier 1794, MH, no. 322.

43. Min. de la Guerre, AH, MH, no. 322.

44. Min. de la Guerre, AH, Armée des Pyrénées orientales campagne de 1793, MH, no. 474.

45. Peter Paret, *Internal War and Pacification, The Vendée 1789–1796*, chap. 4.

46. Ibid.

47. On the fall of Lyons see Palmer, *Twelve Who Ruled*, chap. 7. On the general question of executions see Donald Greer, *The Incidence of the Terror during the French Revolution*. On the recapture of Toulon see the 1852 French staff study, Min. de la Guerre, AH, Précis historique sur le siège de Toulon en 1793, MH, no. 400. For a more recent account see D. G. Chandler, *The Campaigns of Napoleon*, pp. 15–29.

48. For the Background of the Polish Revolution see Jacques Godechot, *La Grande Nation*, 1: 182–87; and R. R. Palmer, *The Age of the Democratic Revolution*, 2: 146–56.

49. See General M. Kukiel, "Koscuiszko and the Third Partition," *Cambridge History of Poland*.

50. Ibid.; and K. Osipov, *Alexander Suvorov*. Suvorov led the Russian forces that took Warsaw.

51. See Vivenot, *Quellen zur Geschichte*, 4: 355–58; and Fedor Martens, *Recueil des traités et conventions conclus par la Russie avec les puissances étrangères*, 2: 238–48.

52. As early as July 1, 1793, the foreign minister noted the growing hostility between Austria and Prussia. See AAE, Mémoires et documents, vol. 321. Carnot decided to launch offensives in the north on February 2, 1794. See Min. de la Guerre, AH, Inventaire analytique, armées du Nord et des Ardennes, janvier–mars 1794.

53. Étienne Charavany, *Correspondance générale de Carnot*, 4: 279–80.

54. Charavany, *Correspondance*, pp. 282–83; see also the Committee's instructions to Jourdan of May 23 in Min. de la Guerre, AH, Mémoires militaires du Maréchal Jourdan, campagne de 1794, MH, no. 6082.

55. For negotiations concerning the subsidy to Prussia see Vivenot, *Quellen zur Geschichte*, 4: 100–101, 107–12, 121–23.

56. See Min. de la Guerre, AH, Exposé des opérations des Armées du Nord et de Sambre Meuse, 1794–95, MH, no. 280. For general secondary accounts see J. W. Fortescue, *A History of the British Army*, vol. 4, pt. 1; M. H. Coutanceau, *La campagne de 1794 à l'armée du Nord;* Louis Jouan, *La conquête de la Belgique, mai–juillet 1794;* and R. W. Phipps, *The Armies of the First French Republic*, vol. 1.

57. Min. de la Guerre, AH, MH, no. 280.

58. Ibid.

59. Min. de la Guerre, AH, MH, no. 6082.

60. Ibid.

61. Ibid.; and Min. de la Guerre, AH, Armées du Nord et de Sambre et

Meuse, Correspondance 1–13 juin 1794, carton B133. See also Min. de la Guerre, AH, Diverses sur les armées de la République, carton XP81.

62. Min. de la Guerre, AH, MH, no. 280.

63. Ibid.

64. Min. de la Guerre, AH, MH, no. 6082.

65. Min. de la Guerre, AH, Relation de la bataille de Fleurs livrée le 8 messidor an 2 (26 juin 1794), MH, no. 274; Min. de la Guerre, AH, Campagnes des armées du Nord des Ardennes et de Sambre Meuse (5 mai 1794–18 mars 1795), MH, no. 293; and Min. de la Guerre, AH, Armées du Nord et de Sambre et Meuse, Correspondance 16 au 30 juin 1794, carton B134.

66. Min. de la Guerre, AH, carton B134.

67. Ibid.

68. Min. de la Guerre, AH, MH, no. 280.

69. See Carnot's orders to Pichegru of June 18 in Min. de la Guerre, AH, carton B134.

70. Min. de la Guerre, AH, MH, no. 280.

71. Ibid.

72. Min. de la Guerre, AH, carton XP81.

73. Ibid.

74. Ibid.

75. See Joseph Ferval, Campagne de la Révolution française dans les Pyrénées orientales; Édouard Duceré, L'armée des Pyrénées occidentales; Fortescue, History of the British Army, vol. 4, pt. 1; A. T. Mahan, The Influence of Sea Power upon the French Revolution and Empire, vol. 1; and Louis Chevalier, Histoire de la marine française sous la première République.

76. Vivenot, Quellen zur Geschichte, 4: 130.

77. Friedrich von der Goltz, Militarische Schriften von Scharnhorst, pp. 35–36, 52–53, 223–26.

4

Muted Victory

The fall of Robespierre's government and the dismemberment of the Terror's administrative apparatus led to a steady decline of the army's strength. Supplies and pay became sporadic, desertions increased, and the *levée* no longer worked effectively. Consequently, the army's rolls shrank rapidly. By the end of 1795 there were but 450,000 men ready for action and only 346,000 by the winter of 1796.[1] Nevertheless, the momentum of earlier victories enabled the Republic to maintain the military initiative.

Late in the summer of 1794 the army of the North invaded the United Provinces. The Dutch army, its morale shattered, collapsed. Strong fortresses surrendered after *pro forma* resistance, and the French traversed strong river lines against minimal opposition. Nor did the coming of winter halt the republicans. They continued to push ahead against ever weakening Dutch resistance while the British army with its German contingents retired to Hanover, leaving the United Provinces to their fate. A widespread network of Dutch revolutionary societies assisted the French advance. In January, 1795, republican cavalry charged across the ice and captured the Dutch fleet and Amsterdam; Stadtholder William V fled to England and local revolutionaries proclaimed the birth of the Batavian Republic[2].

The French then forced the new regime to declare war on England, maintain a French army on Dutch soil, accept *assignats*, cede Flushing and the mouth of the Scheldt to France, and pay

88

a large war indemnity.[3] The treaty was unpopular, but the stadt-holder's actions forced most Dutchmen to accept their alliance with France. Upon arriving in England, William authorized the British to occupy all Dutch colonies and in secret correspondence with Dutch moderates refused to offer any political concessions in return for his restoration.[4] Consequently, the Dutch concluded that they could regain their colonies and preserve the gains of the Revolution only by fighting on the side of France.

France scored a second victory in 1795 when Prussia decided to leave the war. Alarmed by the Austro-Russian alliance, angered by their virtual exclusion from the final Polish partition, and anxious to ease the financial strain caused by the war, the Prussians opened secret talks with the French at Basel on November 24, 1794.

At first, Prussian councils were divided between those who sought peace in the west, even at the price of extensive concessions, in order to free the state's resources for use in the east, and those who opposed any treaty that did not include the rest of the Empire.[5] The French were also divided. Royalist deputies tried to win popular support by capitalizing on the nation's growing war weariness. They became the party of peace and called for renunciation of all conquests coupled with a restoration. A faction of moderates and constitutional monarchists advocated limited annexations but were willing to sacrifice most of the nation's territorial gains in return for peace. Republicans and regicides, on the other hand, sought a victorious peace. They needed victory to maintain popular support and to justify to the public the years of sacrifice and bloodshed. Republicans also believed that the expansion of the nation's frontiers would bring economic benefits, improve France's strategic security, and balance Austrian, Prussian, and Russian gains in the east.[6]

At the outset the Prussians hesitated to make large concessions in the west, but upon learning the details of the third Polish partition treaty, Frederick William decided to break the deadlock in the Basel talks in order to obtain a rapid peace in the west. On April 5, 1795, French and Prussian diplomats signed a treaty wherein France agreed to abandon all conquests on the Rhine's right bank but retained control of the left bank except for Mainz, which the Austrians controlled. In a secret article the two powers agreed that if France kept the left bank after concluding peace with the rest of the Empire, Prussia and other princes, who sacrificed provinces in the Rhineland, would take compensations on the right bank. A supplementary agreement to the Basel treaty signed on May 17 provided for the neutralization of German territory north of the Main River. Prussia was to guarantee the neutral status of northern Germany.[7]

By the Treaty of Basel the Republic obtained recognition from one of Europe's major powers. The Republic also concluded a peace with this power, ruptured the Coalition's unity, and received a promise of Prussian backing for claims to the Rhineland. Prussia failed to alter the situation in Poland and finally had to adhere to the Third Partition. On the other hand, Berlin ended a serious financial drain and gained a dominant position in northern Germany for the next decade.

Prussia's defection from the Coalition was but the first of a series. Tuscany left the war, and Spain also decided to conclude a treaty of peace with France. By mid-1795 Madrid was alarmed at the growth of British economic and political influence in the Mediterranean and Caribbean. The Spanish felt that England posed a threat to the security of South and Central America and might also challenge Madrid's claims to a number of provinces in Italy. Spain therefore opened negotiations with the French at Basel.

The Spanish first proposed the creation of a kingdom for Louis XVII south of the Loire River. The French countered this incredible notion by demanding extensive colonial concessions including Louisiana. Paris also unleashed an offensive that quickly penetrated to the Ebro. The French did not, however, pursue their success, for at this juncture they crushed an *émigré* expedition at Quiberon Bay. Although they defeated the royalist attempt to rekindle civil war in the Vendée and Brittany, the French began to worry about a revival of counterrevolutionary activity. Therefore, they decided to reduce the number of their enemies as quickly as possible. The Republic then modified its terms and on July 22, 1795, signed a treaty calling for the evacuation of Spanish territory and the retention of a single Spanish colony—Madrid's portion of Saint-Domingue. Spain in turn recognized the Republic, left the war, and by their defection administered still another blow to the Coalition.[8]

Encouraged by its diplomatic victories yet worried about the continuing possibility of renewed counterrevolutionary activity, the Convention decided to increase its popular prestige by settling Belgium's fate. On October 1, 1795, the deputies annexed Belgium.[9] They did not incorporate the Rhineland at this time, preferring to wait until they could tie the left bank's fate into a general settlement with the Empire.

Despite these French triumphs Austria and England continued to fight. In May, 1795, Pitt granted a large subsidy to Francis II, and in September Catherine joined the Coalition. The czarina made no military contribution save for a small naval squadron sent to cruise the North Sea, but her formal adherence to the Coalition reduced Vienna's concern over the balance of power in eastern Europe. Moreover, Prussia concluded that since England and Russia would support their ally, it was no longer possible to alter the third Polish partition. Berlin therefore accepted the treaty, a move that allowed Vienna to employ the bulk of its troops in the west.[10]

The French, meanwhile, decided to drive Austria out of the war by launching a large-scale offensive in Germany in the late summer of 1795. Carnot played a major role in devising the strategy for the forthcoming operation. Although he had left the Committee of Public Safety after Robespierre's fall, he continued to exercise his influence through a friend who took his place on the Committee. Since he had succeeded in 1794 by hammering at his enemies' flanks, he decided to pursue a similar policy in 1795. The government, therefore, ordered Jourdan to lead his ninety-one thousand-man Sambre-Meuse army across the Rhine. He was to take Dusseldorf and lay siege to Mainz. Pichegru was to lead the Rhine and Moselle army. His missions were to assist in the attack on Mainz and advance with the bulk of his ninety-six thousand-man army on Mannheim and Heidelberg.[11]

With both flanks in danger Carnot assumed that the entire Austrian army would have to retreat. The campaign itself was a disaster. The troops, lacking pay, supplies, and munitions, were ill-prepared for arduous campaigning. The operational armies were too far apart to support one another, and the commanders failed conspicuously to coordinate their movements.

Engaged in secret talks with the royalists, Pichegru refused to advance despite repeated orders from Paris to cross the Rhine. Jourdan also remained inactive. He felt that his men were not fit for combat and was reluctant to invade Germany without the support of the Rhine and Moselle army. Consequently, aside from the capture of Luxembourg, French armies achieved nothing during the summer of 1795.[12]

In September Jourdan undertook to act alone, and on September 6 the Sambre-Meuse army crossed the Rhine and advanced on Dusseldorf. Outnumbered, the Austrians fell back, and the city capitulated after a brief bombardment. Jourdan then led his army south, and by September 20 his forces stood on the Lahn River, a tributary of the Rhine lying north of the Main. Pichegru, after repeated orders from Paris, also began to move. His army crossed the Rhine and took Mannheim on September 20.[13]

Caught between two forces the Austrians decided to withdraw their right wing behind the Main, hold back Jourdan's army with a covering force, and attack Pichegru's divisions on the Neckar River. They crossed to the south bank of the Main on September 22 to 23. Jourdan followed and proceeded to invest the Mainz garrison from the right bank, but Pichegru failed to move rapidly and decisively. Instead of sending a strong force along the Neckar to take Heidelberg, the gateway to south Germany and the main Hapsburg supply depot, he dispatched only two divisions. Moreover, he directed these formations to move along both banks of the river despite the fact that Heidelberg lay on the southern bank. Separated by the river, the divisions could not support each other, and the Austrians were quick to seize their opportunity to defeat the French in detail. On September 24 they crushed both divisions and, having secured Heidelberg, concentrated men for a thrust at Jourdan.[14]

Jourdan and Pichegru met on October 2 to devise a new battle plan. Jourdan agreed to stand on the Main while Pichegru moved north from Mannheim, but once again Pichegru failed to support his fellow general. The Austrians advanced against Jourdan and turned his left flank by marching through neutralized Germany. Pichegru remained inactive, and Jourdan had to retreat. He began his withdrawal on October 16, abandoned his blockade of Mainz, and recrossed the Rhine.[15]

The Austrians then struck at Pichegru. On October 18 a surprise attack hurled the Rhine and Moselle army all the way back to Mannheim. The Austrians next reinforced Mainz and on October 29 struck into the Rhineland. Taken by surprise, the French lost three thousand men and retreated back to Worms. On November 10 seventy-five thousand Austrians struck again and forced the French all the way back to Landau and Kaiserlautern. The Austrians also attacked Mannheim, forcing the nine thousand-man garrison to surrender on November 21. Jourdan attacked the Austrian bridgehead in the Rhineland, but upon hearing of Mannheim's fall, he canceled further attacks and pulled back behind the Nahe River, a tributary of the Rhine flowing northeast and entering the Rhine north of Mainz.[16] When both sides agreed to an armistice on December 15, the Austrians held a firm position in the Rhineland stretching from Mannheim in the south to Kaiserslautern in the west and along the Nahe to the north and east. Launching a blow against the enemy's flanks with two widely separated armies enabled the Austrians to operate on interior lines and strike with superior forces against each French army in turn. Pichegru's constant refusal to support Jourdan had compounded the problems inherent in Carnot's original plan and produced a severe setback for French arms in Germany.

The French had better success in Italy. Two armies, the Alps and Italy, with thirty thousand men fended off Austrian and Sardinian attacks throughout the summer. In late autumn after the Austro-Sardinian army went into winter quarters, Barthelemy Schérer, commander of the army of Italy, launched a surprise attack against Loano, an Austrian depot on the Mediterranean coast. On November 23 André Masséna, who knew the area well, led a division through the mountains north of Loano, and the following day another division moved to attack Loano from the east. The assault succeeded, and, leaving eight thousand casualties behind, the Austrians pulled back to Genoa.[17] The French had captured positions from which to launch offensives into Piedmont but lacked the men to follow up their victory. Furthermore, triumphs on a secondary front did not offset the grave defeats in Germany.

Military defeat also ruined the plans of the newly installed Directory to negotiate with Austria and England. Threatened by monarchists and Jacobins, the Directory sought a victorious peace to rally popular support for the regime, but neither Austria nor England were willing to make concessions. Encouraged by the results of the recent campaign, Vienna decided to continue fighting.[18] London, despite growing popular hostility to the hardships of war, also decided to fight rather than consent to French expansion.[19]

In the forthcoming campaigns of 1796 the Directory planned to strike at both Austria and England by launching expeditions in Germany, Italy, and Ireland. Having joined the Directory, Carnot again played a major role in devising French strategy. In Germany he decided to repeat his typical approach of striking at his enemy's flanks. Although a similar plan failed in 1795, he nevertheless ordered the Sambre-Meuse army to advance along the Main, and the Rhine and Moselle army with Moreau in command to attack along the Danube. The two armies were to drive in the Austrian wings, combine their forces, and move toward Vienna. The Directory also commissioned a secret agent to organize revolutionary conspiracies in south Germany in an attempt to frighten local princes into leaving the war and perhaps convince the Hapsburgs to negotiate to avoid subversion in their own lands.[20]

Although it regarded Italy as a secondary front, the Directory ordered General Bonaparte, the new commander of the army of Italy, to attack Piedmont, force the court of Turin out of the war, and invade Lombardy.[21] The army of Italy was then to advance into the Tyrol and join the armies operating in Germany for a final thrust at Vienna. As in Germany, the Directors planned to employ political subversion as part of their strategy. Charles Delacroix, the foreign minister, held secret talks with Italian radicals early in 1796. He promised to assist them, but instructed Bonaparte to direct subversive activities only against those states actually at war with France.[22] The Directory also told the civilian commissioner with the army of Italy to make extensive requisitions in northern Italy. Requisitions would hamper French relations with Italian democrats but would assist the Republic's armies and damage Hapsburg resources.[23] On July 25, 1796, Delacroix presented a policy paper to the Directory outlining a settlement with Austria. France would compel Vienna to recognize the Republic's conquest of Belgium and the Rhineland. In return Austria would take Bavaria; the duke of Bavaria would receive Tuscany, Modena, Ferrara, and part of the Papal States, and the duke of Parma would obtain Milan.[24] The Directory then told Bonaparte that while working with Italian radicals he should not create permanent republican regimes because France intended to use Italian provinces as bargaining counters in a broader settlement with Vienna.[25]

Military developments, however, radically altered government policy. In Germany, the main front, French armies collapsed, while in Italy, the secondary zone of operations, Bonaparte scored a brilliant series of victories and proceeded to change the Directory's plans to suit his own wishes.

On May 31 Jourdan led 78,000 men across the Rhine and marched for the Lahn. By June 6 most of the Sambre-Meuse army had arrived on the Lahn. Archduke Charles, one of the most able Hapsburg generals, decided to withdraw from the Rhineland and meet Jourdan's army on the Lahn. Leaving a garrison in Mainz, the Austrians moved quickly to the south bank of the Lahn. Jourdan then withdrew back across the Rhine. The archduke followed and thereby weakened his forces south of Mannheim at the moment when Moreau's 79,500 men were preparing to cross the Rhine.[26]

On the night of June 23 Moreau began his crossing around Strasbourg, but he was too late to take advantage of Jourdan's retreat that pulled Charles north. Jourdan recrossed to the French side of the river on June 22. If Moreau had advanced while Jourdan was still on the right bank, he would have placed the Austrians in a dangerous position. By moving so late, he enabled the archduke to withdraw from the Rhine and march against the Rhine and Moselle army with 85,000 men.[27]

Despite the looming danger of Austrian counterattacks, Moreau, who usually alternated periods of intense activity with long spans of sloth, chose to linger in the Rhine Valley. By July 5 his army had gotten only as far as Rastadt, where the archduke attacked and routed several divisions. Four days later the French won a minor clash near Rastadt, and the archduke, fearing that

Moreau might swing north and pin his army against the Neckar River, retreated eastward.[28]

The Austrian retreat enabled Jourdan to cross the Rhine again. The Sambre-Meuse army crossed the river on June 28, reached the Lahn on July 7, crossed the river on July 9, and took Frankfurt on July 16. Jourdan then detached 28,500 men to blockade Mainz and other fortresses along the Rhine and led the rest of his army along the north bank of the Main toward Nuremberg. By August 18 Jourdan's men had taken Bamberg, Nuremberg, and Amberg.[29]

The Rhine and Moselle army also began to advance. One wing moved south to push into Bavaria while the rest moved due east. The French took Ulm on August 8 and clashed with Charles's army north of the Danube on August 11. Moreau's southern wing, meanwhile, achieved significant political victories by forcing Baden, Württemberg, Swabia and Franconia to conclude peace with the Republic.[30]

On the Danube the archduke crossed to the south bank, intending to draw Moreau after him and then swing rapidly north and fall upon Jourdan. Had Moreau pursued closely, he could have frustrated this scheme, but he waited until August 19 to follow the Austrians north of the Danube, and it was not until August 22 that he entered Augsburg, where his southern wing rejoined him. Moreau then moved toward Munich on August 24, but by this time the archduke with sixty-two thousand men had outdistanced the Rhine and Moselle army and was ready to attack Jourdan.[31]

The Austrians struck at the Sambre-Meuse army's right flank and sent additional regiments to take Nuremberg and cut the French off from the Rhine. Jourdan retreated quickly and avoided the trap. Jourdan, however, was unwilling to retire from Germany without a fight. Moreover, the Directory ordered him to remain on the right bank of the Rhine as long as possible in order to support Moreau. He therefore concentrated his army north of the Main around Würzburg and on September 3 prepared to offer battle. Charles was also anxious to fight, and his superior numbers enabled him to win. Leaving two thousand casualties behind, the French had to retreat back to the Lahn, enabling the Austrians to raise the sieges of the Rhine forts.[32]

Moreau, meanwhile, did nothing to relieve the pressure on the

Sambre-Meuse army, thereby enabling Archduke Charles to continue his offensive. On September 16 the Austrians fought their way across the Lahn, forcing the French to retreat to the Rhine. By September 20 Jourdan was back on the left bank, where he resigned his position in disgust at Moreau's refusal to act decisively to help his battered divisions.[33]

Having defeated Jourdan, Charles next turned on Moreau, who had begun to retreat to the Rhine on September 19. The French on October 2 defeated Austrian units that had remained in Bavaria while Charles moved north, and by October 12 the Rhine and Moselle army had traversed the Black Forest, reached the Rhine, and turned north to cross the river at Strasbourg. Charles's troops also reached the river north of the French and moved to defeat the republicans before they reached Strasbourg. Clashes on October 19 and 20 between the city and the Swiss frontier were indecisive, but Moreau grew disheartened. He retreated south and crossed the Rhine on October 24 just north of the Swiss border.[34]

At this point Charles wanted to send reinforcements to Italy and drive the French from the Po Valley, but Vienna ordered him to remain in Germany and reduce French bridgeheads on the Rhine's right bank. The French garrison in Mannheim held, but troops in Kehl across the river from Strasbourg suffered heavy losses. On January 9, 1797, the Republic signed an armistice with the Austrians to end fighting on the Rhine until spring. The terms included the evacuation of Kehl. Another fortress near Switzerland fell on February 5, providing a gloomy finish to a disastrous campaign.[35]

Carnot, inflexibly reproducing the strategic approach of 1794 and 1795, provided his commanders with a flawed battle plan, because the two armies operated at too great a distance from one another to be mutually supporting. Moreau's persistent failure to act quickly prevented any tactical rectification of the poor strategic situation. French strategy and tactics enabled the archduke to operate from an interior position and to defeat each army separately. The defeat in Germany in turn dislocated the Directory's diplomatic policy, and enabled Bonaparte to play a critical military and diplomatic role as his army scored brilliant triumphs in Italy.

When he took command of the army of Italy, Bonaparte had at

his disposal some forty-five thousand men and sixty field guns. His divisional and brigade commanders, including Masséna, Berthier, Joubert and Augereau, were able veterans, but his soldiers were ill supplied, unpaid, and demoralized. The army of Italy faced forty-five thousand Sardinian and thirty-seven thousand Austrian troops.[36]

Since he lacked numerical superiority, Bonaparte decided to wage a hard-hitting, fast-moving campaign relying on shock and surprise to offset lack of mass. He, therefore, assigned seven thousand men to make demonstrations near Genoa to attract the Austrians while the rest of the army raced north from the Riviera into Piedmont. His immediate objectives were to split the allied armies, drive Piedmont out of the war, and then invade the Lombard plain where supplies were plentiful.[37]

On April 12, 1796, the Austrians advanced to counter the French moves near Genoa, and Bonaparte struck north at Montenotte. The army of Italy shattered a six thousand-man Austrian force, and leaving a division to guard their right, the French continued north. The next day, however, Austrian and Sardinian troops halted the army of Italy at Cosseria. With Sardinians in front and Austrians concentrating on the right, Bonaparte had to move quickly to avoid destruction. Since the Austrians were not fully prepared, the Corsican shifted reserves to his right, struck at Dego on April 14, drove the Austrians from the town, and took nearly five thousand prisoners. Reinforcements stormed back into Dego, but renewed French assaults on April 15 retook the village. On the same day Cosseria's garrison surrendered, thus opening the way into Piedmont.[38]

As the French resumed their northward advance the Sardinians fell back to guard Turin. After a number of heavily contested rearguard actions that cost the army of Italy more than one thousand men, the French by April 21 were nearing Turin.[39] The king of Sardinia-Piedmont then appealed for an armistice, which Bonaparte granted on April 28. The Armistice of Cherasco required Sardinia to conclude peace with the Republic, to allow the French to garrison several important fortresses, and to grant the army of Italy free passage into Lombardy. On May 15 Sardinia-Piedmont signed a definitive peace treaty with France. The monarch ceded Nice and Savoy to the Republic, accepted the continued presence of French detachments in his cities, and paid a heavy indemnity to Paris.[40]

Meanwhile, Bonaparte was advancing into Lombardy. The Austrians had taken up positions behind the Ticino River, a tributary of the Po. To avoid a costly frontal attack Bonaparte decided to march along the Po's southern bank, cross to the north bank behind the Austrians, and cut them off from Milan. On May 7 the army completed its dash and began to cross the river at Piacenza.[41] The Austrians, however, had already begun to withdraw behind the Adda, another tributary of the Po. The Hapsburg commander intended to cover Milan and left a strong rearguard at Lodi to hold the main route across the Adda. Anxious to capture Milan and defeat the Austrian army, the Corsican tried to rush the bridge. On May 10 French troops swarmed onto the bridge, but Austrian artillery slaughtered them. Officers rallied their men and, covered by sharpshooters who picked off the Austrian gunners, led a second assault. The French took the bridge and drove off an Austrian counterattack. Although Bonaparte failed to crush the Hapsburg army, he did dislodge them from the Adda and opened the way to Milan. On May 15 French troops entered the city.[42]

After occupying the city, the Corsican lost little time in pursuing his foes. At the end of May the army of Italy crossed the Mincio River and forced the Austrians back behind the Adige. The army of Italy then advanced to Mantua. The Austrians left a twelve thousand-man garrison and three hundred artillery pieces in the city and retreated north along the shores of Lake Gardia. Bonaparte sent detachments to observe the Tyrol and established a blockade of Mantua.[43]

Bonaparte also sent troops into central Italy to force princes there to come to terms with the Republic.[44] Terrorized by the French advance, the king of Naples sought an armistice with France in June, and Venice agreed to allow the French to enter Verona. The army of Italy then invaded the Papal States, levied contributions amounting to more than a million francs, and seized hundreds of cannon and thousands of muskets from Papal arsenals. On June 23 the pontiff signed an armistice with the invaders and promised to conclude a peace treaty with Paris, to close his ports to ships belonging to states at war with the Republic, to surrender the citadel of Ancona, to hand over numerous works of art, and to pay an indemnity of fifteen million francs in cash and five million in goods. Millions of francs flowed west to refill the Directory's treasury, but additional millions remained in Italy to enrich the French generals and, to a much lesser degree, the common soldiers. The army of Italy also forced Parma and Modena to disgorge huge sums, invaded Tuscany, occupied Leghorn, and seized British goods in the port. At Milan the Austrians in the citadel surrendered. The French extracted twenty-five million francs from Lombardy and crushed antirepublican uprisings in Milan and Pavia.[45]

As he conquered north and central Italy Bonaparte began to organize the newly won regions. He worked closely with Italian republicans largely because representatives of the old regimes had either fled or refused their cooperation. To secure their political objectives Italian radicals had to help the French keep order and obtain supplies. Moreover, Bonaparte hoped that his cooperation with democrats in Italy would frighten Vienna into negotiating to avoid the spread of revolutionary ferment into Hapsburg crown lands. Bonaparte also realized that he could enhance his growing prestige by adding political accomplishments to his impressive military record.[46]

His first step was to establish a Lombard provisional government run by Italian democrats. In Central Italy rebellions broke out as the French advanced, and the old order collapsed. Bonaparte then set up additional republican-dominated regimes and, at the end of 1796, united Bologna, Ferrara, Modena, and Reggio into a single entity known as the Cispadane Republic.[47] The new republic and the Lombard regime were provisional governments, but their creation marked the first steps in the establishment of a permanent French presence in Italy.

The Hapsburgs, meanwhile, organized a counteroffensive, appointing Count Würmser to lead the attack. An Alsatian who had been battling with remarkable success against republican generals since 1793, Würmser gathered a force of fifty thousand men in Trent by the end of June. The count planned to relieve Mantua by sending units down each shore of Lake Gardia and a third corps down the Brenta Valley. By July 29 Austrians on the eastern shore of the lake had driven Masséna's division from

Verona, and on August 1, Würmser's men on the western shore arrived at Brescia. Bonaparte realized that he had to strike quickly before Würmser united his forces, broke through to Mantua, and obtained an unbeatable numerical superiority. He, therefore, took a bold decision to abandon the siege of Mantua and concentrate all his manpower against the divided Austrian forces.[48]

Leaving one division to check the Austrians on Lake Gardia's eastern shore, Bonaparte attacked the enemy on the western shore and on August 3 defeated them at Lonato. He then sent Masséna's division east to reinforce Pierre Augereau, and the combined force, thirty thousand strong, defeated twenty-five thousand Austrians at Castiglione on August 5. With two of his three columns defeated Würmser had no choice but to fall back into the Tyrol, and on August 7 the French reentered Verona. Würmser had managed to slip reinforcements into Mantua, but Bonaparte quickly renewed his blockade and prepared to advance into the Tyrol.[49]

The Austrians, however, readied another offensive of their own. Würmser assembled twenty thousand men and led them down the Brenta Valley toward Mantua, avoiding his earlier mistake of scattering his forces. Bonaparte left ten thousand men to watch Austrian forces in the Tyrol and led twenty-two thousand troops south in order to circle around Würmser's force and hit it from behind. On September 8 the French inflicted a sharp defeat on Austrian rearguards at Bassano, taking four thousand prisoners and thirty-five guns. Würmser escaped annihilation and reached Mantua, but Bonaparte's men were close behind, and no sooner had Würmser entered the city than the French closed in and renewed their investment. Instead of serving as a base for offensive operations, Mantua became a giant trap for twenty-three thousand Hapsburg troops. Short of rations, the garrison began to suffer from starvation, and hundreds started to perish from disease and hunger.[50]

Victorious in Germany, Vienna resolved to launch a third offensive to regain its dominant position in Italy. Forty-six thousand reinforcements marched to Italy where Baron Joseph d'Alvintzy planned to lead twenty-eight thousand troops to Bassano and from there to Verona. At Verona eighteen thousand men from the Tyrol would join him, and the united force would then relieve Mantua. Bonaparte responded by concentrating the bulk of his army before Verona, leaving covering units in the Tyrol. On November 4, however, the Austrians routed the French blocking detachments near Rivoli, and the Corsican had to weaken his striking force to reinforce his shaken left wing. Bonaparte then assailed Alvintzy's troops, but on November 12 the Austrians

ITALY AND SWITZERLAND 1796-99

inflicted twenty-seven hundred casualties on the army of Italy and forced it back to Verona.[51]

The French position was desperate: Alvintzy was ready to advance, and the force in the Tyrol was also pushing forward. Defeat in either sector would result in the army of Italy's destruction. In adversity Bonaparte resolved upon a desperate plan. Leaving a small force in Verona, he withdrew across the Adige and then marched south intending to recross the river, circle behind the Austrians, and seize their convoy and field park. Robbed of food and munitions Alvintzy would have to abandon his offensive.[52]

By November 15 the army of Italy was crossing the Adige and moving on the Austrian encampment located at Arcola. Croatian light infantry with artillery support stopped the French at a causeway leading into Arcola. The French suffered heavy losses, but their attack frightened Alvintzy, who abandoned his advance on Verona and withdrew to the east. New attacks on November 16 failed to take Arcola, and both sides lost heavily. Bonaparte attacked again on November 17. Masséna's division moved into a swamp west of Arcola. Masséna then exposed a demibrigade to lure the Austrians into a trap. The Austrians rushed the lone unit, and the rest of Masséna's troops ambushed the unsuspecting enemy and then fought their way into Arcola. Meanwhile, Augereau's division also advanced on the town, while a flanking unit moved to strike the Austrians from behind. As these units advanced, Alvintzy decided to flee. The army of Italy lost forty-five hundred men but inflicted seven thousand casualties on the Austrians and fended off still another Hapsburg offensive.[53] Bonaparte then raced north to strike at the Austrian units coming from the Tyrol, but they retreated without offering battle.

Determined to drive the French from Italy, Vienna ordered another advance to relieve Mantua and recover Lombardy. Alvintzy gathered twenty-eight thousand men in the Tyrol and prepared to march to Mantua by way of Rivoli. Separate detachments totaling fifteen thousand men were to mount diversionary attacks in the Brenta and Adige valleys. This division of effort gave Bonaparte still another opportunity to concentrate and strike against a single segment of the Austrian army. The Corsican had, meanwhile, received reinforcements and left three thousand men at Verona, ten thousand before Mantua, and ten thousand along his supply lines, and led over thirty thousand men to Rivoli.[54]

On January 14, 1797, the army of Italy met Alvintzy's main force. Ably supported by light artillery that poured withering fire into the advancing Austrians, the French infantry stemmed their advance. An Austrian unit then outflanked Bonaparte's battle line, but reinforcements coming up from the south crushed Alvintzy's flanking column. The next day the French attacked and sent the Austrians reeling back into the Tyrol with a loss of fifteen thousand men. The victory at Rivoli also sealed Mantua's fate. Bonaparte led his men back to the city, beat off a sortie, captured a relief column, and tightened his siege lines about the city. On February 2, 1797, Würmser capitulated. Only sixteen thousand men of a garrison of thirty thousand were fit to march out of Mantua and into captivity.[55]

After Mantua's fall, Bonaparte, acting on orders from Paris, sent troops into the Papal States to force Pius VI to sign a treaty with France. On February 19 the pope, his army unable to resist the French advance, signed a treaty giving up Ancona, Bologna, Ferrara, and Romagna in Italy and Avignon in France. The pontiff also agreed to pay a thirty million franc indemnity.[56] Bonaparte then unleashed an offensive into Austrian territory, while in Germany French armies were also on the move.

The Directory gave General Hoche command of the Sambre-Meuse army in February and ordered him to lead his seventy-eight thousand men across the Rhine, blockade the Austrian fortresses, and march to the Danube. Moreau's Rhine and Moselle army, fifty-seven thousand men strong, was also to advance to the Danube. The combined force was then to march toward Bohemia and, in conjunction with the army of Italy, threaten the Hapsburg crown lands.[57]

On April 15 the Sambre-Meuse army crossed the Rhine, and three days later Hoche attacked the Austrians near Bonn. Making good use of his artillery, Hoche dislodged the Austrians from their field fortifications, inflicting five thousand casualties on them. He then pushed north to the Lahn and wheeled east in pursuit of the retreating Austrians. He also directed other units to advance on Frankfurt. Meanwhile on April 20, Moreau's army crossed the river and, in two days of bitter fighting that cost the

French three thousand and the Austrians six thousand casualties, took Kehl. The Rhine and Moselle army then began its eastward drive, but halted upon receiving word that Bonaparte and the Austrians had concluded an armistice.[58]

The successful double assault convinced Vienna to seek an end to hostilities. They asked Bonaparte for a truce, and the Corsican, anxious to pull back from his exposed position in Austrian territory and determined to enhance his fame by concluding peace with the Hapsburgs, agreed to negotiate. The Directory had earlier sent a political agent to Italy. He was to conduct talks with the Austrians and secure Belgium and the Rhineland for France, giving up the Republic's Italian conquests in return. Bonaparte, however, altered this policy to gain a quick peace and retain parts of Italy. He dropped Paris's demand for the Rhineland and asked instead for Belgium and Milan, granting to Austria the Venetian Mainland, Istria, and Dalmatia. Venice in turn was to obtain compensation from the Cispadane Republic. Bonaparte and the Austrians signed the preliminary Treaty of Leoben on April 18, 1797, and the Directory, in need of military support against a rising tide of domestic royalist sentiment, reluctantly ratified the agreement.[59]

Bonaparte then transformed the provisional regime in Lombardy into the Cisalpine Republic and shortly thereafter merged the Cispadane Republic into the new state. Next he transformed Genoa into the Ligurian Republic, conquered Venice in order to facilitate its transfer to Austria, and concluded a final peace with the Hapsburgs.[60]

Because of the creation of the Cisalpine Republic, the Treaty of Campoformio, signed on October 18, 1797, differed in detail from the earlier agreement. France and Austria obliterated Venice entirely. Austria took Dalmatia, Istria, the city of St. Mark, and the Venetian mainland up to the Adige. The Cisalpine Republic took the rest of the mainland, and France obtained the Ionian Islands. Vienna also agreed to give up Belgium and call an Imperial Diet to conclude peace between the Republic and the Empire. In a secret article Francis agreed to use his good offices to secure the Rhineland for France, while Austria and princes with Rhennish provinces took compensations in Germany.[61]

The Directory again accepted Bonaparte's unilateral changes

in its foreign policy because it needed military support and lacked firm control over its generals. The Republic abolished the use of representatives on mission after Thermidor. Civilian commissioners replaced the deputies but lacked the authority to control the military. The power of strong-willed generals grew rapidly after 1794. Moreover, the republican directors in September had relied upon officers and men from Bonaparte's army to purge royalists from the Directory and the legislative councils. The directors, therefore, were in no position to repudiate the general who had just saved the regime and won great popularity by forcing Austria out of the war. France thus obtained Belgium, but received only vague and unenforceable promises about the Rhineland's fate, and had to accept the burden of protecting Bonaparte's Italian conquests. The Hapsburgs had no intention of permanently sacrificing either the Rhineland or central Italy. Vienna was willing and anxious to renew the struggle at the first favorable opportunity, and the Campoformio treaty was therefore merely an armed truce.

The French were no more successful in forcing England to come to terms. The Directory did strike a number of telling blows against Great Britain, but none were sufficient to compel Pitt's government to conclude peace.

The first French victory came in August, 1796, when Spain, fearing the continued growth of British imperial power and needing an ally that would support Spanish pretensions in Italy, joined the Directory and declared war on England. Madrid's move altered the power balance in the Mediterranean. The British had to evacuate Corsica and pull naval squadrons in the Mediterranean back beyond Gibraltar.[62]

Even more alarming than the setback in the Mediterranean was the growing French threat in Ireland. Irish discontent with British domination had been increasing for several years. The vast majority of the island's three million Catholics had long been hostile to their foreign Protestant overlords. Middle-class Catholics objected to their exclusion from political power, and the Catholic peasantry disliked the steadily rising rents common in the last decades of the eighteenth century.[63] Many among the nine hundred thousand Dissenters (Protestants who were not members of the established Church of Ireland) objected to their economic and political inferiority. Even within the ranks of the six hundred thousand established church members distaste for the landowning aristocrats, who dominated the Irish government, was spreading rapidly by the 1790s.[64]

In 1791 thirty-six men, drawn from the middle class and including both Dissenters and members of the Church of Ireland, established the United Irish Society at Belfast. A reformist group, the Society advocated enfranchisement for Roman Catholics and reform of the Irish Parliament. The Society grew rapidly. Lodges spread throughout Ireland, and members of the Catholic middle class joined in large numbers. At the same time a Catholic peasant organization, the Defenders, founded in 1784 during an agrarian civil war with Protestant landlords, renewed demands for lower rents and abolition of tithes paid to the Church of Ireland. In 1794 the Defenders agreed among themselves to cooperate with a French army if one ever landed in Ireland.[65]

The British responded to these threats with a mixture of reform and repression. In 1793 Britain granted suffrage to Catholics possessing a forty-shilling freehold but continued to refuse them access to high civil and military posts. Nor did the reform permit Catholics to sit in the Irish Parliament. In May, 1794, the government, after discovering correspondence between a French agent and some members of the Society, suppressed the Dublin lodge and began to treat other lodges as criminal organizations. An immediate result of this policy was a secret meeting of United Irish Society leaders. They decided that one of their number, Theobold Wolf Tone, a Protestant lawyer, would appeal to France for help in casting off British domination. Tone went first to the United States and from there set out for Paris. The British, meanwhile, suspended the *habeas corpus* act in Ireland, and the United Irishmen reconstituted themselves as a secret organization. Local lodges communicated with each other through roving deputies, and the Ulster lodge began to function as a *de facto* national directorate. The Society also created a secret military organization and in the summer of 1796 sent two representatives to France to assist Tone in his dealings with the Directory.[66]

Tone had already obtained interviews with Carnot, the minister of war, and General Hoche. As part of their strategy for 1796 the French agreed to help the Irish establish their independence and, as a sign of good intent, made Tone a brigadier general in the French army. Hoche then went to Switzerland where he met secretly with the two agents from Ireland and promised them that French help would arrive before the year's end.[67]

The directors then placed Hoche in command of a 13,900-man invasion force and ordered him to proceed to Ireland, where he was to assist Irish democrats in driving the British from the island and help establish an Irish Republic. In a set of secret orders the directors revealed their real objectives. They told Hoche to establish an Irish Republic *but* to keep control of the government in his own hands, because the Directory intended to employ Ireland as a pawn in subsequent negotiations with England. Paris wanted to use Irish radicals to drive the British from Ireland and then return Ireland to England once Pitt recognized French continental conquests.[68] The French also planned a subsidiary venture: a Black Legion, composed of several hundred convicts and adventurers led by an American soldier of fortune, was to land in Wales and create a republican Vendée as an additional lever against the British.[69]

Before embarking on the Irish venture, the Directory tried to negotiate with England, whose leaders, alarmed by setbacks in the Mediterranean, the defection of Spain, Austria's defeats, a steady financial drain, and a growing threat of revolt in Ireland, agreed to exploratory talks. On October 15, 1796, James Harris, first earl of Malmesbury, arrived at Lille, but in the ensuing talks neither side was willing to grant any major concessions. Consequently, in December the Directory ended the discussions, seeking instead a military solution to force its terms upon the British.[70]

In strategic terms the French expeditions failed, but on the diplomatic level they did coerce the British into serious negotiations. Hoche set sail from Brest in December, but storms dispersed his fleet. Some units reached the Irish coast at Bantry Bay, but Hoche remained at sea. The commander at Bantry Bay refused to attempt a landing in the rough seas, and the whole force eventually returned to France. The Black Legion did land in Wales in February, 1797, but surrendered immediately to the local militia.[71]

Despite its failure, Hoche's expedition convinced the Irish revolutionaries that the French were actively on their side, and they resumed their preparations for an armed uprising with renewed confidence. In 1797 the Society's lodges began to gather pikes and muskets and to drill secretly, and the Society also gained the support of the Defenders by adding the peasant's economic demands to its political program.[72] The Wales fiasco also had serious repercussions. When news of the raid reached London, thousands panicked and rushed to convert their paper currency into gold. On February 27 the government had to suspend specie payments on Bank of England notes.[73] News of Admiral Jervis's victory over the Spanish fleet near Cape St. Vincent on February 14 led to a temporary restoration of confidence, but soon new problems swept in upon the Cabinet.

Catherine of Russia died in November, 1796, and her successor, the half-mad Paul I, ceased to support the Coalition. The Leoben Treaty drove Austria, Britain's last important ally, out of the war, and sailors at Spithead mutinied. After the admiralty had heard their grievances and rectified some of them, the Spithead mariners returned to duty, but almost immediately afterward, seamen at the Nore rebelled against poor pay, bad food, brutal punishments, and bestial living conditions. The government did manage to restore order, but its confidence in the navy as the bulwark of Britain's security was severely shaken.[74]

Faced with defeat, Pitt and most of his colleagues concluded that it was necessary to reopen serious negotiations with Paris. The British did not, however, negotiate solely from fear. The Cabinet knew of the revival of French royalism and of the royalist electoral victories in balloting for seats in the legislative corps. The British hoped that the royalists would gain control of the Republic and make significant concesssions in return for peace. Pitt was willing to grant some continental gains to France but intended to retain most of Britain's extensive colonial conquests.[75]

When Malmesbury reopened peace talks with France at Lille on July 7, 1797, he discovered that the Republic's masters were indeed deeply divided. Republicans wanted a victorious peace and demanded that the British accept French annexation of Belgium and recognize the various satellite republics. Furthermore, the republicans wanted England to return colonies taken from the Dutch and Spanish. The republicans were willing to sacrifice some French colonies and contemplated giving part of

Portuguese Brazil to England or giving Britain several Batavian colonies and using portions of Brazil to indemnify the Dutch.[76] They were not, however, willing to give up Belgium or ruin their relations with their allies by signing away Batavian or Spanish colonies without compensation.

Royalists soon undermined the official royalist position. Under royalist pressure Talleyrand replaced Delacroix at the foreign office. Anxious to be on the winning side, the unscrupulous former cleric adopted the royalist diplomatic stance, which called for extensive concessions to England. At Lille Talleyrand and a royalist member of his delegation informed the British of the Directory's plans and assured them that royalism would shortly triumph in France and the new government would sign a treaty acceptable to Britain. Malmesbury, therefore, refused any concessions. Informed of the Directory's plan to use Portugal's colonies as bargaining counters, the British put pressure on Lisbon, and prevented the king from ratifying a peace treaty with France. Confident of an impending royalist triumph, the British sabotaged the Portuguese exchange plan and refused to deal seriously with the republicans.[77]

The coup of 18 Fructidor Year V (September 4, 1797) placed the republicans back in power. They firmly reasserted their original position, demanding the continental *status quo* of 1797 and the return of Spanish and Batavian colonies.* Malmesbury left Lille on September 15, and on October 6 Pitt officially announced the end of negotiations.[78] On October 11 the British fleet defeated a Batavian flotilla in the hard-fought battle of Camperdown. Reassured of the fleet's recovery from the recent mutinies, the Cabinet gained confidence in the country's ability to fight on alone.

By the end of 1797 France had won numerous military victories but had failed to conclude a successful peace. Lacking a broad basis of popular support, the Directory was unable to control effectively its generals and diplomats. Consequently, Pichegru in 1795 and Moreau in 1796 foiled Carnot's plans to defeat Austria in Germany and force Vienna out of the war. Bonaparte was able to devise his own political schemes in Italy and imposed them on the government, which relied upon his army to maintain the regime. Thus victory over Austria only set the scene for new

---

* Talleyrand again switched sides and become an ardent republican.

hostilities with the Hapsburgs. Telling blows against England convinced Pitt to negotiate, but again the Directory's internal weakness foiled chances to end the war. Royalists within the government convinced the British to refuse concessions, and the republican triumph in the Fructidor coup came too late to influence Pitt's policy. To win a victorious peace France had to continue fighting and defeat England before Pitt could form a Second Coalition. Victory was no closer in the winter of 1797 than it had been four years earlier.

NOTES

1. For the problems besetting the French armies see the reports of the minister of war in Archives nationales, AF III, cartons 149, 331, 332, 333, and AF III, carton *202 (hereafter, AN).

2. See R. R. Palmer, *The Age of the Democratic Revolution*, vol. 2, chap. 6; R. R. Palmer, "Much in Little: The Dutch Revolution of 1795," *Journal of Modern History;* and Petrus Blok, *A History of the People of the Netherlands*.

3. André Fugier, *Histoire des relations internationales*, vol. 4, *La Révolution française et l'Empire napoléonien*, p. 93.

4. H. T. Colenbrander, *Gedenkstukken des Algemeene Geschiedenis van Nederland van 1795 tot 1840*, 2: 831; and Palmer, *Democratic Revolution*, p. 188.

5. Fugier, *Révolution française*, pp. 92–93.

6. Raymond Guyot, *Le Directoire et la paix de l'Europe*, pp. 111, 114, 115–19; and Philippe Sagnac, *Le Rhin français pendant la Révolution et l'Empire*, pp. 118, 126.

7. Reports on the negotiations may be found in Archives des affaires étrangères, Correspondance politique, vol. 668 (hereafter, AAE). Terms of the treaty may be found in Fugier, *Révolution française*, p. 93. See also AAE, Correspondance politique, vol. 364.

8. See AN, AF III, carton 61, for the negotiations with Spain. On Quiberon Bay see Georges Lefebvre, *Les Thermidoriens*, chap. 8.

9. Fugier, *Révolution française*, p. 95.

10. A. W. Ward and G. P. Gooch, eds., *The Cambridge History of British Foreign Policy*, 1: 255; and Guyot, *Le Directoire et la paix*, pp. 94, 100–101.

11. See Ministère de la Guerre État-Major de l'Armée Archives historiques, Inventaire analytique Armées du Rhin et de la Moselle janvier-juin 1795

(hereafter, Min. de la Guerre, AH). This volume contains orders, troop strength, and action reports of the armies.

12. Min. de la Guerre, AH, Inventaire analytique Armées du Rhin et de la Moselle juillet–décembre 1795. Deeply involved with the royalists, Pichegru may well have delayed his advance purposely in order to assure Jourdan's defeat.

13. Ibid.

14. Ibid.

15. Ibid.

16. Ibid.

17. Min. de la Guerre, AH, Armée d'Italie, Campagnes de l'an IV et de l'an V, Mémoires historiques, no. 417 (hereafter, MH).

18. AN, AF III, carton *20; and Guyot, Le Directoire et la paix, pp. 133–37.

19. Guyot, Le Directoire et la paix, pp. 146, 155.

20. See Min. de la Guerre, AH, Précis de la campagne de l'armée de Sambre et Meuse pendant l'an 4, MH, no. 298; and S. S. Biro, The German Policy of Revolutionary France, 2: 573.

21. Antonin Dubidour, Recueil des actes du Directoire exécutif, 1: 717 ff. Bonaparte lost his command after Thermidor but restored his career after crushing a royalist uprising in Paris and marrying a former mistress of one of the directors.

22. Palmer, Democratic Revolution, pp. 269–70.

23. AN, AF III, carton 333.

24. See the secret deliberations of the Directory in AN, AF III, carton *20.

25. Ibid.; and AN, AF III, carton 442.

26. Min. de la Guerre, AH, MH, no. 298; and Min. de la Guerre, AH, Journal de la Campagne de l'an IV sous le commandement du général en chef Jourdan, MH, no. 287.

27. Min. de la Guerre, AH, Précis des opérations des armées de Rhin et Moselle et de Sambre et Meuse pendant la campagne de 1796, MH, no. 342.

28. Ibid.

29. Min. de la Guerre, AH, MH, no. 287.

30. Guyot, Le Directoire et la paix, p. 221. After concluding treaties with the south German Princes, the Directory abandoned further efforts to create revolutions on the Rhine's right bank.

31. Archdukes Albrecht and Wilhelm, eds., Ausgewählte Schriften des Erzherzogs Karl, 2: 219–20; Min. de la Guerre, AH, MH, no. 342; and Min. de la Guerre, AH, Campagne de 1796 sur le Rhin, MH, nos. 301–2.

32. Min. de la Guerre, AH, Campagne de 1796 sur le Rhin, MH, no. 333; Min. de la Guerre, AH, Précis des opérations des armées de Rhin et Moselle et de Sambre et Meuse pendant la campagne de 1796, MH, no. 342; and Min. de la Guerre, AH, Bulletin des operations de l'Armée de Rhine et Moselle,

MH, no. 348.

33. Min. de la Guerre, AH, MH, no. 342.

34. Ibid.

35. Ibid.

36. Min. de la Guerre, AH, Armée d'Italie campagnes de l'an IV et de l'an V, MH, no. 417.

37. Ibid.

38. Ibid.

39. Ibid.

40. Guglielmo Ferrero, *The Gamble Bonaparte in Italy 1796–1797*, pp. 18, 46.

41. Min. de la Guerre, AH, MH, no. 417.

42. Ibid.

43. Ibid.

44. Debidour, *Recueil des actes*, 2: 329–30.

45. Min. de la Guerre, AH, MH, no. 417; and Min. de la Guerre, AH, Inventaire analytique armées des Alps et d'Italie, mai–juin 1796, which contains detailed summaries of correspondence between the Directory and Bonaparte and Bonaparte's orders to his subordinates.

46. Ibid.

47. Palmer, *Democratic Revolution*, chap. 10.

48. Min. de la Guerre, AH, Campagne de l'an V en Italie, MH, no. 423; Min. de la Guerre, AH, Journal historique de quelques opérations militaires de l'Armée d'Italie, MH, no. 426; and Min. de la Guerre, AH, Inventaire analytique armées des Alps et d'Italie, juillet–septembre 1796.

49. Min. de la Guerre, AH, MH, nos. 423, 426.

50. Min. de la Guerre, AH, MH, no. 423.

51. Ibid.

52. Ibid.

53. Ibid.

54. Min. de la Guerre, AH, MH, no. 426.

55. Ibid.

56. Ibid.; and Ferrero, *The Gamble*, p. 155.

57. Min. de la Guerre, AH, MH, no. 348.

58. Ibid.

59. AN, AF III, carton 59.

60. Ibid.; Palmer, *Democratic Revolution*, chap. 10; and J. H. Rose, *The Life of Napoleon I*, chap. 7.

61. AN, AF III, carton 59.

62. AN, AF III, carton 56.

63. Constantia Maxwell, *Country and Town in Ireland under the Georges*, pp. 117, 139.

64. Ibid.

65. Richard Madden, *The United Irishmen, Their Lives and Times*, 1: 222–23, 233, 236; and William Lecky, *A History of England in the Eighteenth Century*, 7: 11–16.

66. Frank MacDermot, *Theobold Wolfe Tone, A Biographical Study*, pp. 116–17, 174; Madden, *United Irishmen*, pp. 389–90; and Rosamond Jacob, *The Rise of the United Irishmen 1791–1794*, pp. 230–31. See also *Report of the Committee of Secrecy to the House of Commons* (London: 1799), pp. 9–10; and Charles Vane, ed., *Memoirs and Correspondence of Vicecount Castlereagh, Second Marquess of Londonderry*, 1: 360.

67. Madden, *United Irishmen*, 2: 389–90.

68. AN, AF III, carton *20.

69. E. H. S. Jones, *The Last Invasion of Britain*, gives a complete account of this aspect of the Directory's plan. See also AN, AF III, carton *20.

70. Guyot, *Le Directoire et la paix*, pp. 288, 293–98.

71. See Jones, *Last Invasion*, and his work *An Invasion that Failed*, for an account of Hoche's expedition.

72. Lecky, *History of England*, 7: 224.

73. Jones, *Last Invasion*.

74. James Dugan, *The Great Mutiny*; and Christopher Lloyd, *St. Vincent and Camperdown*, chap. 6.

75. Guyot, *Le Directoire et la paix*, pp. 379, 389; Ward and Gooch, *British Foreign Policy*, 1: 274; and Charles Ballot, *Les négociations de Lille (1797)*.

76. Guyot, *Le Directoire et la paix*, pp. 412–15, 429–30.

77. Ibid., pp. 431–32, 438, 440–41, 447, 450–51, 454–55.

78. AN, AF III, carton 57.

5

Devising Global Strategy

By October, 1797, France, despite her failure to conclude a peace with England, was the dominant power in western Europe. On the shores of the North Sea, the armed forces of the Batavian Republic stood ready to cooperate with the Directory. From the Batavian border to the Main River, the French military frontier on the Rhine was safe, because neutral Prussia had guaranteed the neutrality of northern Germany. French troops protected the rest of the Rhine barrier from the Main to the Swiss border. Further south Bonaparte had forced Austria to sign the Treaty of Campoformio, wherein the Hapsburgs had recognized the French annexation of Belgium and agreed to call a Congress of the Empire at Rastadt to negotiate a final settlement with the German princes. In a secret article, Vienna agreed to support the Directory's demand for the left bank of the Rhine. The Congress would thus have the additional task of providing compensation to those princes who had given up territory in the Rhineland, and the French were confident that these negotiations would provide them with an opportunity to increase their influence in Germany.

The Campoformio treaty had also given France control of northern Italy, because Bonaparte had compelled Austria to recognize the French-dominated Ligurian and Cisalpine republics. Sardinia had capitulated in 1796, and a French garrison occupied the Citadel of Turin. The remaining independent rulers in the Italian peninsula lived in constant fear of seeing their states turned into "sister republics" through the actions of local revolutionaries aided by the French army of Italy.

The Republic in conjunction with its Spanish ally also dominated the Mediterranean, and together they had forced Pitt to evacuate Corsica and withdraw British naval units back into the Atlantic. No other power had sufficient naval strength to challenge the French position.

Russia and the Ottoman Empire had remained aloof from the First Coalition. Russia was hostile to the principles of the revolution and alarmed by the growth of French influence in the Balkans, but the czar was reluctant to face the Directory's armies alone. The Ottoman Empire was also hostile to the revolution, but the sultan's fear of Russia and Austria caused him to maintain correct if not cordial relations with France. Thus, from the North Sea to the Adriatic, France reigned supreme.

The only remaining enemy was England, and the Directory's political objective at the end of 1797 was relatively simple: to force England to capitulate before Pitt could organize a Second Coalition. To implement this policy, the French had two strategic alternatives. The first was an invasion of the British Isles. The second was an attack on England's colonies, which would ruin British trade and force Pitt to sue for peace because he could no longer finance his country's war effort.

The cross-Channel attack was the most decisive method of defeating England, but it involved grave risks. The French would have to concentrate an invasion fleet in the Channel ports and launch it against the most powerful navy in the world. The Royal Navy consisted of 120 ships of the line and 382 frigates and light craft served by 100,000 sailors and 20,000 marines.[1] The crews were well trained, and the officers were of the highest quality. The French fleet was simply no match for the British. It was vastly outnumbered, having but 57 ships of the line and 65 lesser craft.[2] The sailors, though brave, were poorly led because most of the officers of the Bourbon navy had emigrated. Those remaining were inexperienced and lacked the years of practical training that made their British counterparts so expert. Nor could the French call upon the Spanish and Batavian fleets, because at the end of 1797, the British had inflicted serious defeats on both of them. Thus despite the fact that the British had to maintain squadrons from Newfoundland to Bombay, they could still muster vastly superior forces in the Channel.

A French invasion was not, however, intrinsically impossible. Prior to the Revolution, the Bourbon monarchy had drawn up invasion plans.[3] The revolutionary government continued to believe in the possibility of invading England despite the decline in size and efficiency of its navy. In September, 1793, the Committee of Public Safety had instructed the minister of marine to prepare plans for an attack on the British Isles, and in October, General Hoche had advocated the descent of a 40,000-man expedition on England.[4] In December, 1796, he had led a 13,900-man force to the coasts of Ireland, and only bad weather had prevented his landing. In February, 1797, a small force had executed a successful landing in Wales. These events indicate that the Royal Navy was not infallible and that a landing in England, though dangerous, was feasible.

If the naval aspects of a cross-Channel expedition seemed dangerous, the directors and their advisors could look at the military side of the picture with much greater confidence. If a French army could land in England, it would in all probability be able to crush the British. The Directory had at its disposal 110 demibrigades of the line, 31 dragoon regiments, 25 chasseur regiments, 13 hussar regiments, 8 regiments of foot artillery, and 8 of horse artillery, a total of 365,000 men.[5] Despite a lack of supplies and money, and a growing weariness with years of constant fighting, the French army was still the most formidable fighting machine in Europe. The men were well trained, and many were veterans of numerous campaigns. The junior officers were excellent, and the Republic had at its disposal numerous competent and experienced army, divisional, and brigade commanders.[6] Since there was no longer any active campaigning on the Continent, the Directory could use a large percentage of these troops for an invasion of England. To face this threat, the British could muster about 342,000 men, but Pitt's government had to use some 103,000 militia and regulars to hold Ireland. Another 34,300 served in the West Indies, and 22,100 more were in India. Of the remaining troops in England, 62,200 were half-trained militia and 75,000 were untrained additional militia, both groups probably useless in combat. Thus the British had at their disposal only 46,000 regular troops for the defense of England, and if the campaigns of 1793 to 1795 were to serve as a basis of judging their worth, they would be no match for the French army.[7] Unable to face the French army in combat, England had to rely exclusively on her navy to protect her from invasion. The Directory for its part had to decide whether or not to take the risk of sending a large fleet composed mainly of troop laden transports into an area in which the British navy was generally dominant. The possibility of a disaster was present, but there was the chance of landing an army in England and dictating a final peace in London.

The second alternative, the destruction of England's commerce by an attack on her colonies, offered fewer risks of a major defeat but was not as potentially decisive as a march on London. If the French decided upon a colonial expedition, their logical objective would be the wealthy British holdings in India. To attack India, however, the French would first have to seize an advanced base in the Middle East, because their naval inferiority precluded them from employing the sea lanes around Africa. The best advanced base would be the Turkish province of Egypt, because it offered a route to India by way of the Red Sea. In addition, possession of the Egyptian coast would strengthen French influence throughout the Levant. A successful thrust from Egypt to India might also convince Pitt to reopen peace talks and give the directors excellent bargaining counters that they could trade for important continental concessions.

The French could not, however, be sure that colonial defeats would force the British to sue for peace, because England had suffered overseas disasters in past wars without surrendering. Furthermore, any overseas venture risked ripostes by the Royal Navy. Finally, any colonial expedition to the Middle East would alarm both the Turks and the Russians, because the two powers had vital interests and ambitions in the eastern Mediterranean. On the other hand a rapid conquest of Egypt might leave the sultan and the czar too shocked and intimidated to react. The promise of relatively easy victories in the Near East attracted many, and by the fall of 1797, several groups were already advocating an eastern expedition.

The first group consisted of merchants and consular officials directly involved in trade or official business in Egypt. Since the Middle Ages, the French had maintained extensive contacts with the Levant, and by the time of the Revolution, there were many French merchants and consular officials residing permanently in the major Egyptian cities. The government at Constantinople was unable to exert much influence over the Mamluk beys, the former slaves who had become the real rulers of Egypt. The merchants desired French control of the country, if only to obtain a stable regime that would let them carry on their trade in peace. French consular officials supported the merchants but also tended to take a broader view of the issues involved. In June, 1795, the French consul at Cairo, had written to the Republic's ambassador at Constantinople recommending that the French occupy Egypt to obtain commercial benefits and a base for operations against the British East India Company. The ambassador had sent a copy of the report to Paris.[8] In October, 1795, he sent another memo, this time to the Committee of Foreign Relations, again advocating the seizure of Egypt. The occupation of Egypt, he asserted, would not only bring France great commercial advantages, but would also provide a base for an assault upon British holdings in India. Control of the Red Sea by ships operating from Suez would enable France to get control of the Indies trade, and ten thousand troops leaving from Suez would, he assumed, be sufficient to take Bengal. Delacroix, the minister of foreign relations, showed some interest in these schemes and ordered inquiries as to their feasibility, but at this early date, France was too deeply involved in continental warfare to seriously contemplate an eastern expedition.[9]

Others besides those with direct local concerns took an interest in the possibilities of an eastern expedition. Talleyrand was one. Under the old regime, he had been interested in the Levant, and during the Revolution, he had realized the need for new colonies to increase French foreign trade. On July 3, 1797, he presented a paper to the Institute, in which he pointed out that in 1769 the ministers of Louis XV had planned to annex Egypt to replace the trade lost by giving up the North American colonies. The Republic, he said, could restore her trade by following the same plan.[10] On July 23 he presented a memorandum to the Directory, enlarging this concept by suggesting an attack on India in cooperation with local princes. Noel, the ambassador to the Hague, also favored an eastern expedition. At one point he recommended that the French and Batavians align themselves with the anti-British sultan of Mysore and launch a combined attack on English possessions in the East Indies.[11]

Several military men also expressed an interest in undertaking operations in the east. General Jourdan suggested that the Directory launch an attack on British India in conjunction with anti-British rulers. Admiral Villaret de Joyeuse also favored such a venture.[12] General Bonaparte had for many years been interested in the possibilities of an eastern venture, and as a young officer had been interested in the history of Egypt and the Levant.[13] During the period between the armistice at Leoben and the rupture of peace negotiations with England in October, he was temporarily inactive, and once again turned his attentions to schemes for campaigns in the east. He even commented to his secretary that, "there have never been great empires and revolutions except in the east."[14]

His interest in the east was more than reflective. While at Milan, he took books relating to the Near East and Egypt from the libraries and carefully underscored those passages relating to Egypt. He also discussed plans for invading Egypt with his divisional generals and obtained maps of the area, plus a collection of memoirs of voyagers in Egypt from the naval map section. On May 26, 1797, he sent a memo to the Directory recommending the seizure of Malta.[15] On August 16 he further advised Paris that to defeat England, France should occupy Egypt, a move that would also place control of the commerce of the Levant in French hands. He went on to say that the recently acquired Ionian Islands were worth more than all of Italy, because the Turkish Empire was on the verge of collapse, and from bases in these islands, France would be in an excellent position to seize a share of the spoils. On the same day, he wrote to the minister of foreign relations, telling him that by holding Corfu, France dominated the Adriatic, could contact Greek and Albanian malcontents, and could persuade them to call upon the Republic for aid when the Ottoman state collapsed. To implement this plan, he sent a flattering letter to the pasha of Albania, who was at the moment in revolt against the sultan.[16] Bonaparte had meanwhile taken practical measures to establish French influence in the islands, and on June 28, 2 battalions of infantry, 50 artillerymen, and 750 Italian troops landed on Corfu. They proclaimed a constitution modeled on the French constitution of the Year III, planted liberty trees, and established a departmental system. The French then installed a council under the leadership of a leader of the Corfu's democratic party.[17] The republicans next proceeded to prepare these islands plus Nicopoli and other ports on the Albanian coast as bases from which to launch propaganda or military operations in the Balkans. The advice and activities of Bonaparte and Talleyrand were also having their effect on French policy, because identical recommendations from two important figures in the government convinced the directors to consider seriously the idea of an eastern campaign.

Bonaparte wrote to Talleyrand on September 13. The memorandum, obviously meant for the directors, reiterated his earlier advice that France should never give up the Ionian Islands, went on to suggest the occupation of Malta in order to guarantee French control of the Mediterranean, and concluded with the suggestion that the loss of the Cape Colony could be replaced by the seizure of Egypt, an operation that could be carried out with twenty-five thousand men.[18] Talleyrand, speaking for the Directory, replied ten days later. He told Bonaparte that the government wished him to take Malta, and added that an attack might then be made on Egypt in cooperation with the Porte. The idea behind this seemingly outlandish notion was that the French would invade Egypt in the name of the sultan, and in return for crushing the Mamluks and restoring the sultan's authority, the Porte would grant France *de facto* control of the province. Talleyrand concluded his message by stating that from Egypt France could gain control of the Indies trade, because by using the Suez-Red Sea route, a merchant could make five trips to India in the same time that his competitor using the Cape route made three. On September 27, Talleyrand again wrote to Bonaparte, telling him that the Directory wished him to establish contact with friendly elements in the Balkans and Egypt. The Directory, he stated, also desired to keep Malta from falling into the hands of Austria or Russia and was therefore giving him authority to order Admiral Brueys, commander of the French fleet units

in the Adriatic, to attack the island.[19] Since the French were
still negotiating with the British at Lille, a direct assault on
England was for the moment out of the question. Bonaparte,
ambitious as always, had therefore adopted the idea of an eastern
expedition. His urgings, coupled with those of Talleyrand, merchants, and consular officials, finally convinced the directors, who
wanted to keep pressure on Britain while the talks progressed, to
sanction a colonial venture. Thus by the end of September, 1797,
it appeared as if France had committed itself to a policy of
expansion in the Near East.

    In October, however, events took another turn as the Lille
negotiations collapsed. There had existed throughout the spring
and autumn of 1797 a great number of people who opposed the
commitment of French strength in the east and who favored instead a cross-Channel attack. Reubell, the director generally in
charge of foreign affairs, opposed any eastern ventures. He felt
that to defeat England, France had to attack her directly.[20] Barras
claimed to have supported his colleague, and commented later,
"neither Reubell nor I approved of the expedition to Egypt."[21]
Admiral Bruix, the minister of marine, also opposed an expedition to the Levant.[22] While peace negotiations continued at Lille,
there had been no point in advocating an immediate cross-
Channel attack, and the field had been left open to those who
favored an expedition in the east. The final breakdown of peace
talks, however, forced the government to reconsider its position.
The directors had to consider an eastern expedition not only as
a means of pressuring the British, gaining new colonies, and
increasing French trade, but also as a method for rapidly defeating England. In this new context, the government decided to
drop plans for a descent on Malta and Egypt and rely instead
on the risky but potentially decisive method of a cross-Channel
attack.

    On October 25–26 the directors received a copy of the Treaty
of Campoformio. They signed the treaty the next day, officially
ending the war with Austria and freeing many troops for use
elsewhere. On the same day, they created the army of England,
placing Bonaparte in command.[23] They dropped all plans for an
eastern venture, and on November 23, in a proclamation to the
French people, they announced and explained their decision by

saying that the quickest way to defeat England was by means of a descent on her coasts followed by a peace dictated in London by the army of England.[24] Bonaparte had meanwhile departed for Rastadt, where on December 1 he signed an agreement with the Austrians, providing for the withdrawal of their troops from several imperial fortresses, including Mainz. On December 5 he was back in Paris ready to take command of his new army. The Directory began to issue orders on December 13 for the collection of an invasion fleet, and on December 16 Bonaparte wrote to Rome, cancelling previous orders to send an agent to Malta.[25]

In the following weeks the government withdrew units from the various field armies and concentrated them near the main embarkation ports on the Channel. In December, 36,000 men moved from Italy to the Channel ports, and on January 12, 1798, the Directory decreed that the invasion force was to comprise twenty-nine demibrigades of the line, eleven light demibrigades, four artillery regiments, and thirty-two cavalry regiments, a total of about 50,000 troops. The concentration of troops was accomplished with little difficulty, and by May, the army of England reached its peak strength of 56,400 men.[26] The government also made great efforts to build an invasion fleet. The minister of marine issued orders for warships to concentrate at Brest to provide escorts for the troop ships. Brueys received instructions on December 14 to bring his squadron from Corfu to the Atlantic while warships at Toulon proceeded to the Channel and while ships that were out of commission were prepared for sea duty. The French requested the Spanish to send their navy to assist in the forthcoming invasion. The Spanish reluctantly agreed, and from Cadiz twenty-two ships of the line and six frigates managed to escape Jervis's blockade squadron and put to sea. The Spanish, however, feared a fight with the British squadron blockading Brest and made no efforts to break through to the French ports. They returned to Cadiz without a fight, and by the end of the first week in March, Jervis had firmly re-established his blockade.[27]

Undaunted by this setback, Bonaparte continued his preparations. He sent orders to the Channel ports to prepare transports by adapting merchant ships into armed transports and by constructing new ships. The Dunkirk area was to prepare sixty ships;

Havre, sixty; Granville, twenty; and St. Malo, thirty. The ships were to be ready to sail by March 22, a date that he soon advanced to February 28. To hasten these preparations, Bonaparte commissioned Forfait, an officer of the engineers, to supervise the preparation and provisioning of transports in all Channel ports. On January 11, the Directory extended his authority to include supervision of ship construction and the preparation of armed ships for sea duty. Forfait reported to the Minister of Marine on January 28 that there was sufficient shipping to transport twelve hundred horses and ninety-eight hundred men, and that he had organized preparations to build ships for fifteen thousand more troops in the near future.[28]

The British, learning of French preparations from agents on the Continent, became seriously alarmed. Secretary of State Grenville wrote to the duke of Buckingham in February, telling him that the French were pushing their preparations with great vigor.[29] The Marquis Cornwallis wrote to General Ross in Ireland that Dundas, the secretary of state for war, expected a French invasion in the near future.[30] To meet the invasion threat, parliament passed a law on January 11 authorizing ten thousand militiamen to join the regular army, and the army moved fifty-four hundred infantry and twenty-four hundred cavalry into the London area. Pitt asked the House of Commons to treble the assessed taxes to pay increased war costs, and on March 27 Dundas proposed a bill to indemnify people whose property had been damaged while resisting an invasion.[31] In a speech to the House of Commons on April 20, King George III told the members that,

> from various advices received by his majesty it appears that the preparation for the embarkation of troops and warlike stores are now carried on with considerable and increasing activity in the ports of France, Belgium and Holland with the avowed design of attempting the invasion of his majesty's domains.[32]

He asked the House to take all necessary measures to put the realm in a state of readiness to resist attack. The government ordered the construction of a system of beacon masts, watchtowers, and semaphore telegraphs to cover south England, and in April the duke of York completed his military survey and drew up a plan for the defense of London.[33] Dundas requested the House of Commons to consider arming the people, adding that despite the fact that there were many who subscribed to French principles, the risk of putting arms in their hands was less than the risk of being unprepared if the French should land. Meanwhile numerous volunteer corps mobilized and began to drill.[34] Despite these extensive efforts, it was still doubtful that the English armed forces could face the republican demibrigades with any hope of victory. Britain's best defense was still her navy.

The British situation was not, however, totally gloomy, because the French soon began to encounter grave difficulties in assembling their invasion flotilla. On December 20 the minister of marine reported to Bonaparte that only twenty-five ships could be gathered at Brest and that even these lacked sufficient men and supplies.[35] On February 12, in an effort to have the fleet ready by the end of the month, the government directed a second engineer officer, Caffarelli, to work on the invasion plans. He went to Boulogne to prepare that port to receive and supply fifty armed sloops and fifty fishing boats that had been converted into transports. Caffarelli's instructions also included the preparation of four hundred transport sloops at Calais, but these efforts were insufficient, for on February 20, he told the Directory that the available shipping could accommodate only 24,250 men and 1,200 horses.[36] Two days earlier the Prussian ambassador at Paris had reported to Berlin that the minister of marine had stated publicly that the navy lacked the means for an invasion of England.[37] In attempting to rectify this situation, the French appealed to the Batavians, who wanted to recover the Cape Colony and Ceylon. Bonaparte sent Forfait to the Hague with a request that Batavia supply two hundred fishing boats and twenty or thirty sloops to the French navy, but before the results of this mission were known, the government received still another discouraging appraisal of the situation.

Bonaparte himself had set out on a special inspection tour of the Channel ports on February 9. He was back in Paris by February 21, and on February 23, presented a memorandum to the Directory that painted a bleak picture of the state of the navy. Bonaparte noted that the French had to attack at the end of

March or the beginning of April in order to take advantage of the long nights that would hinder the blockaders. The state of French naval preparations, however, forced the general to conclude that the invasion fleet might not be ready in time. He commented, "The invasion of England does not appear to be possible before next year; and then it is probable that encumbrances which crop up on the Continent will stop it. The moment to prepare this attack is lost, perhaps, forever."[38] He went on, however, to qualify this statement—by adding that he could launch his assault if the government devoted immediate and massive efforts to the organization of the fleet. He insisted that the government spend 1,500,000 livres plus 300,000 francs per *decade* on naval preparations. In addition, the government would have to equip as transports all gunboats between Ostend and Bayonne, charter all ships capable of carrying horses, and requisition all available transport ships between Antwerp and Cherbourg. Finally, the navy would have to get ships from the Batavians, and press into service the best equipped sloops between Bordeaux and Antwerp. If the government did not attain these goals before the end of March, it would have to renounce the expedition to England and seek another way to strike at the British. He suggested an attack on Hanover and Hamburg as one possibility, and also revived his old plan of an expedition to Egypt.[39]

The purpose of this report was twofold. First, he wanted to get the Directory to devote greater energies to the preparation of the invasion of England. The fact that Forfait and Caffarelli were hard to work while Bonaparte was making his gloomy prognosis indicates that he still took seriously the cross-Channel venture. If at this point he were already committed to an eastern expedition, he would not have kept two of his best and most important engineer officers occupied in the Channel ports. Thus the pessimistic nature of his report was primarily a means of scaring the government into greater activity.

Bonaparte's second object was to present the Directory with alternatives in case the renewed efforts to prepare the fleet failed. Seeing the chances of an invasion of the British Isles becoming more and more problematical, it is not surprising that he suggested other possibilities of action. Nor is it surprising that he emphasized the line of action that had so greatly attracted him earlier in the year. His report of February was then primarily an attempt to force the government to step up its efforts to attack England while at the same time presenting alternative policies if the first course of action became impossible, as it ultimately did.

The reaction of the government to Bonaparte's report indicates that this interpretation of his motives is correct. The Directory went to great lengths to fulfill the conditions for launching at attack on the British Isles, and only after the failure of these efforts did they agree to a change of plans. The government issued orders to commandants of the Channel ports on February 25, directing them to put an embargo on privateers and force their crews to join the regular navy. Two days later the Directory ordered all sloops in ports from Bayonne to Ostend to proceed to Le Havre and Dunkirk.[40] On March 1 Forfait reported from the Hague that the Batavians had agreed to place transport for ten thousand men at the disposal of the French navy, but even these efforts were insufficient. The minister of marine had previously reported that only thirteen ships of the line were ready at Brest, and doubts as to the feasibility of the invasion grew.[41] As these doubts grew, the idea of adopting the alternative of an Egyptian expedition became more attractive.

Meanwhile, Talleyrand, independently of Bonaparte, continued to press for an invasion of Egypt, and while Bonaparte was inspecting the Channel ports, Talleyrand, on February 14, submitted a long report to the Directory in which he forcefully presented the views of those who favored an attack on Egypt. He asserted that, "Egypt was a province of the Roman Republic; it must become one of the French Republic."[42] Egypt would, he insisted, make a rich colony, and was well situated to serve as an *entrepot* for trade with Africa, Europe, and the Indies. As France profited, English commerce would decline, for from Egypt, France could capture the India trade. The Porte would not go to war if France took Egypt for fear that the Republic would create revolutions in Greece and Albania. Nor would England take any action, because all her efforts were directed towards the protection of her home islands. He assured the government, "The Executive Directory need fear no obstacle or opposition to its possession of Egypt."[43] He concluded his report with a prognosis of future action after the conquest of Egypt. He claimed that twenty-five thousand troops could conquer and hold Egypt and that fifteen thousand additional troops would suffice for an expedition against India. These troops could reach India by commandeering ships in the Red Sea.[44]

On the first and second of March, the Directory met in secret session to review the possibility of launching the invasion, and to discuss a possible change of strategy. At this critical juncture, the minister of marine again reported that preparations were insufficient to transport an expeditionary force to England.[45] It was probably this report that finally forced the directors to give up hope of carrying out the cross-Channel attack, for it was at these meetings that the government decided to adopt the policy of attacking Egypt. The desire to get Bonaparte out of the country might also have played a role in influencing the directors' decision, but as Larévellière-Lépeaux pointed out, if the government wished to get rid of a dangerous general, it could have found a way to do so without dispensing with the services of thousands of good troops.[46] Evidently the directors were less influenced by fear of Bonaparte than by the failure to obtain enough ships to invade Britain and the consequent necessity to strike at her in another area.

On March 5 the Directory ordered troops to concentrate at Toulon. The minister of marine directed the Toulon squadron to prepare for action, and the government appointed Bonaparte to supervise all military and naval preparations in southern France.[47] Bonaparte told the government on the same day that he would require twenty to twenty-five thousand infantry, two to three thousand cavalry, one hundred cannon, and two companies of miners and two of sappers for an invasion of Egypt.[48] On April 12 the Directory issued a series of decrees that gave the expedition its final form and defined its goals. The first decree created the army of the East, consisting of both land and naval units. The land units consisted of those troops stationed in the eighth and twenty-third military districts of France, units of the army of Italy stationed at Genoa and Civita Vecchia, and the garrison of the Ionian Islands. The sea forces comprised all naval units in the Mediterranean, and Bonaparte led both the army and naval contingents.[49] The second decree gave a justification of the expedition and also set forth its strategic goals. Following closely the reasoning of Talleyrand's February memoire, the government asserted that the Mamluk beys were cooperating with the English against the French and had to be punished. Further, the English, by their seizure of the Cape of Good Hope, had made access to India very difficult for French arms and trade, and it was therefore vital to obtain another route to the Indies to enable the republican forces to reach this area, defeat the English, and ruin their commerce. To carry out this mission, Bonaparte was to lead the army of the East to Egypt and, with the cooperation of the sultan, take control of the country and dominate the Red Sea. He was then to cut through the isthmus of Suez to create a short sea route to India. A third decree charged Bonaparte with the additional task of conquering Malta.[50] The final directive sought to provide the means to enable Bonaparte to control the Red Sea and to transport his army to the Indies. To accomplish this object, the Directory called the forces of the French possessions in the east into action. The government instructed

the frigates of the Republic which find themselves at the Isle of France . . . to go to the port of Suez where they will be under the orders of Citizen Bonaparte, general in chief of the Army of the East. To this effect they will set sail immediately after the receipt of this order. They will bring with them all transports capable of making the trip which can be found in the ports of the Isle of France and Réunion.[51]

Using the extended powers granted him by Paris, Bonaparte began to choose his subordinate commanders from the various armies of the Republic. A partial list of them comprised a galaxy of the best officers of the day plus many who were later to gain fame and glory. Berthier became chief of staff. Divisional commanders included Kléber, Bon, Reynier, and Desaix. Murat, Leclerc, and Marmont served as brigadiers, and Junot and Bonaparte's brother Louis served as aides-de-camp. In addition, Bonaparte collected a group of savants from the Institute, including an astronomer, an artist, a chemist, a minerologist, a zoologist, and an Arabist to accompany the army, indicating that he was also concerned with developing Egypt's potentialities as a colony.[52]

Nor did the general neglect the naval aspects of the expedition. On April 2, Brueys arrived at Toulon, where he found orders directing him to prepare his fleet to set out again in the near future. Two weeks later the government informed him of the creation of the army of the East and told him that he would be operating in the Mediterranean. During this period the army of the East began to collect transports and supplies, paid for in part by money seized from Switzerland, which the French had transformed into a satellite republic in April. Brueys brought his crews up to full strength. He had serious doubts about their efficiency and their ability to face the English in battle, but since there were no British ships in the Mediterranean, this worry was hypothetical, at least for the present.[53]

Talleyrand was also hard at work preparing the diplomatic groundwork for the expedition. He appointed Ruffin as *chargé d'affaires* at Constantinople and instructed him to assure the Porte of France's peaceful intentions. On March 16 he proposed a truly grandiose scheme to the Directory, suggesting that after Bonaparte had established himself firmly in Egypt, Paris would send a special envoy to Sultan Selim III with an offer of alliance against Russia. Talleyrand's aim was to distract the Turks' attentions from Egypt by involving them in a war with the Russians. To obtain French aid, the Sultan would have to agree to any demands Bonaparte might make concerning the fate of Egypt. Talleyrand optimistically assumed that since Austria was at peace with the Republic, she would not aid Russia, and that if the czar did declare war, the Russian armies would be unable to strike directly at France. Involved in a war with each other, neither Russia nor Turkey would be able to interfere with French plans.[54]

In pursuit of this goal, Talleyrand wrote to Ruffin on May 11, telling him that French policy was to occupy Egypt only for the purposes of subduing the Mamluks and obtaining a base from which to strike at British holdings in the East Indies. He told Ruffin that a special envoy was about to leave for Constantinople to explain these matters to the sultan. In fact, Talleyrand himself was to fulfill this vital role, and the Directory told Bonaparte that the minister of foreign affairs would leave for Constantinople shortly after the expedition set sail from France.[55]

While the government prepared its preliminary diplomatic moves, Bonaparte's army completed its preparations. On May 19, thirteen ships of the line, seven frigates, eighteen sloops and gunboats, and three hundred transports carrying the thirty thousand infantry, twenty-eight hundred cavalry, sixty field and forty siege guns, and two companies of sappers and miners of the army of the East left Toulon for Egypt. Bonaparte assured his troops that they were acting as a wing of the army of England and in addition were about to spread the doctrine of liberty to the non-European world.[56]

Convinced that they could not prepare an invasion fleet in time to invade England before the weather turned against them, the Directory decided to invade Egypt as the first step in a thrust at British India. Although an overseas expedition involved grave diplomatic risks, it did offer the French an opportunity to strike at one of Britain's wealthiest possessions while simultaneously extending their influence into the Near East and Asia.

NOTES

Chapter 5

1. William Clowes, *The Royal Navy*, 4: 153.

2. Edouard Desbrière, ed., *1793–1805 projets et tentatives de débarquement aux Iles britanniques*, 1: 287.

3. Edouard Guillon, *La France et l'Irlande pendant la Révolution*, pp. 55–71.

4. Ibid., pp. 73–75.

5. Patrice Mahon, *Études sur les armées du Directoire*, pp. 32–33, 40.

6. Georges Lechartier, *Les soldats de la Révolution et de l'Empire*, pp. 12–13.

7. J. W. Fortescue, *A History of the British Army*, 4, pt. 2: 939.

8. François Charles-Roux, *Les origines de l'expédition française en Égypte*, pp. 271–73.

9. Ibid., pp. 276–79.

10. Ibid., pp. 294–95.

11. Ibid., p. 320; and H. T. Colenbrander, ed., *Gedenkstukken des Algemeene Geschiedenis van Nederland van 1795 tot 1840*, 2: 28–29.

12. George Duruy, ed., *Mémoires de Barras*, 3: 90; and Guillon, *La France et l'Irlande*, p. 202.

13. Georges Douin, *La flotte de Bonaparte sur les côtes d'Égypte*, p. 27.

14. L. A. Bourrienne, ed., *Memoirs of Napoleon Bonaparte*, 1: 122.

15. Douin, *La flotte de Bonaparte*, pp. 28–29; and C. de la Jonquière, ed., *L'Expédition d'Égypte 1798–1801*, 1: 25–26.

16. Henri Plon and J. Dumaine, eds., *Correspondance de Napoléon Ier*, 3: 235–37.

17. Paul Pisani, "L'expédition russe-turque aux Iles ioniennes en 1798–1799," *Revue d'histoire diplomatique*, 2: 194–97.

18. Plon and Dumaine, *Correspondance de Napoléon Ier*, pp. 293–94.

19. Jonquière, *L'Expédition d'Égypte*, pp. 37–38.

20. Bernard Nabonne, ed., *La diplomatie du Directoire et Bonaparte d'après les papiers inédits de Reubell*, p. 156.

21. Duruy, *Mémoires de Barras*, p. 162.

22. Guillon, *La France et l'Irlande*, p. 202.

23. Jonquière, *L'Expédition d'Égypte*, p. 41.

24. *Réimpression de l'Ancien Moniteur*, 29: 68.

25. Jonquière, *L'Expédition d'Égypte*, pp. 51–52, 73.

26. Ibid., pp. 95–96, and Desbrière, *Projets et tentatives*, p. 370.

27. Desbrière, *Projets et tentatives*, p. 287.

28. Ibid., pp. 288–89, 295, 307–10, 315.

29. Duke of Buckingham and Chandos, *Memoirs of the Court and Cabinet of George the Third from Original Family Documents* (London: 1853), 2: 388.

30. Charles Ross, ed., *Correspondence of Charles, First Marquess of Cornwallis*, 2: 330.

31. J. Holland Rose and A. M. Broadley, *Dumouriez and the Defense of England against Napoleon*, p. 106; and William Cobbet, ed., *The Parliamentary History of England from the Earliest Period to the Year 1803*, 33: 1066, 1358.

32. Ibid., p. 1422.

33. Ross, *Correspondence of Cornwallis*, pp. 334–35; and Wheeler and Broadley, *Napoleon and the Invasion of England*, 1: 227.

34. Wheeler and Broadley, *Invasion of England*, pp. 124–26, 132.

35. Desbrière, *Projets et tentatives*, pp. 298–99.

36. Ibid., pp. 320–21, 327.

37. Paul Bailleu, ed., *Preussen und Frankreich von 1795 bis 1807 Diplomatische Correspondenzen*, 1: 172.

38. Ministre de la Guerre, ed., *Correspondance Militaire de Napoléon Ier* (Paris: 1876), 1: 464.

39. Ibid., pp. 467–68.

40. Desbrière, *Projets et tentatives*, pp. 325–26.

41. Ibid., p. 305.

42. Jonquière, *L'Expédition d'Égypte*, p. 124.

43. Ibid., p. 162.

44. Ibid., pp. 162–65.

45. Ibid., p. 187.

46. David d'Angers, ed., *Mémoires de Laréveillière-Lépeaux*, 2: 341.

47. Napoléon Bonaparte, *Correspondance inédite officielle et confidentielle de Napoléon Bonaparte, Égypte* (Paris, 1819), 1: 4, 5, 10.

48. Plon and Dumaine, *Correspondance de Napoléon Ier*, 4: 2; and Bonaparte, *Correspondance de Napoléon Bonaparte*, 1 :4.

49. Bonaparte, *Correspondance*, pp. 12–13. France was divided into twenty-four military districts. A commander of such a district was essentially an inspector-general with control over all troops stationed in the district. Combat divisions had a separate organization and often an army commander had control over both combat divisions and military district, especially if his troops were concentrated in or defending such a district.

50. Plon and Dumaine, *Correspondance de Napoléon Ier*, 4: 53.

51. Ibid., p. 54.

52. P. G. Elgood, *Bonaparte's Adventure in Egypt*, p. 54.

53. Douin, *La flotte de Bonaparte*, pp. 34, 49.

54. Jonquière, *L'Expédition d'Égypte*, 2: 591–92.

55. Ibid., pp. 593–94, 605.

56. Henri Galli, ed., *Journal d'un officier de l'armée d'Égypte, l'armée française en Égypte 1798–1801*, pp. 15–16.

6

Egyptian Fiasco

The army of the East sighted Malta, its first objective, on June 9. The military position of the Knights of Malta was very weak, for Baron Hompsech, the Grand Master, could muster only 332 Knights and 2,000 local militia to defend the island. Because of their taxation policy, control of the university, and refusal to let natives join the order, the Knights were very unpopular and could not rely on the support of the native militia and civilians.[1]

Hompsech, nevertheless, decided to resist, called out the militia, and rejected a French request to allow their fleet to enter Valetta to obtain fresh water. These actions gave Bonaparte the excuse he needed to attack, and on June 10 two demibrigades landed and began to advance on the capital. Resistance was feeble, and the natives, supported by some of the Knights, demanded that Hompsech surrender. The next morning the Grand Master asked for an armistice, and on June 12 signed a formal surrender renouncing the order's sovereignty over the isle.[2]

Bonaparte spent the next few days organizing a government for the island and its smaller neighbor, Gozzo. He chose a nine-man commission to govern the islands, reorganized the courts on the French model, divided the islands into cantons, and turned the holdings of the Knights into national lands. He abolished slavery and all remnants of feudalism and annexed Malta to the Republic. He also issued orders to establish a school system, a taxation system, and a militia. Finally, he placed General Vaubois

in charge of the French garrison, a force sonsisting of some three
thousand infantry and four hundred gunners. Vaubois was to
support his troops by means of a special tax of fifty thousand
francs per month, and he held a veto power over any act of the
Maltese civil authorities.[3] These tasks completed, Bonaparte resumed his voyage to Egypt on June 19.

After sailing eastward toward Crete and then turning south in
the direction of Egypt, the fleet reached the coast near Alexandria
by July 1. Four miles west of Alexandria, Bonaparte sent a four
thousand-man advance guard ashore, and the following morning
grenadiers stormed the town walls, which they easily breached, but
heavy fighting developed inside the town as the garrison put up
a stout resistance from fortified houses. Reinforcements moved up
from the beach, and after several hours of bitter house-to-house
fighting, the Mamluk commander capitulated. Wasting no time,
Bonaparte ordered Desaix's division to set out for the Nile, and
instructed the rest of the army, which was preparing to disembark
in Alexandria the next day, to follow as soon as they landed. He
directed Brueys to take the fleet to Abukir Bay, where it could
maintain communications between Alexandria and the newly
captured town of Rosetta.[4]

Before joining his troops in the field, Bonaparte made his first
effort to obtain the support of the local population. On July 3 a
proclamation printed in Arabic and dated 1213, Year of the
Hegira, informed the people of Egypt that the French had no
intention of destroying the Islamic faith. In fact, Bonaparte insisted that they respected "more than the Mamelukes do, God,
His Prophet, and the Koran."[5] The French, he asserted, would
free the Egyptians from Mamluk tyranny and allow them self-
government. He also told the natives that the French, having
destroyed the power of the pope and the Knights of Malta, were
friendly to the sultan.[6] He gave Moslem prisoners, whom he had
freed from captivity on Malta, copies of the proclamation and
sent them back to their homes to spread this propaganda.[7] Bonaparte then turned his attention to the major task of defeating
the Mamluks and establishing himself in Egypt.

The advance to Cairo, beginning on July 6, occurred in two
stages. First, the army moved to the west bank of the Nile and
then turned south toward Cairo. The local population offered

little resistance and regarded the French with a mixture of hope and suspicion. The natives were happy enough to be rid of their Mamluk rulers, but since they were devout Muslims, they did not support their "infidel" liberators wholeheartedly. Bedouins and Mamluk cavalry pickets harassed isolated French units, but failed to delay the general advance. Heat and lack of local supplies were the main obstacles, but the veterans of the Italian and German campaigns were equal to the task, and by July 13 the French stood on the west bank of the Nile.[8]

On July 14, Bastille Day, ironically enough, the army began to move on Cairo. Since the Mamluk army was mainly a cavalry force, Bonaparte devised a special formation to combat it. Rather than marching in columns, the French marched in divisional squares three ranks deep with the staff and baggage in the middle and artillery at the angles. On the first day of the advance, a fifteen hundred-man cavalry force attacked the French squares, but Bonaparte's soldiers drove them off and inflicted heavy losses. After this defeat, the Mamluk commanders, Murad and Ibrihim, returned to their old tactics of attacking isolated units and harassing the flanks of the main body of troops. Such tactics did make the French march somewhat more difficult but failed to slow their advance. If the Mamluk generals wished to save Cairo, they would soon have to abandon their harassing tactics and face the French in open combat, for by July 20 Bonaparte's army had reached the plain of the Pyramids on the west bank of the Nile, a bare fifteen miles north of the city.

It was here that Murad finally decided to fight and on July 21 drew up fifteen thousand native infantrymen, three thousand Bedouin light cavalry, and six thousand Mamluk heavy cavalry in a line running from the Nile to the Pyramids. Bonaparte drew up his five divisions by echelons with their right refused so as to flank each other, and both leaders prepared to attack.[9] The Mamluks moved first, rushing the divisions of Reynier and Desaix on the French right and center. The assault was bravely executed, but discipline and firepower proved superior to untrained ardor. Well-aimed musket fire quickly emptied the Mamluk saddles, and the cavalry broke and fled. Meanwhile on the other flank, the divisions of Bon, Menou, and Kléber rushed forward. Kléber's division assaulted a fortified village held by the native infantry, the key to Murad's position. The village fell after a brief but bitter fight, and the Egyptians broke and fled for the river, where they attempted to swim across to Cairo, but most of them drowned in the swift current or fell victim to French sharpshooters. Murad's defeated cavalry had meanwhile fled south, and Ibrihim, gathering the Cairo garrison, began to retreat into Sinai. At the day's end, the French were in complete control of the battlefield, having killed about 2,000 of the enemy at a cost to themselves of only thirty dead.[10] The next morning the civil authorities of Cairo, wishing to avoid useless bloodshed, surrendered, and the first French units began to enter the city. Five days later Bonaparte himself made a grand entry into the new capital of the French eastern empire.[11]

Having entered the city, Bonaparte ordered Desaix to pursue Murad and sent Bon and Reynier after Ibrihim.[12] He then turned his attention to organizing the administration of his newly conquered domain and to gaining the support of the local population, a necessary prerequisite for any future campaigns. With the population on his side, his army would be able to draw on the natural resources and perhaps even the manpower of Egypt, and Bonaparte would be able to spare many of his own troops from the tasks of guarding bases and lines of communication. That Bonaparte was indeed thinking of further operations may be demonstrated by the fact that after the battle of the Pyramids, he told his troops that his aims were to free Egypt from the tyranny of the Mamluks, to strike a blow at England's maritime prosperity, and to open the shortest invasion route to India.[13]

On July 25 Bonaparte established a local government for Cairo consisting of a nine man *divan* responsible for police, food supply, and sanitation. Two days later he organized provincial governments, giving each district a seven-man *divan* headed by an *aga* and an intendant to collect taxes.[14] Bonaparte, however, kept the real power in his own hands, and in the provinces the local French military commanders held a veto power over the acts of the native governments. In August, Bonaparte created a health commission and established a printing press, library, laboratories, and a postal system.[15]

Nor were these the only methods used by Bonaparte to gain popular support. He gave military escorts to caravans going to

Mecca and opened discussions with Muslim leaders concerning the conversion of the French army. He promised to build a new mosque, and ordered the entire French garrison of Cairo to turn out to celebrate the birthday of the Prophet. The French confiscated Mamluk property but not that of the natives, and Bonaparte ordered his troops to respect the lives, property, and faith of the Egyptians. The French assured the bey of Tripoli that the Directory had nothing but friendly intentions toward the Islamic powers, and Bonaparte continued earlier negotiations with the pasha of Albania.[16]

The result of these efforts to gain popular support was, however, minimal. The majority of the population continued to regard the French as infidels and soon came to regard them as exploiters as well, because to obtain funds for the army, Bonaparte had retained the old Mamluk taxes. To the deeply religious Egyptians, there seemed little difference between French and Mamluk rule except that the Mamluks were at least of the same faith. Bonaparte also failed to take advantage of the land hunger of the peasantry. He passed no land reform laws, thereby losing an opportunity to gain the backing of at least one important segment of the population.[17] In the provinces, attacks on French patrols soon became common, and the practice of taking hostages from among the local notables did nothing to halt them. The populations of Cairo and the other large cities were quiet and submissive but hardly enthusiastic supporters of French domination. Nevertheless, the situation by the end of July was still quite favorable for the French.

The army of the East was the undoubted military master of Lower Egypt, and although the countryside was restive, the cities were tranquil. The new administration functioned adequately. Furthermore, the French could count on the passivity of the vast majority of the population as long as there was no drastic alteration of the overall military situation. The British, however, were about to alter this situation with results more far reaching than either they or the French could have expected.

From numerous sources—secret agents, diplomats, and journalists—the British learned of the French preparations at Toulon, but they did not know the destination of the expedition. In fact, both the majority of the Cabinet and the admiralty made entirely wrong assumptions as to Bonaparte's ultimate goal. The Cabinet assumed that the French were going to attack Ireland, and on June 10 Pitt proposed the recall of troops from Portugal to strengthen the Irish garrison.[18] The navy for its part was too concerned with the protection of the British Isles to take seriously any notion that the French might be planning to invade Egypt. On April 6, Spencer, the first lord of the admiralty, told Grenville that England did not have enough ships to protect the home isles and station a fleet in the Mediterranean.[19] The next day, however, Pitt told Grenville that Spencer's figures indicated that in an emergency some units could be detached for service in the Mediterranean but that the risks involved in such a course of action were grave.[20] On April 26 Spencer reaffirmed his view that the navy should stay out of the Mediterranean, because he felt that the French and Spanish were too strong to be challenged in their own home waters unless the Royal Navy could destroy one of their fleets.[21]

Given the strategic situation at the time, such views are understandable, even though Grenville had reliable information as to the desination of the French fleet. Earlier, Grenville had sent a special agent to the Continent to negotiate with the duke of Brunswick and the king of Prussia for a renewal of the coalition. The agent, de Luc, had many contacts, one of them with Dolomieu, a French naturalist, who was one of the experts going to the east. In a dispatch to Grenville dated May 7, de Luc enclosed two letters that he had received from Dolomieu. The first of these letters, written on March 28, said that the expedition was destined for Africa or Asia, and the second letter, dated April 11, was even more specific, stating that the French planned to conquer Egypt, cut a canal at Suez, build a fleet on the Red Sea, and attack India.[22] Grenville, however, chose to ignore this unsupported evidence and never informed the admiralty.

The only Cabinet member to divine the true goal of Bonaparte's venture was the secretary of state for war, Dundas. He had long been interested in eastern affairs and had been a member of the East India Company's Board of Control since 1784. As secretary of state for war he was also responsible for colonial affairs, and his policy was imperialist rather than continental. His chief aim was to reduce Britain's military commitments in Europe

while using her naval superiority to expand her trade and overseas possessions.[23] With such an outlook, it was not unnatural
that he would assume that the French would do what he himself
might well attempt if he were in their position. Realizing that
if the French were to attack India, Egypt would be their first
goal, he wrote to Spencer on April 17 telling him that Egypt was
probably the goal of the French fleet.[24]

At the same time the rest of the Cabinet was beginning to
contemplate the possibility of sending a fleet into the Mediterranean. Although they did not share Dundas's opinion concerning
the destination of the French expedition, diplomatic considerations encouraged them to resume naval activities in the Mediterranean for the first time since 1796. Pitt and his colleagues in
their search for continental allies concuded that only some forceful
and victorious naval action would convince other powers to
resume hostilities against France. Consequently, on April 29,
Spencer instructed Admiral St. Vincent, commander of the squadron blockading Cadiz, to send naval vessels into the Mediterranean to protect Naples, Portugal, and Ireland from invasion
and by a decisive show of force to encourage the Austrians to
act.[25]

The admiralty gave Horatio Nelson command of fourteen ships
of the line, and on May 1 Spencer told St. Vincent, Nelson's immediate superior, that the object of the Mediterranean squadron
was to protect Naples and blockade Spain in order to prevent the
French and Spanish fleets from uniting and entering the Atlantic.
He concluded his message by adding that there was a remote
possibility that the French were planning to invade Egypt.[26] On
May 21 St. Vincent gave Nelson his final instructions. His mission
was to find and destroy the French Toulon fleet. Since the destination of this fleet was not precisely known, the admiralty gave
Nelson a free hand in his search.[27] Again Dundas warned the
admiralty that Egypt was probably the objective of the French
fleet, but he wrote to Spencer on June 9, and by this time Nelson
had already entered the Mediterranean.[28]

By May 21 the British squadron had arrived before Toulon,
where Nelson discovered that the French fleet had already departed. He ordered an immediate pursuit, but storms delayed him

until June 7. During this period, St. Vincent sent him further orders, informing him that the French objectives were Sicily and Naples, and when the weather cleared, he set off immediately for Naples, arriving there on June 17.[29] Not finding the French, Nelson next proceeded to Messina, where on June 20 he learned of the French seizure of Malta. Two days later a scout ship reported sighting the French sailing southeast. Since the French were obviously not headed for Spain, Portugal, or Ireland, Nelson began to divine the real aims of their expedition. As early as June 15 he had written to Spencer saying, "If they pass Sicily, I shall believe that they are going on their scheme of possessing Alexandria and getting troops to India—a plan concerted with Tippoo Saib, by no means so difficult as might at first view be imagined."[30] The route taken by the French evidently convinced him that his assumption was correct, and he asked his captains for their views, telling them, "Should the Armament be gone to Alexandria and get safe there our possessions in India are probably lost. Do you think we had better push for that place?"[31]

Nelson's officers agreed with his analysis, and the fleet headed for Egypt. While en route to Alexandria, Nelson on June 24 wrote to the British consul, telling him that he was now absolutely certain that the French intended to attack India by way of Egypt. Two days later he wrote again to the consul stating that the French objective was to capture a port in Egypt in order to transport an army into India. He concluded by asking the consul to discover if any French vessels had been seen in the Red Sea, but when his fleet arrived at Alexandria on June 28 both the British consul and the French fleet were absent.[32]

Nelson had in fact beaten the French to Alexandria, but failing to find them did not alter his judgment. The day after his arrival, he wrote to St. Vincent to tell him that he was sure that the French were now planning to strike in the eastern Mediterranean and that Alexandria was their destination.[33] On the same day, he set off to continue his search in the eastern Mediterranean and headed for the coast of Anatolia, arriving there at about the same time that the French reached Egypt. Finding nothing in Asia Minor, he returned to Sicily for supplies, reaching Syracuse on July 19. Still convinced that the French were heading for

Egypt, Nelson ordered the fleet to sea on July 25 to carry out a second, more thorough search of the Levant. His first objective was the Bosporus, and he planned to work south from there.[34]

By July 18 he was near the coast of Morea, where he captured a French ship and learned that the enemy fleet had been seen in the vicinity three weeks before heading southeast. A few hours later a passing ship corroborated this piece of information. Nelson then headed directly for Egypt and by July 31 was cruising near Alexandria. In the first light of dawn on August 1, two frigates set out to locate the French, and by the afternoon Nelson knew that the whole of the French fleet was anchored in Abukir Bay.[35] He ordered his captains to attack at once.

The French fleet, anchored in a line running from northeast to southwest across the bay, consisted of thirteen ships of the line. Their position was, however, quite weak. Despite a numerical advantage of three ships and possession of a 120-gun flagship, the *Orient*, the largest vessel in either fleet, the French lacked mobility, and the British stood between them and the high seas. To make matters worse, the leading ship on the northwest part of the line was not close enough inshore to prevent the British from turning the whole line, and the land batteries that could have covered this gap were not yet in place. Finally, many of the French seamen were ashore on supply details and consequently unavailable for combat.[36]

If Brueys was responsible for the weak tactical disposition of the fleet, the responsibility for keeping the fleet in such a bad position lay with Bonaparte. After the battle, Bonaparte claimed that he had warned Brueys not to remain at Abukir, but the evidence tells a different story. The Corsican had originally wanted the fleet to enter Alexandria, but the harbor was too shallow, and on July 1 Brueys took the fleet to a deeper anchorage in Abukir Bay.[37] Brueys wished to leave Egyptian waters, but Bonaparte wanted to keep the fleet in the Levant to support his army. Brueys did have an order dated July 3 allowing him to proceed to Corfu if necessary, but since Bonaparte was the commander in chief of both land and naval forces in the area, Brueys could not take advantage of this permission without more explicit instructions. Moreover, Bonaparte also told Brueys that the departure of his fleet was dependent upon the overall military situation, which only the commander in chief could judge, and he never issued a direct order to proceed to Corfu.[38] Thus, when Nelson arrived, he found the French fleet in a weak position primarily because of Bonaparte's wish to keep naval support close at hand.

The battle itself was exceptionally hard fought. Nelson directed the ships of the line to attack the French van and center. Coming in from the northwest, five British ships, acting on their own initiative, crossed the French line and attacked from the inshore side. They instantaneously destroyed the two leading French ships with withering broadsides. Soon five French ships closed with eight British men of war, five of which were inshore and three on the ocean side of the French vessels. A ninth British ship attacked the French flagship, and a tenth entered the engagement farther down the line. The battle raged all afternoon and on into the night. Three more British ships that lagged behind in the voyage from Morea arrived after dark, and two of them joined in the attack on the flagship. At about 9:00 P.M., the *Orient* caught fire, but its crew continued to man their guns. The fire spread rapidly; at about 9:45 P.M., it reached the magazines, and the flagship exploded. The fighting then died down due to the fatigue of both French and British craws.[39]

Next morning the results of the battle became apparent. The British had captured the first six ships of the French line, completely destroyed the flagship, dismasted another, driven two others aground, and forced still another to run aground while trying to escape. Only two ships of the line and two frigates managed to reach the high seas. The British had lost 895 men, but the French losses amounted to 8,930.[40] In less than twenty-four hours, Nelson had altered the entire strategic picture in the Mediterranean, but this was not the only result of the Battle of the Nile. The effects of this battle would eventually influence developments in Turkey, Europe, and India, and in none of these areas would the ensuing events be favorable to the Republic.

The most immediate effect of Nelson's victory was to give the British control of the Mediterranean and isolate Bonaparte's army from the Metropole. The Directory, unable to reinforce and supply this army, could not coordinate it as part of a broader strategy. Furthermore, other powers became convinced that they could strike at France with a reasonable chance of success.

The first of these powers to strike at the Republic was the Ottoman Empire. French activities in the Mediterranean had alarmed the Turks for some time. As early as September, 1797, the Russian ambassador at Constantinople noted that the Porte was worried about the French occupation of the Ionian Islands and that Ottoman officials even went so far as to cooperate with Russia in disarming Denisco, a Polish revolutionary who had fled to Moldavia after 1795 and was raiding Galicia and Bukovina with the aid and encouragement of the French envoy at Constantinople. A month later the ambassador reported that the Turks feared that the French would spread Jacobin sedition in Morea.[41] The Turks took no action at this point, for although they were worried about French ambitions, they were even more afraid of the Republic's military might. They were equally fearful of Austrian ambitions in the Balkans and of Russian designs on Constantinople, and they wanted to maintain good relations with the Directory as a counterweight to the eastern European powers.

As the threat of a French invasion became more probable, the Turkish position gradually changed. Ruffin, the French *chargé d'affaires* at the Porte, reported on June 1 that the Turks were alarmed by French preparations at Toulon. On June 19, he met with the Turkish foreign minister, and in his report of June 20 he noted that the Turks expressed anxiety for the safety of Egypt.[42] Rumors of Bonaparte's invasion reached Constantinople by July 17, and on August 10 Ruffin wrote that public opinion had become very anti-French. On the same day, the Porte called upon provincial governors for troops and began to prepare a fleet of six ships of the line and eight frigates, but the Turks were still not ready for a complete rupture with France because they feared to face Bonaparte's forces alone.[43]

News of Nelson's victory reached Constantinople on August 12 and encouraged the Turks to further action. They placed French residents in the city under house arrest, and held anti-French demonstrations in the streets.[44] Paris was unable to control or influence the situation because the directors lacked sufficient information. Even under the best of circumstances communications with the Levant were slow, but Nelson's control of the Mediterranean served to make contact virtually impossible. Lacking basic information, the Directory was unable to frame a realistic policy, and as late as August 15, Talleyrand was writing that he was sure of continued Turkish neutrality.[45] It was not until September 2 that the Directory decided to send a special ambassador to Constantinople. Talleyrand was originally supposed to go, but the British captured the ship that Bonaparte sent to take him to Constantinople, and the Directory suspended the mission. Hearing nothing from Bonaparte for several months, the Directory eventually decided to act on its own and in early October appointed a special envoy. His instructions included an offer to the Porte of an offensive and defensive alliance in return for recognition of French control of Egypt, but the government canceled the mission a fortnight later upon learning of the course of events in the Levant.[46] However, even on October 3 the instructions were hopelessly out of date, because the Turks, having received the promise of Russian aid against the French, were preparing for war.

Russian hostility toward the Republic had also been building up for several years, and by 1798 the czar was sufficiently alarmed at French expansion to drop his long-standing enmity toward the Ottoman Empire and unite with the sultan against a common danger. Czar Paul I feared and hated the principles of the French Revolution, and like many of his fellow monarchs he feared internal revolt, because the number of revolutionaries in Europe was, according to a contemporary English journal, greater than any royalist would have cared to admit.[47] For Russia, Poland was a particular worry, for although their political independence had been obliterated in 1795, the Poles were still restive. There were émigré Polish brigades in the Cisalpine army, and Polish refugees in Paris were constantly urging the French to attack Russia and liberate Poland.[48] In November, 1797, at Vilna, the Russians had uncovered a French-financed plot to liberate Poland.[49] Paul had already demonstrated his hostility to the French by receiving Condé in St. Petersburg, escorting his émigré army through Germany, and allowing it to stay in Poland. The czar had also recognized the count of Provence as Louis XVIII.[50]

It was, however, French expansion in the eastern Mediterranean, an area in which Russia had long-standing ambitions, that led the czar to contemplate active hostilities.

The French, after their occupation of the Ionian Islands in 1797, had opened negotiations with the pasha of Albania and with Greek leaders. Bonaparte sent a Greek living in Corsica to hold talks with the patriarch of the Greek Church, and the Russian reaction was to enter into the current English, Austrian, and Prussian negotiations, and he offered Berlin a defensive alliance.[51] The Prussians, however, were too afraid of France and too suspicious of Austria to take any positive action, and Haugwitz told the Russian envoy that Frederick William III was determined to maintain his neutrality.[52] The failure to find an ally in central Europe plus the French seizure of Malta and Egypt forced the Russians to turn their attentions to the Near East. The czar ordered six ships of the line and seven frigates from the Black Sea fleet to proceed to the Bosporus and activated a corps of sixteen thousand men for action against the French. To gain the cooperation of the sultan, he signed a military assistance convention with him on August 20. Assured against the possibility of Russian aggression, the sultan felt that the time had come to strike at the French invaders. On September 2 he placed Ruffin under arrest. Three days later the Russian fleet arrived at the Golden Horn, and on September 9 the Ottoman Empire issued an official declaration of war against France.[53]

Turkish units gathered at Rhodes and Syria to prepare for an assault on the Ionian Islands. On October 14 advance units of the combined Turko-Russian fleet under the command of a Russian admiral reached Cerigo, and the next day the one hundred-man French garrison capitulated. The fleet next sailed to Zante; troops landed, and the garrison surrendered on October 25. The bulk of the fleet then made for Corfu, while other units went to Albania to make contact with Ali Pasha, who had already begun hostilities with the French in order to be on the winning side. He had on November 1 taken the French base of Nicopoli on the Albanian coast, inflicting eight hundred casualties on the defenders.[54] By November 5, twelve thousand Albanians, Turks, and Russians had invested Corfu. The Directory issued orders for the reinforcement of the garrison, but the blockade was so efficient that the task was impossible. It was only a matter of time before the French would be forced to surrender. That they held out until March, 1799, was a remarkable but strategically futile exploit.[55]

The French military defeats in the eastern Mediterranean were matched by new diplomatic setbacks. The czar opened negotiations with Austria and England to form a new coalition against France. He also continued diplomatic talks with the sultan, and on December 23, 1798, the Turks and Russians concluded a treaty of alliance against France. For the first and only time in the eighteenth century, these two hereditary foes agreed to a mutual guarantee of each other's possessions. Further, they promised that neither contracting party would conclude a separate peace with a common foe and that both would give military assistance in case of aggression on the part of a third power. Other powers were invited to adhere to this treaty—a clear invitation to England. Pitt for his part was not slow to seize the opportunity to find allies in the Mediterranean, and on January 5, 1799, England acceded to the Russo-Turkish treaty.[56]

Thus in both military and diplomatic terms, the eastern expedition proved to be an unmitigated disaster for the French. They had lost a fleet and with it control of the Mediterranean. The British isolated Bonaparte's army and rendered it strategically useless, and the Turks and Russians destroyed the French foothold in the Balkans. Russia and Turkey temporarily ended their age-old rivalry and together went to war against France, and the English found themselves in an excellent position to devise a new coalition dedicated to the destruction of the Republic.

NOTES

Chapter 6

1. Jacques Godechot, *Histoire de Malta,* p. 65.

2. Désiré Lacroix, *Bonaparte en Égypte (1798–1799)* , pp. 46–47; and William Hardman, *A History of Malta,* pp. 52, 55, 58–61.

3. Henri Plon and J. Dumaine, eds., *Correspondance de Napoléon Ier,* 4: 143–44, 156, 159, 172, 175; and Ministère de la Guerre État-Major de l'Armée, Archives historiques, Armée d'Orient Situations, carton B^{6}190 (hereafter, Min. de la Guerre, AH) .

4. Louis Alexandre Berthier, *Relations des campagnes du général Bonaparte en Égypte et en Syrie*, pp. 4–9.

5. Plon and Dumaine, *Correspondance de Napoléon Ier* p. 191.

6. Ibid., pp. 191–92.

7. Edmund Ferry, *La France en Afrique* (Paris: 1905), p. 7.

8. Commandant P. G. Guitry, *L'Armée de Bonaparte en Égypte 1798–1799*, p. 95.

9. Min. de la Guerre, AH, Mémoires historiques, no. 9081, Bataille des Pyramides le 3 Thermidor an 6 (27 juillet 1798) par le général Berthier (hereafter, MH).

10. Ibid.

11. Berthier, *Rélations des campagnes*, p. 22.

12. Ibid., pp. 24–25.

13. Henri Galli, ed., *Journal d'un officier de l'armée d'Égypte, l'armée française en Égypte 1798–1801*, p. 53.

14. Plon and Dumaine, *Correspondance de Napoléon Ier*, pp. 255, 266.

15. François Charles-Roux, *Bonaparte, gouverneur d'Égypte*, pp. 57–59: and Plon and Dumaine, *Correspondance de Napoléon Ier*, pp. 301–3.

16. Ferry, *La France en Afrique*, pp. 11, 14; and Napoléon Bonaparte, *Correspondance inédite officielle et confidentielle de Napoléon Bonaparte, Égypte* (Paris: 1819), 1: 260–64, 349.

17. Charles-Roux, *Bonaparte*, pp. 50–55, 65.

18. François Charles-Roux, *L'Angleterre et l'expédition française en Égypte*, 1: 10.

19. Julian Corbett, ed., *Private Papers of George, Second Earl Spencer, First Lord of the Admiralty 1794–1801*, 2: 433–34.

20. Historical Manuscripts Commission, *Report on the Manuscripts of J. B. Fortescue, Esq., preserved at Dropmore*, 4: 166.

21. Corbett, *Private Papers of Spencer*, pp. 192–93.

22. *Manuscripts of Fortescue*, pp. 192–93.

23. Cyril Matheson, *The Life of Henry Dundas First Viscount Melville, 1742–1811*, pp. 130, 190.

24. Corbett, *Private Papers of Spencer*, p. 318.

25. Ibid., pp. 437–41.

26. Ibid., pp. 444–46.

27. Thomas J. Pettigrew, ed., *Memoirs of the Life of Vice-Admiral Lord Viscount Nelson, K. B.*, 1: 119.

28. Corbett, *Private Papers of Spencer*, p. 448.

29. A. T. Mahan, *The Life of Nelson*, 1: 327–29.

30. Nicholas H. Nicolas, ed., *The Dispatches and Letters of Vice-Admiral Lord Viscount Nelson* (London: 1845), 3: 31.

31. George P. Naish, ed., *Nelson's Letters to His Wife and Other Documents*, p. 407.

32. Nicolas, *Dispatches of Nelson*, pp. 36–37; and Mahan, *Life of Nelson*, p. 338.

33. Naish, *Nelson's Letters to His Wife*, p. 411.

34. Mahan, *Life of Nelson*, pp. 339–40, 342.

35. Ibid., p. 343.

36. Ibid., p. 346.

37. Bonaparte, *Correspondance*, p. 201. After becoming First Consul, Bonaparte destroyed much of the evidence.

38. Georges Douin, *La flotte de Bonaparte sur les côtes d'Égypte*, pp. 77–78.

39. Oliver Warner, *The Battle of the Nile*. Witnesses differ as to the precise time that the *Orient* exploded.

40. Ibid.

41. Peter I. Bartenev, ed., *Papers of Mikhail Larionovich Vorontsov and Other Members of the Family*, 14: 89–91.

42. Clément de la Jonquière, ed., *L'expédition d'Égypte 1798–1801*, 2: 594, 596.

43. Ibid., p. 601; and Paul Pisani, "L'expédition russo-turque aux Iles ioniennes en 1798–1799," *Revue d'histoire diplomatique*, 2: 202.

44. Pisani, "L'expédition russo-turque," p. 203.

45. Jonquière, *L'expédition d'Égypte*, pp. 608–9.

46. Ibid., pp. 605–7, and 3: 257–60.

47. *The Annual Register or a View of the History, Politics and Literature for the year 1798*, p. 91.

48. See Leonard Chodzko, *Histoire des légions polanaises en Italie*, vol. 2.

49. Bartenev, *Papers on Vorontsov*, 11: 6–7.

50. Ernest Daudet, *Les émigrés et la Seconde Coalition*, pp. 37–38.

51. *Annual Register*, pp. 137–38.

52. *Manuscripts of Fortescue*, p. 213; and Bartenev, *Papers of Vorontsov*, 11: 6–7.

53. Jonquière, *L'expédition d'Égypte*, 3: 230.

54. Min. de la Guerre, AH, Correspondance, Armée d'Italie, novembre 1798, carton B356bis.

55. Min. de la Guerre, AH, Correspondance, Armée d'Italie et de Rome, décembre 1798, carton B357 and mars 1799, carton B359.

56. Annual Register, pp. 237–40.

7

India and Syria

The French venture in the Near East had a marked influence on events in Asia as well as in Europe. Even before Bonaparte landed in Egypt, the French had upset the balance of power between the British and the princes of the Indian subcontinent. Operating from their colonies in the Indian Ocean, privateers and units of the French navy struck continuously at English commerce. At the same time, French adventurers, who had remained in India after the Seven Years' War, adopted the principles of their mother country's revolution and worked to convince the native rulers to align themselves with the Republic in the struggle against Britain. The arrival of a French army in the Levant convinced many British officials of the existence of a grand design that threatened the security of their Indian possessions. The success of the French freebooters in influencing the Indian princes, the threat posed by the sultan of Mysore's overtures to the French for an offensive alliance against the British, and the danger of concerted action between Mysore and Bonaparte's army of the East convinced Richard Wellesley, earl of Mornington and governor-general of India, that it was necessary to take energetic action to halt the French, eliminate hostile native powers, and expand the empire.

In 1798, Britain was by far the most powerful of all the colonial nations. On the east coast of India, Calcutta dominated the Ganges River basin and was the seat of government for

Bengal, as well as for the other British holdings in India. Further south on the Coromandel Coast, Madras controlled the land approaches to Bengal and served as a naval base for the British fleet, while on the west coast, Bombay served as the main trading port of the East India Company.[1]

Originally, the East India Company ran the Indian colonies. The proprietors and a board of twenty-four directors controlled the company, but thirteen standing committees conducted the day-by-day operations. The most important of these was the Secret Committee, which directed the company's naval and military operations, gave sailing instructions to ships in time of war, and represented the company in dealing with the British government.[2] In 1784, the Government of India Act gave Parliament a great deal of power in the affairs of the company. The act left nomination to the posts of governor-general, governors, other high civil posts, and army commands in the hands of the company but made them subject to government approval, and in fact the ministry usually made the appointments. The government could also recall any of the appointed officials. The act also set up a Board of Control consisting of a secretary of state, the chancellor of the Exchequer, and four privy councilors, whose job it was to supervise the civil and military government of the company. The board could issue secret orders concerning war, peace, and negotiations with Indian princes. The company's Secret Committee relayed the board's orders to officials in India.[3]

The military establishment was also of a dual nature, consisting of king's regiments and the company's European and native troops. The government could send troops to India at the company's expense whether or not the company requested their services. In 1798, there were about eighty thousand soldiers in India, of which twenty-two thousand were king's troops. The Royal Navy also cooperated in the protection of British India. It was assisted by the company's merchant ships, specially built for the Asiatic trade and large enough to be converted into warships. There were seventy companymen in commission in 1798.[4]

British possessions in India produced great wealth. In Bengal during 1795, the company's imports totaled £246,731, while exports amounted to £1,406,490. From 1796 to 1797, the figures were £249,391 and £812,831, and from 1797 to 1798, they were £254,605 and £1,809,273. The figures for private merchants in Bengal from 1795 to 1796 amounted to £246,731 in imports and £1,406,490 for exports. From 1796 to 1797, the totals were £380,828 and £797,999, and from 1797 to 1798, they were £522,000 and £573,308. The combined totals show that from 1795 to 1796, Bengal imported £527,818 worth of goods and exported £2,828,930. From 1796 to 1797, imports amounted to £630,219 and exports to £1,610,830, and from 1797 to 1798, the figures were £776,605 and £3,382,581. In the following year, exports amounted to £7,367,727. In Bombay, exports during 1795 amounted to £204,676; in 1796 they were £143,925, and in 1797, £342,945.[5] In 1798 the total taxable revenue from rents, trade, and industry in England amounted to £102,000,000, of which £17,000,000 was derived from foreign trade.[6] Of this £17,000,000, over forty percent was derived from profits of the India trade, giving both the company and the government a great interest in preserving and expanding the Indian Empire.

In marked contrast with the British holdings, French colonies in the area were small, produced little wealth, and had only small garrisons. On the subcontinent itself, the British had taken the small French enclaves of Pondicherry, Mahe, and Chandermagore by 1794. The only remaining French colonies were their island holdings in the Indian Ocean. The largest of these, the Isle of France, had a population of ten thousand whites and mulattoes and fifty-five thousand slaves. Trading in sugar, coffee, cotton, indigo, and cloves, the island derived an annual income of about forty to fifty thousand pounds. The Isle of Bourbon, lying 130 miles to the southwest, with a population of eight thousand free men and forty-eight thousand slaves, exported grain to the Isle of France. Roderigue, 375 miles east of the Isle of France, was mainly a watering place for ships, as were the Seychelles, 800 miles north of the Isle.[7]

French naval forces stationed at the Isle of France at the outbreak of the war numbered only four frigates, soon outmatched by Admiral Ranier's five ships of the line that arrived to blockade the small colony in February, 1794. After an indecisive action forced Ranier's fleet to return home for repairs, the French were able to raise the blockade. The Batavian Revolution and consequent shift of the Dutch to the French side gave the Republic's colonies a further respite, because the British turned their attention away from the small French islands toward the more alluring prospects of conquering the Cape Colony, Ceylon, and Java. They took the Dutch colonies by the middle of 1796, and in August the British captured a Batavian fleet, sent to retake the Cape Colony. The concentration of British naval strength against the Dutch had, however, enabled the French to reinforce the Isle of France.[8]

In July, 1796, twelve hundred infantry under the command of General Magallon, and Rear-Admiral Sercey's naval squadron of four frigates arrived to strengthen Governor-general Malartic's local forces. By 1797, however, the British had reinforced their Indian Ocean squadron and had again isolated the French colonies.[9] Since communications between Paris and the Isle of France were at the mercy of the British, it was almost impossible for the Directory to coordinate Malartic's actions with its overall strategy. The refusal of the colonies to obey those few orders that they did receive further weakened the French position. Malartic had refused to enforce a decree abolishing slavery in all French possessions, and when the Directory sent agents to apply this law, he forced the agents to leave the island.[10] After this clash, the local officials were able to exercise almost complete independence, and Malartic acted like a sovereign ruler. His freedom, however, was limited because he could expect little help from Paris. Nor could he turn to France's allies for aid. The Dutch colonies were in British hands, and the Spanish had but a single Mexican regiment, three thousand native militia, and thirty small gunboats to protect the Philippines. The Spanish authorities in Mexico, who governed the Philippines, were far too worried about British attacks to contemplate undertaking offensive operations.[11] Sercey's ships did raid British commerce with some success, but the French could hope to do little more than annoy the British unless they could cooperate with the native princes in a concerted drive against the British Indian colonies.

The three main independent states of India, the Mahratta Confederacy, Hyderabad, and Mysore, were engaged in a constant round of hostilities against each other with the British holding the balance, a fact that made a French-Indian alliance difficult to arrange. Such an alliance was not, however, impossible, because although the princes were often willing to align themselves with the English to defeat their rivals, they were all suspicious of the growth of British power. By 1798, the independent rulers were becoming increasingly hostile to the presence of the British in India. French influence was growing rapidly on the subcontinent, and Paris was well aware of the possibility of striking at British commerce through India.

The Mahratta Confederacy, the weakest of the major native powers, was a union of princes that had established a Hindu state in 1707 upon the ruins of the disintegrating Mughul Empire. The Confederacy itself soon lost much of its power because of defeats suffered in clashes with Afghanistan. In the 1770s, the Mahrattas regained some cohesion and conquered the remnants of the Mughul domains around Delhi, but in 1794 the head of the Confederacy was a fifteen-year-old boy, and the princes began to struggle among themselves for power.[12] In 1795 a French officer obtained command of the army from one of these feuding princes, but he was isolated in northern India and could not hope to influence events in favor of the Republic without outside assistance.[13]

The nizam of Hyderabad had for many years been closely allied with the British and had signed defensive treaties with them in 1766 and 1768. He had even joined England in a war against Mysore in 1790. In 1795, however, the British had remained neutral in a war between Hyderabad and the Mahrattas, and Hyderabad lost. After his capitulation in March, 1796, the nizam held British neutrality to be the principal cause of his defeat. In revenge, he dismissed the British trained battalions and British officers from his army and turned to the French. He placed a republican French officer, Raymond, in charge of his army, and soon had fourteen thousand men armed and trained in the republican manner.[14]

The situation in Mysore was even more alarming for the British. Mysore had traditionally been hostile to the English, and the sultan was more than willing to undertake direct negotiations with the French to obtain an ally for an attack on British possessions. The state had originally risen to power through the efforts of Hyder Ali, a Muslim adventurer who had overthrown the original Hindu ruler. Hyder had fought the English to a draw

SOUTHERN   INDIA

1792 – 99

in 1769, but they defeated him ten years later. After his death
in 1782, his ambitious son, Tippoo, continued the war, and in
1784 obtained a treaty restoring the *status quo ante*. Wishing to
gain control of Deccan, Tippoo regarded the treaty as nothing

more than a truce. In 1789 he began a new round of hostilities, but Cornwallis, aided by the nizam and the Mahrattas, inflicted a crushing defeat upon him. In 1792 Tippoo had to sue for peace and surrender about half his territory to the victorious coalition. But he immediately began looking for a way to renew the conflict on favorable terms.[15]

Tippoo realized that he could not fight the British alone and that he needed the support of a major power. The advent of Anglo-French hostilities presented him with his long-sought opportunity to find an ally, but the actual opening of negotiations with the French was more a matter of chance than of conscious design. On May 5, 1797, François Ripaud, a French privateer, arrived at Tippoo's capital at Seringapatam. Ripaud claimed that he was an official of the French Republic, and at Seringapatam he organized a primary assembly, a revolutionary tribunal, and new laws in keeping with revolutionary principles for the French troops in the sultan's service. On May 15 he raised a tricolor flag and swore eternal friendship with Tippoo, to whom he gave the complimentary title of Citizen Prince.[16]

Tippoo was not so foolish as to take Ripaud at his word, and from the moment of the Frenchman's arrival on his shores, he and his advisors had been debating the wisdom of using him in order to establish direct contact with France. On March 24, the head of Tippoo's Commercial Department advised his master that although Ripaud was a liar and a fraud, the sultan should, nevertheless, employ him as an agent in opening negotiations with France. The French were not trustworthy, the advisor added, but sufficient promises of territorial gains at the expense of the British should guarantee their loyalty to any alliance. The next day, the heads of the Naval and the Military departments agreed with their colleague's analysis and stated that although Mysore could not trust France, the two states could work together for the limited objective of attacking the British in India. The heads of the Fortification and Garrison departments also agreed. On March 27 Tippoo decided to undertake official negotiations with the French, for although Ripaud's false claims did not fool the sultan, they presented him with the opportunity of dealing with the French on a serious basis.[17]

On April 2 Tippoo designated five ambassadors to arrange a

treaty of alliance with the French. The sultan directed them to proceed to the Isle of France and open discussions with Malartic. If Malartic was unable or unwilling to conclude a treaty, three of the ambassadors were to go to Paris and conduct negotiations with the Directory. Tippoo gave his envoys copies of a proposed treaty, the terms of which included provisions that neither party would in case of war make a separate peace and that they would divide any spoils of victory equally. Tippoo went on to propose that the French supply forty thousand men for a campaign against the English, while Mysore contributed eighty thousand troops. The combined forces would attack the English possessions in India and the Portuguese colony of Goa. After the victory, France would obtain all the territory from Madras to Pondicherry, Bombay, and half of Bengal. Tippoo would take the rest of Madras and Bengal, and Goa.[18]

Tippoo's agents arrived at the Isle of France on January 19, 1798, where Malartic gave them a public reception despite their wish to keep the entire proceeding secret. Malartic then told the ambassadors that only Paris could ratify the proposed accords, but that he would ask for volunteers to serve in the sultan's army. He issued a proclamation calling for recruits, but only eighty-six men answered the appeal. These plus the ambassadors then returned to Mysore on a French frigate.[19] Malartic also agreed to send Tippoo's proposals on to Paris, and a French naval officer, commissioned as the sultan's ambassador to the Directory, set off for France on February 5. On July 20 two more ambassadors from Mysore set out for Paris, and Tippoo continued earlier negotiations with Zemaun Shah, the ruler of Afghanistan. He hoped to convince the shah to attack the Mahrattas, depose their king, set up a puppet government, and then join France and Mysore in attacking the English.[20]

Meanwhile, in Paris, the Directory was beginning to take an interest in the possibilities of opening direct negotiations with the Indian princes. Although they placed most of their hopes for an attack on India on Bonaparte's army, they also tried to arrange direct action between France and India. On January 21, 1798, Sercey told the minister of marine of the arrival of Tippoo's ambassadors at the Isle of France and suggested that the Republic take advantage of the sultan's offer of alliance. By means of an alliance with Mysore, France would be better able to strike at England's resources and at the same time expand her colonial empire.[21] On February 22 another naval officer, Piveron, told the directors that the best way to force the English from India was by means of an alliance with Tippoo Sultan. Piveron said that the French should send ten thousand infantry and four thousand light cavalry directly to Mysore to cooperate with Tippoo's army. He admitted that the voyage would be long and difficult, but he went on to point out that in the 1780s Suffren had made just such a voyage, and there was a good naval base at the Isle of France where a fleet could obtain supplies and make repairs, and that Mysore also had a good harbor. Piveron concluded by telling the directors that negotiations should also be opened with other Indian rulers and that a French seaborne invasion of India would take the British completely by surprise.[22]

After arranging for the Egyptian expedition, the Directory decided to undertake direct negotiations with Tippoo. The government directed Piveron to go to India and open talks with the sultan. He left Toulon on August 16, but his ship foundered and he had to go ashore at Genoa. He continued his voyage by the overland route going from Genoa to Ancona and from there to Corfu, but by this time the situation in the Mediterranean had drastically altered. He was trapped on Corfu by the Russo-Turkish siege and eventually taken prisoner.[23] The directors did not, however, abandon hopes of arranging an alliance with Tippoo, because a copy of the sultan's proposed treaty eventually reached Paris. Noting Tipoo's willingness to fight the British, the French became more determined than ever to establish direct contact with Mysore.

On October 26, 1798, the Directory chose Louis Monneron as agent to the Isle of France and Réunion and ordered him to secure the submission of these two islands to the Constitution and the laws, and in general to make these colonies subject to control from Paris. The Directors then instructed him to report on the financial and military situation of the colonies, send ships to the Red Sea to open communications with Bonaparte's army, and increase corsair warfare against British commerce. Finally, Paris told him to attempt to procure information on the position of the princes of India, particularly on that of Tippoo Sultan and undertake friendly relations with him. He will give to him assurance that the Executive Directory counts on him, when it will be possible to act effectively against the English, and that he will be warned of the measures that will be taken so that he can make his own preparations. . . .[24]

The directors also tried to integrate this effort with the larger one of setting strategic objectives for Bonaparte's isolated army. On November 4 they told Bonaparte that because the enemy controlled the Mediterranean, his army could not return to Europe. The Directory then presented him with three alternatives: establish a firm and lasting hold on Egypt; march on Constantinople; or go to India, where preparations were already underway to receive a French force.[25] The directors left the choice up to Bonaparte, but since they told him that Monneron was on his way to India, it seems that the Directory wanted Bonaparte to choose the third alternative. Unfortunately, part of the Directory's plan broke down almost immediately, because on November 18 Monneron was placed under house arrest pending an investigation into charges of treason against his brother and himself.[26] Nevertheless, Bonaparte's army, acting independently, could still pose a serious threat to India, and officials in London and Calcutta were well aware of this fact.

The British were aware, if not in precise detail at least in broad outline, of Tippoo's plans and of French policy. The expedition to Egypt proved to some of the Cabinet members and most of the officials in Calcutta the necessity of taking rapid preventive action. Dundas, the first of the Cabinet ministers to grasp the full implications of the Toulon expedition, continued to press his colleagues for action in India. On June 13 he told the Cabinet that Bonaparte's ultimate aim was an invasion of India by the overland route through Syria, down the Euphrates valley, and from there along the Persian coast to the Indus River, where he would meet Tippoo's army. He suggested that the Cabinet send ships to the Persian Gulf and the Red Sea to hinder communications between Bonaparte and Tippoo, and warn the Turks and Russians of the impending danger in the

East. He further advised the government to send reinforcements to India.[27] After his arrival in the Mediterranean, Nelson, too, became convinced that Bonaparte's final goal was India. On June 15, in a letter to Spencer, Nelson stated that such a plan was not as difficult as some might think, and when writing to the British consul at Alexandria, he expressed the same views.[28] Dundas meanwhile continued to warn the Cabinet about the mounting danger to India, and the news of the arrival of Tippoo's ambassadors at the Isle de France, reaching London on June 14, finally convinced Pitt and Grenville that the army of the East, combined with Tippoo's forces, did indeed pose a serious threat to England's Indian empire. The Cabinet then agreed to take remedial measures, and on June 26 ordered three infantry battalions to proceed from Lisbon to Bombay.[29]

Dundas also warned Mornington of the French threat. He had the East India Company's Committee of Secrecy send Mornington a warning and a policy directive on June 18. The Committee informed the governor-general that a French fleet had left Toulon and that its ultimate objective was to attack British India in consort with Mysore. The Committee then directed Mornington to crush Mysore before the sultan completed his warlike preparations.[30]

But even before the Secret Committee sent their warning, Mornington had been keeping a close watch on events in Mysore and was debating whether or not to attack. On June 23 he received a report from General Harris, commander in chief of the troops in Bengal. Harris favored an immediate attack on Tippoo.[31] Five days later Mornington's brother, the future duke of Wellington, suggested that war be delayed until Royal and company troops were better prepared, but a month later he wrote that the British should attack Tippoo as soon as possible because delay would give the sultan time to get aid from the French and the other Indian princes.[32] On August 12, Mornington wrote a secret minute setting forth his policy. The minute stated that Tippoo planned to act in concert with France against English interests. The governor-general went on to state that French influence in India was growing progressively stronger and that the arrival of even a small body of French troops would create an alarming situation. For these reasons, it was in England's best interest to destroy Tippoo. This was not possible in the immediate future because of the weakness of the British forces, and, until reinforcements arrived, the British would have to continue to balance Mysore, Hyderabad, and the Mahratta Confederacy in such a manner that British intervention in alliance with one of these states could overpower the other two. As the British army grew stronger, the first goal would be the elimination of the French corps in Hyderabad. Since the Mahrattas were weak, Tippoo could not rely on them in case of war, and British control of Hyderabad would place Mysore in an untenable position. Mornington would then insist that Tippoo dismiss the French from his service and accept a resident British ambassador at his court. Tippoo would have to accept these terms, which amounted to surrender, or fight against overwhelming odds.[33]

Mornington's first concern was then to strengthen his army. At the end of 1798, reinforcements began to reach India. In October a battalion arrived from Lisbon, and starting in September, three battalions from the Cape Colony landed. A regiment from England and a battalion from the Mediterranean moved east in December. In India itself, Mornington activated the Calcutta militia and brought European and native artillery units to full strength. In November he raised two new native infantry regiments.[34]

With his strengthened army, Mornington next struck at Hyderabad. A force of four Madras battalions and a Bengal regiment accompanied by sixteen guns arrived before the nizam's capital on October 12. For ten days, the British and the nizam's French-trained troops faced each other, and the nizam's troops finally broke without firing a shot. A mutiny forced Raymond to flee to the British position, and on October 23 the British occupied the nizam's lines, disbanding his French-led contingent. The British then forced Hyderabad to sign a treaty of alliance.[35] Having eliminated the French threat from Hyderabad, Mornington was ready to turn his attentions to the destruction of Mysore. On November 4 he informed Tippoo of the French fleet's defeat in the Levant, and on November 8 he told him that he was fully aware of Mysore's hostile activities. The letter concluded with the proposal that a British envoy come to Mysore to settle all differences. On November 26 Mornington received word from

England that the French were firmly established in Egypt and posed a definite threat to India. This information caused the governor-general to take temporarily a more conciliatory line, and on December 15 he told the sultan that he entertained hopes of increasing the friendship that already existed between England and Mysore.[36] Tipoo had meanwhile responded to Mornington's first letter on December 18, the note reaching Calcutta on Christmas Day. The sultan denied having any dealings with the French. He rejected the idea of a special envoy, claiming that existing treaties were a sufficient guarantee of peace.[37]

Mornington had meanwhile received additional reinforcements and decided to revert to his earlier belligerent policy. In his reply of January 9, 1799, he reiterated his original demands of November. He concluded by saying that he expected a friendly reply and that, "I most earnestly request that your reply may not be deferred for more than one day after this shall reach your presence. Dangerous consequences result from the delay of arduous affairs."[38] On February 3, Mornington, now confident of his ability to decide the issue by force of arms, decided not to wait for a reply and ordered General Harris's Madras army of 5,000 Europeans and 13,900 natives, Stuart's Bombay army comprised of 1,600 Europeans and 4,800 native troops, and the Hyderabad contingent, now under British control, of 6,500 Europeans and 6,500 native soldiers to prepare to march into Mysore.[39]

Tippoo had meanwhile realized the overwhelming nature of the forces arrayed against him and attempted to take defensive measures. He refused to answer Mornington's latest note, hoping to delay the course of events until the advent of the rainy season made campaigning impossible. He also sent a Frenchman and two Muslims to Europe to request aid from the Directory, but they were captured by a British man-of-war near the Seychelles Islands.[40] Tippoo also wrote to Zemaun Shah asking for help in repelling the "infidels" but he received no answer. These moves having failed, Tippoo felt that he had no alternative but to adhere to the British demands, and, in a letter received in Calcutta on February 13, Tippoo stated that he would receive the special envoy.[41] He was, however too late, for Mornington felt that any further delay would only benefit his enemies. The troops from

Hyderabad joined Harris at Vellore on February 20, and the combined force began to move into Mysore. Stuart's army also started moving east from Bombay, and on February 22, Mornington issued a formal declaration of war against Mysore.[42]

Tippoo's forces amounted to thirty-three thousand infantry, fifteen thousand cavalry, and two thousand artillery, but they were no match for the British Cown and East India Company forces. By April 14 the British had arrived before the walls of Seringapatam, and their siege guns began to batter the city walls. On May 4, storming parties pushed through a breach in Tippoo's fortifications and entered the city. Tippoo's army dissolved, and the British slaugtered the disorganized masses. Tippoo himself perished while trying to organize a counterattack.[43] Late at night, one of Tippoo's aides, under armed guard, searched by torchlight through the ten thousand corpses littering the area until he found the sultan's body, which was buried the next day. At the close of the burial ceremony, a thunderstorm of unusual violence burst over Seringapatam, marking with terror the end of the Hyder Dynasty, which in conjunction with the French had posed the greatest threat yet placed in the path of the growing British domination of India.[44]

In the following months, the British stabilized their control of Mysore by annexing the country's coastline and by giving Hyderabad and the Mahratta Confederacy portions of the dead sultan's domains. Mornington also restored the Hindu dynasty of Mysore at Seringapatam and forced the new monarch to sign a treaty with the British providing for an offensive-defensive alliance. The treaty also provided for the maintaining of a British garrison at Seringapatam at the rajah's expense, and for the occupation of other strategic forts throughout Mysore by British or company troops. Finally, the British received the right to introduce any measures they wished for the better ordering of the Mysore government, and the new ruler had to undertake to follow British advice on finance, taxation, commerce, trade, agriculture, and any other objects that the British desired.[45] Thus, Mornington had not only destroyed the strongest native power in India and eliminated French influence on the subcontinent, but he had also extended the area of direct British domination.

After destroying Tippoo, Mornington next turned his attention to securing the British position in the Persian Gulf area. As in India, his motives were based upon the desire to enhance British power and the need to check the ambitions of the French, who had agents operating in this region.

Fortunately for the British, these states were hostile to one another. The Gulf pirates were at war with Muscat, and Oman was also hostile to Muscat because in 1793 Muscat, which had formed a part of Oman, had declared itself independent. The pasha of Baghdad, a Turkish official, was also hostile to Muscat, because he felt that the imam was pro-French. Mornington had become worried about French activities in the area, and had sent his agent at Bushire to negotiate a treaty with Muscat. The imam was happy to get British protection in return for turning against the French. The treaty, signed in October, 1798, required the imam to deny French and Batavian ships admittance to his ports, prevent them from establishing trading posts in his country, and dismiss French and Dutch citizens from his service. In return, Enland promised to arrange a rapprochement between Muscat and the pasha of Baghdad.[46]

The threat posed by Tippoo Sultan turned British attention away from the Gulf area, but after the fall of Seringapatam, Mornington sent John Malcolm, a Persian expert, to Tehran to arrange an alliance with the shah. Malcolm left India in December, and on his way to Persia stopped at Muscat, where he convinced the imam to accept a British resident at his court. His mission in Persia dragged on for several years, and eventually led to the conclusion of an Anglo-Persian treaty.[07]

As a final step, British naval forces secured strategic positions in the Red Sea to protect the approaches to Bombay. On May 7, 1799, two frigates, two gunboats, a bomb ketch, and several transports carrying the Eighty-fourth Regiment and six hundred native troops arrived off the island of Perim, where the troops landed. In July the ships bombarded the French-held Red Sea port of Kosseir, driving the garrison out of the town, and in August the squadron proceeded to Jidda, where their commander convinced the sheriff to forbid trade between his subjects and the French, and he then shifted the troops on Perim to Aden upon invitation from the sultan.[48]

By May, 1799, the British had destroyed the threat of a Franco-

Mysore attack on their Indian possessions, and by August had gained control of the strategic areas of the Persian Gulf and the southern end of the Red Sea. Mornington had successfully frustrated French ambitions, and if the French still hoped to attack India, their only hope lay in Bonaparte's army of the East.

While Mornington extended British power and influence in India and the Gulf, Bonaparte, despite the annihilation of his fleet, maintained firm control of Egypt and began to organize the country as if he expected a long occupation. He issued orders to fortify Rosetta and Alexandria, and he told his divisional commanders that the French in Egypt could, if necessary, beat off one hundred thousand Turks.[49] Bonaparte also started to prepare for an eventual attack on India. On December 1 he ordered General Bon, along with a naval officer and ten men, to proceed to Suez, to set up a shore battery and put the town in a state of defense. He directed a unit of sappers and engineers to accompany Bon's expedition, and decreed that Suez should have a 150-man garrison. He instructed the naval officer to give an account of all ships found in the port and to arm two ships to cruise in the Red Sea. On December 10 he sent a second unit of technical troops to Suez. An armed sloop put out into the Red Sea on a reconnaissance on December 30, and Bonaparte issued orders to build three more sloops and a corvette. In January, 1799, the general visited Suez, and on January 15 he ordered four armed sloops to put out into the Red Sea.[50]

Bonaparte also opened communications with Mysore. Already, on December 17, a ship had arrived at Suez carrying, according to Bonaparte's report, "an Indian who had a letter for the commander of the French forces in Egypt."[51] On January 25 Bonaparte replied to Tippoo, stating that he had come to Egypt as part of a plan to drive Britain from India and asked Tippoo to send a representative to Egypt to arrange concerted action.[52]

Despite these grandiose plans, the French had to cope with problems much nearer home. The Muslim population had never really accepted the French, and after the Turks had entered the war, the sultan sent agents into Egypt to rouse the population against them. Agents of the exiled Mamluks were also active, and on October 21, 1798, they succeeded in igniting the flames of revolt in Cairo itself. The army of the East quickly crushed the

rebellion, but the outbreak, neverthless, alarmed the French, show-
ing them that despite all their efforts to obtain the population's
support, they had failed.[53]

The French received even more alarming news in the first month
of 1799, when they learned that the Turks were gathering their
forces for an attack on Egypt. The sultan was preparing a field
army of twenty-five thousand in Syria, supported by a four thousand-man garrison at Jaffa and a twenty thousand-man garrison
at Saint Jean d'Acre. In addition, he stationed eighteen thousand
troops at Rhodes in preparation for a seaborne attack on Egypt.[54]
A British flotilla of three ships of the line plus lighter craft under
the command of Sir William Sydney Smith supported the Turkish
field army and prepared to transport the Rhodes army to Egypt
in conjunction with the land attack from Syria. At this point,
Bonaparte did not yet know of the Turkish declaration of war, but
he certainly was aware of the hostile preparations in Syria.

Advance units of the Turkish field army occupied El Arish,
a town on the Egyptian-Syrian frontier, in late December. To
prevent a further Turkish concentration on the frontier, Bonaparte
felt it necessary to strike first. The infantry divisions of Kléber,
Bon, Reynier, and Lannes, and a cavalry division under Murat
made up the bulk of the 12,945-man invasion force that also
included a battalion of sappers, a brigade of engineers, and an
artillery brigade. He sent Desaix's 6,500-man division into Upper
Egypt to drive the Mamluks from the area, and assigned 10,000
troops to hold Lower Egypt.[55] On February 4, the advance units
of the expeditionary force drove the Turks out of El Arish, thereby
opening the French campaign in Syria.

On February 10 Bonaparte informed the Directory of his reasons
for moving into Syria. His first was to assure the security of Egypt
by capturing the major cities of Syria, which the Turks would
otherwise use as advance bases for an attack. His second reason
was to force the Porte to negotiate, and the final motive was to
deprive the English of the supplies and bases they had found in
Syria.[56] Bonaparte's objectives appear to be entirely defensive, but
there exists much evidence to indicate that he had in addition
a far more ambitious plan. Despite the fact that he had not yet
received the Directory's recommendations of November 4, he may
well have been planning to march through Syria and attack India

by the overland route in a last desperate attempt to fulfill the original aims of the eastern expedition.

The first piece of evidence to support this assumption is the original plan of the expedition, which was to prepare an invasion of India. In the second place, it is hardly likely that Bonaparte would choose to fight the Turks in Syria if he had only a defensive operation in mind. His army was undoubtedly superior to that of the Turks, and there was little reason to tire his troops by a long march over the bad terrain of Sinai and southern Palestine when he could force the Turks to take this same route in reverse and could meet them on ground of his own choosing. The risks involved in an invasion could be justified only if Bonaparte had plans involving more than a preemptive expedition. Nor does the argument that a campaign in Syria would force the Turks to sue for peace explain Bonaparte's motives. Syria was a long way from Constantinople, and the Turks had more troops than those stationed in Syria. The sultan could also call upon his Russian ally for aid, and even a decisive tactical victory by the French in Syria would not necessarily put the Ottoman Empire out of the war. Furthermore, an overland march to India was within the realm of possibility. It had been done before, and the veteran French troops were past masters at traveling light and living off the country. Finally, the idea of a march to India would appeal to Bonaparte's sense of adventure. It is true that, in his note of February 10, he said he would return to France if there were wars on the Continent, but this may have been an attempt to have an excuse to leave Egypt if things went badly. An overland move to the Indus was of course a difficult operation. The distance involved was great and the logistical problems enormous. He had no guarantee of victory even if he did reach India, because his army would still be isolated from reinforcements from France, and even with the cooperation of the native princes, Bonaparte would have to face a large, well-organized British military machine. Thus the idea of marching overland to India may indeed seem far-fetched, but Bonaparte had done and would do many things equally difficult. Nobody would have believed that a young general in his twenties and holding his first large army command could have conquered most of Italy, defeated Austria, and imposed peace terms on the Hapsburgs in both Italy and Germany. Later it

was to appear equally amazing that Bonaparte could convince a
czar of Russia to turn on his former ally and march on India,
attempt to create a new French empire in America, set up a continental system, and move armies about from Madrid to Moscow.
Yet Bonaparte did all these things and more. Given Bonaparte's
genius and proclivity for grand adventure, it is certainly not too
much to assume that, in addition to his desire to forestall a
Turkish attack, he was also planning to extend the Republic's or
his own authority to the Indus if circumstances provided the
least opportunity.

Even before his troops had entered Syria, Bonaparte had expressed such notions to his officers. After the defeat of Abukir,
he told one of them that

> an army of sixty thousand men mounted on fifty thousand
> camels and ten thousand horses, carrying with it supplies for
> fifty days and water for sixty would arrive at the Euphrates
> in forty days and at the Indus in four months in the Middle
> of Sikhs, Mahrattas, and the peoples of Hindoustan impatient
> to be freed from the yoke which oppresses them ! ! ![57]

Bonaparte also claimed that Egypt was the intermediate base
between France and India, and that since Alexander had marched
to India, the French could do the same thing and achieve the
same and perhaps even greater results than their predecessor. The
French could find transport for the army in Egypt, and could
obtain supplies in Persia. Bonaparte also felt that he could obtain
reinforcements by recruiting among the Syrian peoples like the
Druses and Christians, who were hostile to the Turks. If he could
raise a sufficiently large force, the Porte might even be convinced
to leave its Anglo-Russian connection and join the French in a
march on India.[58] Thus with the definite intention of forestalling
a Turkish attack on Egypt, and with the possible motive of pushing
on to the east in case of success in Syria, Bontparte's army moved
on Gaza.

Kléber's division forced Gaza to surrender on February 26, and
the army then pushed rapidly on to Jaffa, where the Turks offered
more serious resistance. Two divisions entered the city and engaged in house-to-house fighting until the Turks surrendered.[59]
Leaving their wounded at Jaffa, the French moved rapidly through

Palestine and by March 20 stood before the heavily fortified city of Acre. On the way to Acre, Bonaparte signed an armistice with the aga of Jerusalem. The aga promised to protect the Christians of the area, to give no support to the Turks, and, after the capture of Acre, to submit to French rule. Bonaparte also sent agents to Damascus, Aleppo, and Asia Minor to stir up anti-Turkish feelings among the Arabs, Christians, and Druses. The Jews and Christians of Syria gave their wholehearted support to the French, who held out the promise of liberation from Muslim oppression, and Bonaparte wrote to the emir of Belhir, promising the Druse leader to create an independent Druse nation in return for his cooperation against the Turks.[60] If Bonaparte could take Damascus and Aleppo, the Druses and Arabs of the area would probably join him. They hated their Turkish rulers, but would not act unless they saw a good chance of success. If Bonaparte could recruit these elements for his army, a march to India stood a real chance of success, but Acre was the key to Syria, and before all else, the French had to take it.

Such a task was not an easy one, for Acre was an immensely strong fortress. Situated on a peninsula, three sides of the city were covered by water, while elaborate entrenchments protected the landward side. The Turkish field army could support the twenty thousand-man garrison, and Smith's squadron could attack French waterborne transport and send sailors and marines ashore as infantry or artillerymen. Already on March 17, Smith's fleet had struck the first blow by capturing the French heavy artillery that Bonaparte was sending to Acre by sea. He then added these guns to the Turkish artillery park and supplied British seamen to serve them.[61]

The French had, however, brought other guns overland, and on March 20 they opened their attack trenches against the eastern face of the city. By March 28 they had made a breach in the ramparts and launched a picked force of grenadiers in front of a deep moat near the breach. By the time the French had crossed the moat, the Turks had brought up large numbers of reinforcements and drove them back. A second assault also failed. Bonaparte then tried a mining operation, but on April 7 British marines, covered by gunfire from the fleet, attacked and destroyed the mine.[62] In addition to these reverses, Bonaparte received even more distressing news the next day, learning that the pasha of Damascus, at the head of the field army, had crossed the Jordan and was marching to the relief of Acre.

Bonaparte sent out a reconnaissance detachment of six companies under Junot, and on April 8 it repulsed a Turkish cavalry unit near Nazareth. The next day, Bonaparte sent Kléber's division to Junot's aid, and on April 11 Kléber defeated a five thousand-man Turkish force in the same general area. On April 16 Kléber's force came upon the main Turkish army encamped below Mount Tabor, and he decided to attack. He was, however, so vastly outnumbered that he soon had to go on the defensive and retreat up the slopes of the mountain. His troops continued to beat off Turkish attacks, but started to run low on ammunition. Bonaparte, however, realized the gravity of the situation, and leaving Reynier and Lannes to carry on the siege, he set out with Bon's infantry and Murat's cavalry to rescue Kléber. His forces took the Turks by surprise, striking them in the flank and forcing them to fall back. At the same time, Kléber ordered his men to counterattack. This dual attack was successful, and the Turks broke and fled for the Jordan, leaving six thousand dead behind them.[63] The rout of the field army opened all Syria to French conquest if they could first take Acre. Acre held the only organized Turkish army left in Syria, but Bonaparte could not advance unless he eliminated this threat to his rear, which was the only remaining obstacle between him and his plans to push to the Indus.

After the return of the army from Mount Tabor, Bonaparte renewed his attacks on the city with great vigor. In the last weeks of April, he directed three attacks against the breach, but the Turks repulsed them all and, supported by the British, even managed to carry out occasional sorties to keep the French off balance. The attacks continued throughout the first week of May. The Turks threw them back but suffered heavy casualties. On May 7, however, the Turks began to obtain reinforcements from their army at Rhodes, and in the hope of taking the city before the reinforcements had completely disembarked, Bonaparte ordered still another attack. The thirteenth and sixty-ninth demibrigades went forward on May 8 and, despite the heavy casualties, managed to breach a tower on the northeast wall and capture it.

The Turkish reinforcements quickly rushed to the front, but French sharpshooters decimated them. The fate of Acre hung in the balance, but a second attack, covered by the guns of the British fleet, recovered most of the lost ground, and the Turks drove back a final French attack after bloody fighting at close quarters.[64]

May 8 was the crucial day in the defense of Acre. Fighting did go on for another week with both sides suffering heavy losses, but, on the French side, the assaults were carried out with ever-diminishing hopes of success. Never again did they come close to penetrating the Turkish fortifications, and Bonaparte began to worry about the Rhodes army, which was preparing to attack Egypt, and about the fact that plague had broken out in his trenches. Military defeat, plague, and fear of a seaborne invasion of Egypt finally forced the Corsican to raise the siege and begin his retreat to Egypt.[65] The retreat began on May 21, and the line of march was strewn with corpses of soldiers who succumbed to the Black Death. By May 28 the French had passed through Jaffa, leaving more plague sufferers in the lazaretto with a lethal dose of opium to end their miseries. At the beginning of June, Bonaparte's army was back in Egypt, having lost five hundred men in combat, seven hundred to disease, and eighteen hundred wounded.[66]

Bonaparte had suffered the first major defeat of his career, but the French were still capable of holding Egypt, and on July 25 they crushed the Turkish army of Rhodes that had landed at Abukir Bay. Bonaparte, however, realized that his failure to take Acre meant an end to his ideas of forcing the Turks out of the war or of marching on India. He later maintained that if he had been victorious he could "have changed the face of the world. The fate of the east lay in that small town."[67] Even later at St. Helena, he stated that if he had been successful he would have been joined by the Christians of Syria and Armenia and by the Druses, and would have marched to the Indus.[68] The British, too, realized the importance of Bonaparte's defeat at Acre, and in September, King George III told the House of Lords that the French defeat in Syria had also frustrated their ambitious projects in India.[69] Since his army was beaten and isolated and it was only a matter of time before the Allies would overwhelm it, Bonaparte prepared to desert his troops and return to France, where he hoped to find new opportunities for glory and power.*

Whether or not the Syrian expedition had India as its ultimate goal is still a debatable question, but to the people involved the French threats to India had appeared grave. The attempt to cooperate with Mysore had failed partly because of the difficulty of communications that made it impossible for the Directory to coordinate its actions with those of Egypt, the Isle of France, and Mysore, and partly because of the energies of Mornington, who responded rapidly to the dangers besetting British India. The attempt at an overland invasion failed due to the ability of the Turks, assisted by Sir Wiliam Sydney Smith's fleet, in holding Acre against Bonaparte's veterans. The French had failed to damage England's colonial empire, and their general strategic position became even worse because of the isolation of one of their best armies in Egypt. The British for their part had not only staved off the threats to their empire, but had also managed to increase their power and influence in India and the Persian Gulf. In addition, with the colonial empire safe, Pitt was able to turn his full energies to mounting a continental campaign.

NOTES

1. C. Northcote Parkinson, *War in the Eastern Seas 1793–1815*, pp. 11–12.
2. C. H. Philips. *The East India Company 1784–1834*, pp. 2–3, 9–11.
3. Ibid., p. 33.
4. Ibid., pp. 54, 57, 80–81; and John W. Fortescue, *A History of the British Army*, 4, pt. 2: 939.

---

* Bonaparte left Egypt at the end of August. Despite his earlier letter stating that he would return to France if there were a war on the Continent, he had not been officially called home by the Directory, and his departure from Egypt was technically desertion. When he left Egypt, Bonaparte did not know how the war in Europe was progressing and legally could have been court martialed, but his successful coup in November naturally made such an action impossible. The Directory had in fact made plans to bring Bonaparte and his army back to Italy, but they had never contemplated having Bonaparte return alone. The army of the East, under Kléber, and after his assassination, under Menou, continued to hold Egypt until 1801, when it finally surrendered on honorable terms to the British and Turks.

5. *The Asiatic Annual Register; or a View of the History of Hindustan and of the Politics, Commerce, and Literature of Asia for the Year 1799*, pp. 286–87.

6. *The Speeches of the Right Honourable William Pitt in the House of Commons*, 3: 323.

7. Parkinson, *War in the Eastern Seas*, pp. 14–21.

8. Ibid., pp. 67–68, 75–77, 78–81, 85–88.

9. Ibid., p. 122; and S. P. Sen, *The French in India (1763–1816)*, p. 535.

10. Parkinson, *War in the Eastern Seas*, pp. 71, 99.

11. Ibid., pp. 39–40, 43.

12. R. C. Majumdar, H. C. Raychaudhuri, and Kalikinkar Datta, *An Advanced History of India*, pp. 527, 543, 549; and James Grant Duff, *A History of the Mahrattas*, 3: 91–92.

13. Sen, *The French in India*, p. 544.

14. S. J. Owen, ed., *A Selection from the Dispatches, Treaties, and Other Papers of the Marquess Wellesley, K. G. during his Government of India*, p. 32; and Duke of Wellington, ed., *Supplementary Dispatches and Memoranda of Field Marshal Arthur Duke of Wellington K. G. India 1797–1805*, edited by his son, 1: 72.

15. Majumdar, *History of India*, pp. 682–88.

16. *Asiatic Annual Register*, pp. 246–48, 250. The *Asiatic Annual Register* published all of Tippoo's captured documents after the fall of Seringapatam.

17. Ibid., pp. 184–87.

18. Ibid., pp. 194–96.

19. Ibid., pp. 207–17; and Archives nationales, carton BB4129 (hereafter, AN).

20. *Asiatic Annual Register*, pp. 107, 231–32.

21. AN, carton BB4129.

22. Ministère de la Guerre État-Major de l'Armée Archives historiques, Indes Orientales, 1797–99, carton B81 (hereafter, Min. de la Guerre, AH).

23. Clément de la Jonquière, ed., *L'expédition d'Égypte 1798–1801*, 3: 267.

24. AN, AF III*, carton 19.

25. Ibid.

26. Ibid.

27. François Charles-Roux, *L'Angleterre et l'expédition française en Égypte*, 1: 15–20.

28. Nicholas H. Nicolas, ed., *The Dispatches and Letters of Vice-Admiral Lord Viscount Nelson*, 3: 31, 36–37.

29. Fortescue, *British Army*, p. 605.

30. Owen, *Dispatches of Wellesley*, pp. 1–3.

31. R. R. Pearce, ed., *Memoirs and Correspondence of the Most Noble Richard Marquess Wellesley*, 1: 203.

32. Wellington, *Dispatches and Memoranda*, pp. 52–55, 71.

33. Owen, *Dispatches of Wellesley*, pp. 17–56.

34. Fortescue, *British Army*, pp. 718–20; and *Asiatic Annual Register*, pp. 68–69, 102.

35. *Asiatic Annual Register*, p. 83.

36. Pearce, *Memoirs and Correspondence of Wellesley*, pp. 213–17, 225.

37. Owen, *Dispatches of Wellesley*, p. 61.

38. Pearce, *Memoirs and Correspondence of Wellesley*, p. 245.

39. Ibid., p. 247.

40. Parkinson, *War in the Eastern Seas*, p. 122.

41. *Asiatic Annual Register*, pp. 238–39; and Owen, *Dispatches of Wellesley*, p. 74.

42. Owen, *Dispatches of Wellesley*, pp. 88–93.

43. Fortescue, *British Army*, pp. 726–36; *London Gazette. Bulletins of the Campaign, 1799*, pp. 260–61; and *Asiatic Annual Register*, pp. 258–59.

44. Fortescue, *British Army*, p. 744.

45. Owen, *Dispatches of Wellesley*, pp. 160–64.

46. Arnold Wilson, *The Persian Gulf*, p. 231; and A. Azoux, "La France et Muscate aux dix-huitième et dix-neuvième siècles," *Revue d'histoire diplomatique*, 24: 236–38.

47. John W. Kaye, ed., *The Life and Correspondence of Major-General Sir John Malcolm G. C. B.*, 1: 105–10.

48. Parkinson, *War in the Eastern Seas*, pp. 150–52. The French troops at Kosseir were from Desaix's division, which was pursuing Murad Bey and trying to impose French control on Upper Egypt.

49. Napoléon Bonaparte, *Correspondance inédite officielle et confidentielle de Napoléon Bonaparte, Égypte*, 1: 375–76, 394–95.

50. Henri Plon and J. Dumaine, eds., *Correspondance de Napoléon Ier*, 5: 174–76, 197, 233–35, 257.

51. Ibid., p. 213. This was probably the Ambassador sent by Tippoo in July.

52. Ibid., p. 278.

53. Henri Galli, ed., *Journal d'un officier de l'armée d'Égypte, l'armée française en Égypte 1798–1801*, p. 87.

54. Min. de la Guerre, AH, carton Xᴰ3.

55. Min. de la Guerre, AH, Campagne de Syrie an VII, MH, no. 9081.

56. Bonaparte, *Correspondance*, p. 220.

57. Henri Bertrand, ed., *Campagnes d'Égypt et de Syrie 1798–1799, Mémoires pour servir à l'histoire de Napoléon dictées par lui-même à Sainte-Hélène*, 1: 123.

58. Ibid., 2: 20–21.

59. Min. de la Guerre, AH, MH, no. 9081; and Louis Alexandre Berthier,

Relations des campagnes du général Bonaparte en Égypte et en Syrie, pp. 52–53, 55–56.

60. Bertrand, *Campagnes,* p. 66; and Bonaparte, *Correspondance,* 2: 272.

61. John Barrow, ed., *The Life and Correspondence of Admiral Sir William Sidney Smith,* 1: 266–68.

62. Berthier, *Campagnes de Bonaparte,* p. 63, and Barrow, *Sir William Sidney Smith,* pp. 284–85.

63. Min. de la Guerre, AH, MH, no. 9081; and Berthier, *Campagnes de Bonaparte,* pp. 70–77.

64. Barrow, *Sir William Sidney Smith,* pp. 284–89.

65. Berthier, *Campagnes de Bonaparte,* p. 98. The French had already suffered from the plague, but until May such outbursts had been mild and had caused relatively few casualties.

66. Sir John Burgoyne, *A Short History of the Naval and Military Operations in Egypt,* p. 13; and Désiré Lacroix, *Bonaparte en Égypte (1798–1799),* p. 335.

67. L. A. Bourrienne, *Memoirs of Napoleon Bonaparte,* 1: 89.

68. Gerard Walter, ed., Las Cases, le comte de, *Le mémorial de Sainte Hélène,* 1: 454–55.

69. Barrow, *Sir William Sidney Smith,* pp. 318, 320.

8

The Irish Rebellion
of 1798—
A Lost Opportunity

The French-Egyptian expedition set forth from Toulon on May 19, 1798, just before the Irish Rebellion, which had been brewing for many months, burst forth and was raging at its height. The invasion of Egypt, a move designed to weaken England by threatening the Indian sources of British wealth, had the opposite effect. Instead of weakening England, it reactivated the war in the Mediterranean and opened the way to the formation of a second coalition. While organizing their eastern venture, the Directory ignored the Irish revolt, although a French invasion of Ireland in conjunction with the actions of the United Irishmen would have been no more costly than the attack upon Egypt in which the French ultimately lost both a fleet and an army. Had a French army landed in Ireland in the spring of 1798—a feat that was far from impossible considering the facts that the French had landed there in 1689 and spent sixteen days in Bantry Bay in 1796—such a force, even with its communications with the Metropole severed, would have been more of a threat to the British than the army of the East, which surrendered in 1801. Had the French occupied Ireland for any length of time, it is doubtful that a viable Irish Republic would have resulted. Such an occupation, however, would have deprived England of Irish exports, English landlords would have lost an annual £1,500,000 in rents, and the British armed services would have lost a valuable recruiting ground.[1] In addition, Ireland would have provided the Directory with a diplomatic bargaining counter far more valuable than Egypt. The French could have traded Ireland away at the peace table just as they had traded Venice to the Austrians at Campoformio, and the British might have been compelled to make peace on terms favorable to the Republic in order to recover Ireland. Furthermore, if the French had landed a force in Ireland instead of Egypt, the Ottoman Empire and Russia might well have held aloof from the conflict. Their vital interests would not have been threatened, and Nelson's fleet would not have entered the Mediterranean to encourage and goad these powers into united action. A successful descent upon Ireland seemingly offered the French a wider range of favorable alternatives than an Egyptian venture.

Militarily an invasion of Ireland was not a difficult operation. Even Pitt recognized this and never even devised a systematic defense plan for the island, because he recognized that his land and sea forces could not possibly interdict all of the approaches.[2] In contrast to England and Egypt, where the populations would be either passive or hostile, the French if they landed in Ireland could rely upon the armed assistance of large segments of the Irish people.

In Ireland the United Irish Society armed themselves and prepared for rebellion, while in Paris Wolfe Tone and Lewins sought to convince the Directory to come to their assistance. In December, 1797, and January, 1798, the two Irishmen obtained a series of interviews with Talleyrand and Bonaparte but received little more than vague promises of assistance at some future date. Meetings with individual directors produced nothing more concrete.[3] Involved with their plans to invade England and, after this scheme collapsed, with preparations for the Egyptian expedition, French officials ignored the strategic possibilities inherent in a blow against British power in Ireland.

That such a blow was not a figment of the fertile Irish imagination is reflected in the drastic actions of the British government. The Cabinet increased the Irish garrison to 103,000 men: 39,500 regulars, 26,000 militia, and 37,500 yeomen recruited from the Protestant gentry.[4] The British also inaugurated harsh repressive measures to stifle revolutionary ferment. Commanders placed whole counties under martial law and seized thousands of pikes and muskets. Irish revolutionaries responded by attacking small detachments and murdering loyalist civilians.[5] By the end of 1797 a state of civil insurrection existed throughout Ireland's northern counties.

The United Irish Society, meanwhile, prepared for their uprising, expecting the French to arrive in the spring of 1798. On February 26, the Leinster Directory appointed Fitzgerald head of a military committee with the task of organizing the revolt and planning measures of cooperation with the French. Fitzgerald reported that the Society had 279,800 members, of whom 100,000 were armed. Other figures credit the Society with a membership of 500,000, with 280,000 of them under arms. Fitzgerald was so confident of success that he felt it unnecessary to wait for the French before starting the rebellion. The Leinster Directory, however, felt it was safer to wait until the French had landed in Ireland before taking any action.[6]

As the danger of rebellion grew, the British concluded that they could do nothing but extend the system of repression to the south, and in April, Lake began to disarm the southern counties. In their search for arms, the troops, many of whom were Protestant militiamen and yeomen, committed numerous outrages against the rebellious Catholic Jacobins. For example, an infantry platoon entered Gardenstown. It approached a seventy-year-old farmer and ordered him to surrender his weapons, and after the farmer had complied, the officer in charge shot the old man, and his men bayoneted the farmer's three sons. The troops then seized three other inhabitants, apparently at random, and shot them. Suspects were flogged, tarred, shot, subjected to half-hangings and forced to wear pitch caps. Under the guise of punishing rebels, officials and militiamen settled many personal grudges, and individual commanders used their authority to vent their own personal or political hatreds on the population.[7] The explanation for this viciousness lies not so much in the barbarity of the government as in the circumstances confronting the British and the loyalists. Like the French in the Vendée, the British in Ireland had to assume that the majority of the native population were actual or potential enemies. In an area overwhelmingly hostile and verging on revolt, the government resorted to repressive measures not so much out of desire but because of necessity.

Military operations were, however, not the only means of repression, and the British had at their disposal an equally effective means of striking at the rebels—spies. Since 1793 the British had maintained paid informers within the ranks of the United Irish Society and from 1797 to 1801 had paid thirty-eight thousand pounds for information from these spies.[8] In England on February 28, officials arrested two agents of the United Irish Society, O'Connor and O'Coigly, a priest, as they were about to depart for France. They discovered incriminating evidence in O'Coigly's possession and jailed the two men.[9] O'Connor's arrest deprived the Society of one of its most able leaders. On March 12 the Society received another crushing blow. The Dublin Directory was meeting secretly at the house of Oliver Bond, one of the directors, but an informer told the authorities of the meeting. Police raided the meeting and arrested thirteen members of the Leinster Directory and three of the national directors. Fitzgerald was the only leading member who escaped, but his freedom was of short duration. On May 19, again with the aid of a paid informer, the British found and captured the head of the United Irishmen's military committee.[10]

Henry and John Sheares and Samuel Neilson, all three of whom had been relatively minor officials in the Society before the March 12 arrests, hastily set up a new National Directory. They were worried by the closing net of arrests and felt they had no choice but to start the revolt before the British completely destroyed their organization. Despite the fact that they would have to act without French aid, they set the date of the uprising for May 23. The rebellion was to begin in Dublin. The signal to the countryside was to be the seizure of the mail coaches leaving the city, their nonarrival in the provinces being the sign to start fighting, but again the British struck first.[11] On May 21, police officials, with the aid of an informer, arrested the

Sheares brothers, and the next day the authorities recognized Neilson in the streets and captured him.[12] Thus even if the revolt had occurred as planned, the British had deprived it of its chief leaders, and it would have resulted in little more than a series of uncoordinated armed uprisings. The British repressive measures had weakened the United Irish Society through the seizure of weapons, arrest of suspects, and seizure of those leaders who could have coordinated the local revolts. Finally, the British forced the revolt to explode prematurely. The hatred generated during the repression, however, guaranteed that the revolt, even if premature and uncoordinated, would rage with great viciousness on both sides.

Despite the great success of British countermeasures, rebels attacked the mail coaches according to plan on the night of May 23, and at the same time they raided military posts throughout Dublin County. On May 24 the rebellion spread to surrounding counties in a growing wave of minor clashes. For example, government troops drove 5,000 rebels out of Dunboyne on May 25, killed 400 rebels in an assault in Carlow on May 27, and on June 4 killed 700 rebels in five separate engagements. A column of 50 yeomen killed 120 rebels, and in a nearby county, 200 militia beat off an attack of 400 rebels killing 130 of them. In addition to these clashes, there were numerous individual terroristic attacks on isolated loyalists.[13]

As these isolated attempts were being crushed, the rebellion suddenly took an unexpected and far more serious turn, when on May 26 the peasants of Wexford County, led by a priest, John Murphy, joined the rebellion. The Wexford revolt was particularly surprising because the United Irish Society had made little progress in spreading propaganda and organizing Wexford, and the priests and peasants there had been particularly docile.[14] The British, however, had not spared Wexford from the rigors of military repression, and had pushed the peasants to the point of desperation. More proximate causes of the uprising were the execution without trial of thirty-four prisoners on May 24, and a similar occurrence on May 25 in which the militia shot twenty-eight prisoners. On May 26 the militia burned the home of Father John Murphy. This priest, who had in the past urged his parishioners to give up their arms to the authorities, became convinced that he could expect neither justice nor mercy from the British. In desperation he turned on them, gathered his followers, and attacked.[15] Other peasants rallied to Murphy's support, and the rebel forces, little more than an infuriated mob, began to march on the town of Wexford. British repression thus had an unexpected effect. The English destroyed much of the United Irish Society's strength but drove thousands of others to rebellion.

The following morning the rebels, now thirty thousand strong, routed the Wexford garrison and entered the town, where they raised the green flag of Ireland. After some initial pillaging, the rebels began to organize their own town government, and at this point the Wexford rebellion began to take on political overtones. The Irish selected a Committee of Twelve to regulate the requisition and distribution of food. The Committee established public stores of provisions and a crude rationing system. It also mitigated the Catholic nature of the rebellion, because the rebels protected Protestants from the vengeance of the Catholic peasants and allowed them to continue holding their services. Bengal Harvey, a Protestant landowner and a United Irishman, took command of the rebel army, and another Protestant, Matthew Keugh, commanded the Wexford garrison. Some weeks later on June 16, the rebels appealed to France to send them one thousand men and five thousand rifles to help establish an Irish republic.[16]

There appear to be two basic reasons for the growing political nature of the rebellion. In the first instance, the rebels had to establish some sort of government. It is not unreasonable to assume that the ideas of the United Irish Society were known to many, although perhaps in a somewhat garbled form. When faced with the necessity of organizing themselves, the rebels adopted the most familiar ideas at hand. In the second place, there were more United Irishmen in Wexford than had been commonly assumed. One rebel claimed that the reason people thought that there were so few United Irishmen in Wexford was because the Wexford delegate to the March 12 meeting escaped, and the British authorities never captured his papers.[17] Thus, despite the fact that the Society did not organize the rebellion, individual members joined Murphy's forces and attained high positions. They were then in a position to influence significantly the nature of the rebel government.

It is probably going too far to assert that all of the peasants adopted republican ideology. Anti-Protestant feelings, desperation, and a desire for revenge all played their part in motivating the rebels, but the leaders and at least some of the rank and file quickly adopted political goals that were almost identical with those of the United Irish Society.

The British soon became very alarmed at the extent of the revolt, and rushed reinforcements to Ireland. By June 9, five thousand troops were on their way. By the end of the month, the British had expanded their Irish garrison to one hundred and thirty thousand men,[18] the largest British force ever to take the field throughout the entire revolutionary and Napoleonic period.

But before these reinforcements could reach General Lake, the revolt spread to the north, and in the south the rebels came very close to success. In Ulster, four thousand United Irishmen attacked the town of Antrim on June 7 but retreated after a sharp fight. The British attacked and defeated seven thousand rebels in County Down six days later, and in Belfast court martials sat in permanent session while patrols were on a constant alert.[19]

IRELAND   1796-98

In Wexford the rebels were much stronger. Having increased their forces to about one hundred thousand men, they inaugu-

rated a serious offensive operation. The rebels divided their army
into two corps. One of them, led by Harvey, advanced to attack
New Ross, while the other, under Murphy, moved in the direction of Dublin by way of Arklow and Wicklow. Harvey's troops
reached New Ross on June 5 and immediately stormed the
British outposts. The rebels, armed mainly with pikes and charg-
ing in dense masses, pushed into the town, where artillery firing
at point-blank range inflicted heavy losses, but the Irish finally
captured the guns after vicious hand-to-hand combat. The British
evacuated the town, but they managed to reform their ranks and
counterattacked just as the rebels were breaking ranks to begin
plundering. With the advantage of surprise, the British forced
the rebels to abandon New Ross and take up a defensive position
near Vinegar Hill. The English had killed over thirty-four hundred Irish in the battle, including many wounded who had been
left behind in the rebel retreat. The Irish removed Harvey from
his command after the battle, replacing him with a priest, Philip
Roache, who could do little to better his corps' position. He
confined his activities to preventing the victorious British from
advancing on Wexford.[20]

Murphy's corps meanwhile had greater success. It defeated a
British attempt to retake Wexford by ambushing and dispersing
one of the assault columns. The other force, hearing of the first
column's defeat, turned and fled. The rebels followed the British
as far as Gorey, which they occupied on June 5. The British
kept on running. They abandoned Arklow and did not halt until
they reached Wicklow. Had the rebels at this point pushed on
to Arklow, they would have been in an excellent position from
which to launch an attack on Dublin. There were large amounts
of small arms and artillery stored in Dublin, a valuable prize for
the under-armed rebels, and a striking success like the capture of
Ireland's capital would not only have aroused the passive elements in Ireland but also alerted the French to the opportunities
awaiting them. Murphy's troops were, however, tired and disorganized. Murphy himself, though a natural tactician, had no
previous military experience and failed to appreciate his strategic
position. Without the enemy facing him, he evidently did not
know what to do, and instead of pushing on to Arklow and
Dublin as fast as possible, he allowed his corps to halt at Gorey.[21]

This halt was to prove disastrous for the Irish, because the British, realizing the importance of Arklow, reoccupied the town on June 6. Murphy had given the defeated British time to rest, reform their scattered units, and fortify the main route to Dublin. To make matters worse, Murphy did not get his troops moving until June 9. The twenty-seven thousand rebels, unable to engage in complicated maneuvers, rushed straight for the entrenchments of the sixteen hundred-man Arklow garrison. As at the battle of New Ross, the British artillery simply cut the Irish to pieces. The rebels failed to penetrate the British trenches and recoiled toward Gorey, leaving behind over one thousand dead.[22] This defeat was in fact a disaster for the Irish cause. The English had forced both corps of the revolutionary army to go on the defensive, and General Lake began to close in on Wexford.

On June 16 Lake issued orders for his twenty thousand men to advance in four columns against the main rebel position at Vinegar Hill. His goal was to surround and destroy the rebel army. By June 19 the British were in position, and the Irish had no choice but to attempt to break out of the closing ring. The next day Roache's corps attacked the British at New Ross, but as in the first battle, Lake's troops repulsed them with heavy losses. On June 21 it was the British who attacked, advancing with three columns against the front and flanks of the Irish position while a fourth moved to cut the rebels' escape route to the rear. For one and a half hours, the rebels held off Lake's men, but upon seeing the fourth column in their rear, they broke and fled. The British pursued them closely, cutting down anybody they caught, giving no quarter even to wounded and prisoners. Roache tried to arrange a capitulation for his men, but upon reaching the British headquarters, he was arrested and hung. By June 22 the British were back in the town of Wexford where they executed Harvey, Keugh, and any other rebels, including the wounded who were still in the town.[23]

Meanwhile, Murphy led the remnants of the defeated rebel army into Carlow and Kilkenny counties and by June 24 was in Queen's County. He seemed to have no other aim but to escape, but on June 26 the militia caught his band and killed over one thousand of their number. The remainder then fled back into Wexford, but Murphy was killed during the retreat. At this point, the leaderless rebels lost all cohesion. Some formed small bands and carried on guerrilla warfare, but most simply fled for their lives. A second group also escaped from Wexford and fled into Wicklow County. On June 30 and again on July 2 this unit defeated elements of the forces that were hunting them, but on July 4 this band fought its last regular battle with the British, and like Murphy's force it disintegrated.[24]

Throughout the summer, the British continued to hunt down fleeing rebels. Court-martials worked overtime handing out death sentences to those captured rebels who were not killed on the spot. Estimates of casualties during the course of the rebellion vary greatly. None can be regarded as entirely accurate, but they range as high as fifty thousand slaughtered in cold blood and dying in the numerous armed clashes.[25] Long after the British had dispersed the major rebel units they had to retain martial law, because guerrilla warfare continued in the rural areas. In 1799 the British felt it necessary to retain sixty thousand men in Ireland, and were still hanging rebels or sending them to the Australian penal colonies. Despite these measures the spirit of revolt continued to infect a few Irishmen, for at the end of 1798 Irish seamen on the HMS *Gladiator,* HMS *Cambridge,* and the HMS *Diomede* were court-martialed for plotting to seize their ships and turn them over to the French. In 1803 the British crushed an uprising in Dublin, and in the following year Irish prisoners in New South Wales rose in revolt,[26] but realistic hopes for Irish independence were doomed by the summer of 1798.

Had the French responded to the Irish appeal of June 16, the rebellion might have been successful, but Wolfe Tone seemed to be one of the few people in France who took the rebellion seriously. On June 20 he had an interview with General Kilmaine, Bonaparte's replacement as commander of the army of England. Tone informed the general that to insure the success of the revolt rapid French action was necessary, but Kilmaine replied that the Directory was not anxious to risk an invasion of Ireland.[27] Doubtless the French were reluctant to commit any more troops to overseas ventures, especially since they had not yet concluded a definite peace with Austria, but the opportunity in Ireland was too great to be completely ignored. Larévellière-Lépaux was in favor of invading Ireland, and Reubell felt that an invasion of Ireland was the first step in a descent upon England.[28] Unfortunately, the French arrived at these conclusions too late. They failed to send a force to Ireland to start the revolt under their own leadership, and failed to act quickly when the revolt broke out on its own. It was not until the receipt of numerous Irish requests for aid that the French decided to act, and by then it was too late.

Originally, the Irish had asked for one thousand men, and on June 19, as Lake was preparing to attack the rebels at Vinegar Hill, Admiral Bruix ordered the commander of the Brest squadron, Bompard, to prepare four frigates (a fifth ship was added on June 20) to carry a battalion of infantry to Ireland. Although speed was vital, it was not until June 25 that the Directory decided to take full advantage of the revolt and expand the size of the expedition.[29] Bruix wrote to General Joubert in Batavia telling him to ask the Batavians to send aid to the Irish, but only on July 18 did the Dutch assign two frigates to the task of landing troops in Ireland. French preparations also proceeded very slowly. Not until July 4, the day on which the last organized resistance in Ireland was crushed, did the Directory learn that twenty-four hundred men were ready to sail from Brest and that another battalion was in readiness at La Rochelle. Two more weeks passed until General Cherin assumed overall command of the expedition. His forces totaling eight thousand men were to sail in three echelons: Humbert from La Rochelle with one thousand men, Hardy from Brest with twenty-four hundred men, and Cherin with the remainder after his subordinates had landed.[30]

Still the French seemed incapable of swift action, and it was not until July 22 that the government allotted funds to pay and supply Humbert's and Hardy's contingents, and another three days elapsed before the Directory ordered funds dispatched to Cherin. This was still not enough, because the money never arrived, and Hardy's force, which was ready to sail by the end of July, remained immobilized. To add to the delays and confusion, the government suddenly transferred Cherin to the army of Italy. He was so angered by previous delays that this action caused him to resign his position.[31] Meanwhile, Humbert's troops, a battalion of the Seventieth demibrigade, were ready to sail by August 5, but like Hardy, Humbert had not yet received any money. Humbert, however, was an ambitious commander and managed to wrangle forty-seven thousand francs from the paymaster of La Rochelle. He paid his men and set sail for Ireland on August 6.[32] Thus only the smallest of the several French forces destined for Ireland had put to sea by August.

After sixteen days at sea, Humbert landed at the small town of Killala in the western county of Mayo. Mayo was the least revolutionary of any Irish county. Protestants were numerous, and the militia was well organized, but, nevertheless, Humbert sent a three hundred-man advance guard ashore, where it routed the garrison of Killala and occupied the town. When the rest of the troops had reached Killala, Humbert raised the green flag of Ireland and issued a proclamation to the populace telling them that France had answered the appeal of Irish leaders and promised them that French arms would be dedicated to aiding the Irish in establishing a government that would guarantee their national dignity and ensure their independence. Humbert issued a second proclamation to his troops enjoining them to treat the Irish as allies and not as a conquered nation. The few local United Irishmen in Killala joined Humbert's forces, and despite the defeats and repression of the past months, about eight hundred peasants volunteered to serve with the French.[33]

Humbert's force was too small to remain stationary; mobility was his only hope of achieving anything at all, and on August 26, leaving two hundred men to hold Killala, he set out for Ballina, a small town on the road to Dublin. The British meanwhile were concentrating their forces with the intention of destroying the French before they could reach an area in which rebel guerrillas were still active. Some six thousand regulars and militia were at Castlebar when General Lake arrived to take command on the night of August 26. Humbert knew of their presence. He marched fifteen miles from Ballina on the following morning and hurled his columns, comprised of seven hundred French infantry and eight hundred Irish volunteers, against the British lines. Halted by the British artillery, the French withdrew, re-formed their columns into lines, and pushed forward in irregular parties. When they were close to the British, they re-formed into lines and rushed forward. The British broke and fled, some cavalry units retreating sixty-three miles in little more than a day, an action that gave the battle its popular name—the races of Castlebar. Humbert reported to the Directory that he had killed six hundred, taken twelve hundred prisoners, and captured ten cannon.[34]

The French remained at Castlebar until September 4, training volunteers and bringing the Killala garrison forward. Humbert also set up a Provisional Government of Connaught, but this regime never really had a chance to function. The Irish in the west were, however, encouraged by the French victories, and on September 4, six thousand of them rose and attacked Granard, while a second group fought the militia near Sligo.[35] These actions were ineffective, but they did indicate what might have happened if the French had arrived earlier. A small force had easily defeated a much larger British army, and many peasants without any previous organization had joined the French. Had this small force arrived before the defeat of the Wexford rebels or had a larger force come in September, the situation might well have proved disastrous for the British. Unfortunately, Humbert was isolated, and despite his victory at Castlebar, it was only a matter of time before the British closed in with overwhelming strength.

Lake gathered his scattered forces south of Castlebar, while Cornwallis with twenty thousand troops moved from Carrick toward Lake Allen. To avoid being trapped between two overwhelming forces, Humbert left Castlebar and moved toward Sligo, where he hoped to join forces with Hardy's troops who were supposed to land there. On September 5 he defeated a militia detachment at Clooney, a small town a few miles south of Sligo. The militia fled to Sligo, where reinforcements joined them, and Humbert, seeing his hopes of joining forces with Hardy dashed, turned west in an attempt to reach Granard, where rebels, despite their defeat of September 4, continued to wage a guerrilla war against the local militia. By forced marches, Humbert managed to cross the Shannon River at Balintra and reached Cloone on September 7, but Lake's troops were close behind. Cornwallis also started to close his trap by occupying Mohill, a move that cut Humbert's escape route to the south. On September 8 Cornwallis occupied St. Johnstown, while Lake pursued the French as far as Ballinamuck, where Humbert, realizing that all avenues of escape were closed to him, surrendered his 844 French and 1,500 Irish troops. The British executed many of the Irish on the spot, while the others fled. The British then advanced on Killala. They retook the town on September 23, hanging those Irishmen whom they were able to capture.[36] County Mayo began to feel the heavy hand of martial law, and the second French invasion of Ireland ended in total failure. Humbert had done the best he could with insufficient forces, and had conducted a brilliant little campaign. He had arrived in Ireland too late to assist the main rebellion, and his defeat was really only a matter of time because he was so vastly outnumbered. The success he did manage to achieve indicates what might have been accomplished had the French acted earlier and with greater strength.

Meanwhile, the Directory, having once decided to aid the Irish, finally realized the extent of the possibilities open to them, and while the British were closing in on Humbert's force, the directors were finally making serious efforts to get more troops to Ireland. On August 14 General Hardy obtained the necessary funds to pay his men and buy supplies, but bad weather intervened to further delay his voyage. When the wind finally changed, it was the British blockaders who continued to hold the fleet in port. On August 20 the fleet made an attempt to put to sea, but was spotted by a British frigate and had to return hastily to port. On September 11 the Batavians reported that the blockade was also preventing their ships from leaving port, but a week before, a single Batavian frigate had managed to get to sea. It had left from Dunkirk and arrived off the Irish coast on September 16. Several Irish exiles landed, but when they heard of Humbert's capture, they reboarded the ship, which then proceeded to return to France by way of Norway.[37] Weather and the Royal Navy had combined to prevent a third expedition to Ireland, but the Directory refused to abandon hope, for on September 13 they ordered Savary, who had commanded the naval portion of Humbert's expedition, to prepare another landing. On the same day, Hardy received instructions to get to Ireland at all costs to aid Humbert, of whose capture the Directory was as yet uninformed. Bompard finally left Brest with Hardy's corps on September 16. Unfortunately, British frigates spotted Bompard's single ship of the line and eight frigates and followed him until October 3 when

they sailed to Ireland to warn the authorities. Commodore Warren, with three ships of the line and six frigates, then put to
sea to ambush Bompard near the Isle of Terry. When the French
appeared on October 11, Warren's fleet attacked them, and after
a hard-fought battle captured the ship of the line and three of
the frigates. Wolfe Tone, who had commanded a battery during
the engagement, was among the prisoners. After being taken
ashore, he was recognized and placed in jail as a traitor rather
than as a prisoner of war. He was taken before a court martial
and tried for treason. Condemned to death, he cut his throat
before the sentence could be carried out. Meanwhile, Savary had
put to sea the day after Bompard. He reached Killala by October 27, but upon discovering that Bompard had not yet arrived
he decided to return to France.[38]

This was still not the end of French efforts to invade Ireland.
On September 18, Kilmaine proposed that he lead an eight
thousand-man expedition to Ireland, and on September 26 the
Directory gave its approval. The Directory, on October 5, placed
six ships of the line, three frigates, and two corvettes (they later
added another ship of the line, three frigates, and two sloops) , a
demibrigade of infantry, two light infantry battalions, three
hundred cavalry, one hundred gunners, twelve guns, fifteen thousand rifles, one million five hundred thousand cartridges, and
six thousand uniforms at Kilmaine's disposal. Five days later
Bruix informed Vice-admiral Martin, who was to command the
naval portion of the expedition, that Humbert had surrendered
but that Bompard and Savary were probably ashore. Kilmaine,
therefore, continued his preparations, and the infantry was
actually on its way to its embarkation port when the government
received news of Bompard's defeat. Realizing that if Kilmaine
landed in Ireland unsupported he would probably suffer the fate
of Humbert, they canceled his expedition on October 29. It was
the Batavians, however, who made the final attempt to invade
Ireland. On the night of October 23 two frigates sailed from
the Texel, but the British caught and captured them the next
morning.[39] With this defeat, France and her allies gave up their
efforts to invade Ireland, and for several years there was no further
challenge to British rule at Dublin.

Since May, the Directory and its Batavian ally had projected seven expeditions against Ireland. Five had gone to sea; two had been defeated while at sea; two had reached Ireland but had not landed any troops; and one had actually landed men in Ireland. The French had failed to grasp the importance and extent of the May revolt and consequently failed to act in time to aid it. It is true that once they had decided to aid the Irish they made significant efforts, but because they lacked the time for careful planning, the efforts were weak, uncoordinated, and doomed to failure. Only a large-scale invasion had any chance of success after the middle of June, and for such an invasion the French had neither the men nor the ships. They had no choice but to settle for several small-scale attempts, and these failed. An expedition the size of Kilmaine's or even of Humbert's landing in Ireland during the course of the Wexford rebellion might well have led to the defeat of the British and their expulsion from Ireland. By not acting soon enough and then by acting on too small a scale, the French lost a great opportunity to strike a serious blow at their major opponent. As Bonaparte commented years later, "If instead of the expedition to Egypt, I had made one to Ireland . . . what would England be today?"[40]

NOTES

1. William Lecky, *A History of England in the Eighteenth Century*, 7: 279–80; and Constantia Maxwell, *Country and Town in Ireland under the Georges*, p. 48.

2. J. Holland Rose and A. M. Broadley, *Dumouriez and the Defense of England against Napoleon*, p. 228.

3. W. T. Wolfe Tone, ed., *Life of Theobold Wolfe Tone*, 2: 454–58, 473–74.

4. John W. Fortescue, *A History of the British Army*, 4, pt. 2: 939.

5. Lecky, *History of England*, p. 209.

6. Richard Madden, *The United Irishmen, Their Lives and Times*, 1: 287, 396–97.

7. Ibid., 1: 308, 313–14; and James Gordon, *History of the Rebellion in Ireland in the Year 1798*, pp. 23–25, 60–61.

8. Madden, *United Irishmen*, 1: 365.

9. *Report of the Committee of Secrecy of the House of Commons*, pp. 23,

61–62. O'Coigly was hung. O'Connor was tried, freed, arrested again, and kept in jail until 1802.

10. Madden, *United Irishmen*, 2: 57.

11. J. A. Froude, *The English in Ireland in the Eighteenth Century*, 3: 345.

12. Madden, *United Irishmen*, 2: 58.

13. Bishop of Bath and Wells, ed., *The Journal and Correspondence of William, Lord Auckland*, 3: 429–30; and Madden, *United Irishmen*, pp. 402–4, 409, 411–12.

14. Lecky, *History of England*, p. 76.

15. Ibid., pp. 79–82.

16. Lecky, *History of England*, pp. 91–93; and Edouard Desbrière, ed., *1793–1805 projets et tentatives de débarquement aux Iles britanniques*, 2: 40.

17. Miles Byrne, *Mémoires d'un exile irlandais de 1798* (Paris: 1864), 1: 51–52.

18. Desbrière, *Projets et tentatives*, 2: 37.

19. Lecky, *History of England*, 7: 129–33.

20. Froude, *English in Ireland*, 3: 407–11; and H. F. B. Wheeler and A. M. Broadley, *The War in Wexford*, pp. 130–33.

21. Gordon, *Rebellion in Ireland*, p. 125.

22. Wheeler and Broadley, *War in Wexford*, pp. 119–20; and Froude, *English in Ireland*, 3: 420–23.

23. Byrne, *Mémoires*, p. 140; Lecky, *History of England*, pp. 150–51, 164, 166; and Froude, *English in Ireland*, pp. 436–37, 443–44, 437.

24. Lecky, *History of England*, pp. 175–78, 180–82; and Byrne, *Mémoires*, p. 241.

25. Madden, *United Irishmen*, 1: 360–61.

26. Fortescue, *History of the British Army*, p. 939; *Report*, pp. 72–75; and Lecky, *History of England*, 7: 250–51.

27. Wolfe Tone, *Life*, pp. 505–7.

28. David d'Angers, ed., *Mémoires de Larevellière-Lépaux*, 2: 185; and Bernard Nabonne, ed., *La diplomatie du Directoire et Bonaparte d'après les papiers inédits de Reubell*, p. 166.

29. Desbrière, *Projets et tentatives*, 2: 42, 50.

30. Ibid., pp. 51, 58, 60, 69–70.

31. Ibid., pp. 75–77. Larevellière maintained that the reason that funds were lacking was because of treason in the treasury department. He said that the Clichy faction had not been cleaned out of the treasury in September, 1797, and they conspired to delay the shipment of funds to Hardy, Humbert, and Cherin in the summer of 1798. See *Mémoires de Larevellière-Lépaux*, pp. 185–86.

32. C. L. Falkiner, *Studies in Irish History and Biography*, p. 257.

33. Édouard Guillon, *La France et l'Irlande pendant la Révolution*, pp. 371–74; and Falkiner, *Irish History*, p. 278.

34. Falkiner, *Irish History*, pp. 286–92; and Guillon, *La France et l'Irlande*, pp. 379–81, 385.

35. Guillon, *La France et l'Irlande*, p. 388; and Falkiner, *Irish History*, pp. 310–12.

36. Charles Ross, ed., *Correspondence of Charles, First Marquess of Cornwallis*, 2: 398–401; and Desbrière, *Projets et tentatives*, 2: 123–28.

37. Desbrière, *Projets et tentatives*, 2: 143–44, 149–50, 155–57.

38. Ibid., pp. 164–68, 170–71, 182–83; and MacDermot, *Theobold Wolfe Tone, A Biographical Study*, pp. 291–92.

39. Desbrière, *Projets et tentatives*, 2: 176–77, 190–95, 207–9, 212.

40. Gérard Walter, ed., *Las Cases, le comte de, Le mémorial de Saint-Hélène*, 1: 646.

9

The Formation of the Coalition

French disasters in overseas ventures had vast repercussions on the balance of power in Europe. Austria saw these French setbacks as an opportunity to reenter the war on advantageous terms. Francis offered Czar Paul an alliance, and the Russians, having committed themselves to hostilities in the Mediterranean, quickly accepted. The British, who were still seeking to revive a coalition, also made overtures to the Russians, and by the end of 1798 London and St. Petersburg had agreed upon a common set of war aims. Thus by the start of 1799, it had become obvious that the main theater of war had shifted away from colonial areas and was moving back to the Continent, where the allies could strike directly at France.

The Austrians took the first steps toward the resumption of war in Europe. Vienna had never accepted the Campoformio treaty as final but had been afraid to renew hostilities without the assistance of other powers. Talks with England had failed, but Russia was more than willing to listen to Austrian proposals. An Austrian offer to Russia was, however, long in coming, for Vienna was playing a double game. Austria, although worried about the spread of revolutionary propaganda and the growth of French power, was, nevertheless, willing to negotiate with the

Republic in an attempt to extend its holdings in Italy. The Hapsburgs, therefore, followed a dual policy of preparing war against France on the one hand while negotiating with the Republic on the other.

Vienna expressed the bellicose side of its policy on February 18, 1798, when the Austrian ambassador to England told Grenville that only the reestablishment of the monarchy in France could bring security to Europe. In April the Austrians suggested the formation of a coalition including Russia, Denmark, Sardinia, and Naples to drive France from the Low Countries and the Rhineland.[1] Austria also showed her hostility to France at the Rastadt Conference by refusing to arrange a definitive settlement of peace terms between the Republic and the Empire. French representatives reported that the Austrians were constantly delaying the negotiations, working to renew a coalition, and preventing a final peace.[2] In Italy, the Austrians also followed a policy of strengthening their military position, and on May 19, signed a treaty with the Kingdom of the Two Sicilies providing for a permanent alliance between the two powers. Vienna promised to keep sixty thousand men in Italy, and Naples agreed to have thirty thousand troops ready for an immediate attack on the French-supported Italian republics. The treaty also stipulated that generals of the two armies would coordinate their actions, and in a secret article Austria and Naples agreed that they would regard only France and the Italian republics as potential enemies. Finally, the treaty stated that a renewal of hostilities in Germany would automatically call for war in Italy.[3] Thus by the summer of 1798 Austria was ready to renew the war in either Germany or Italy.

Two factors restrained the Austrians from immediate action at this time. The first was the lack of allies, for they could reach no financial agreement with Britain, and Prussia was too suspicious of Austrian ambitions and too afraid of the French to join a coalition. The second reason for Austrian inaction was that Vienna had hopes of making substantial gains in Italy without recourse to war. The means of attaining these gains was through direct negotiations with France. The opportunity for such negotiations arose when Viennese crowds on April 14 tore down and burned a huge tricolor flag that Bernadotte, the ambassador, had hung from a window of the French embassy. Despite Austrian notes of apology, Bernadotte left Vienna on April 15. Ten days later the Directory told Vienna that it was sending Bonaparte to Rastadt to negotiate a settlement of the incident, but since Bonaparte was soon to leave for Egypt, ex-Director François de Neufchateau took his place, and the Directory transferred the site of the conference to the Alsatian town of Selz.[4]

Negotiations between François and Cobenzl, the Austrian envoy, opened on June 1. Cobenzl immediately turned to the issues of Italy and Switzerland, claiming that France was threatening Austrian interests in these areas by her occupation of Rome and the Swiss cantons. He gave but a passing reference to the Vienna incident, blaming Bernadotte for inciting the riot, but François insisted that discussions be limited to rectifying the insult to the French flag.[5] Discussions continued to follow this pattern: Cobenzl demanding the reestablishment of equilibrium in Italy by the concessions of certain papal territories and François insisting on confining the talks to the Vienna incident.[6] Since neither side made concessions, the Austrians discontinued the talks on July 5 and returned to their warlike policy. They were doubtless encouraged to pursue this course of action by the facts that Bonaparte and his army had left Europe and the British had isolated them. Since the Russians were already hostile to France, it was to them that the Austrians naturally turned, and on July 8, François informed his government that Cobenzl was on his way to St. Petersburg.[7]

Thugut had been laying the groundwork for a Russian alliance even during the negotiations at Selz. He had sent the emperor's brother to St. Petersburg in June, and on July 7 he told the czar that Austria needed the support of a Russian corps of sixteen thousand men in order to resume hostilities. On August 8 the Austrian ambassador informed Thugut that the czar had agreed to place the required troops at Austria's disposal, and by the time Cobenzl arrived in Russia on August 31, the czar had increased the size of the corps to twenty-four thousand men, and it was already on the march to the west.[8] Austria had only to await the arrival of the Russians before resuming hostilities.

Having agreed to extend the war to central Europe, the czar next attempted to gain more allies. Negotiations with Prussia, however, still failed to convince Berlin to drop its policy of neutrality, and Berlin also rejected a Russian offer of the cooperation of forty-five thousand men.[9] Negotiations with England led to better results. On November 16 Grenville wrote to the British ambassador in Russia, putting forth the conditions for a new coalition that he should present to the czar. England was willing to give Austria Lombardy and Savoy, and wished to deprive France of the Rhineland and the Low Countries. The allies would restore the stadtholder in Holland and add the Austrian Netherlands to his domain.[10] The czar accepted these terms, and on December 29 England and Russia signed a treaty whereby they agreed to cooperate in reestablishing the balance of power in Europe by reducing France to her limits of 1792. The two powers also agreed to further efforts to get Prussia to join the coalition by promising military aid and territorial aggrandizement at the expense of France.[11] England's adherence in January, 1799, to the Russo-Turkish alliance completed the basis of an alliance stretching from St. Petersburg to Constantinople.

The French, meanwhile, sought desperately but unsuccessfully to stave off a new continental war. In late August, reports from the Middle East indicated that the Porte was preparing for war, and on September 4, news of the Abukir disaster arrived.[12] Paris was already suspicious of Austrian intentions, knowing that Vienna had opened negotiations with the Russians, and the Directory also learned that the Austrians were placing their army on a war footing.[13] The government, therefore, felt it necessary to strengthen its army, which had been declining in size for several years due to the failure to replace combat losses and because of increased desertion. In March, 1798, there were still 365,000 men under arms. The army was strong enough to defeat any single power, but it could not face a coalition. The loss of Bonaparte's army made it even more imperative to rectify this situation, and on September 5 the Legislative Corps passed a Law of Conscription, Title III of which stated that all Frenchmen from twenty to twenty-five years of age were subject to conscription and had to report for medical examinations and registration.[14] A military committee headed by General Jourdan had been discussing such a measure ever since 1797, but it took the events of 1798 to speed the act to its final completion and enactment.

On September 23 the Directory requested the Legislative Corps to call up the first 200,000 conscripts to bring standing units up to regulation strength, and form sixteen new demibrigades.[15] Calling for new troops and obtaining them were, however, two very different things, and from the first there was widespread resistance to conscription. In the former states of Belgium and Liège, draftees refused to join their units and ran away to become brigands.[16] Priests often assumed leadership of these deserters and led them on raids against the authorities, destroying draft and tax rolls and burning the homes of those who had purchased nationalized church lands.[17] The government had to withdraw valuable troops from the active field armies to aid the local authorities in hunting the rebels.[18] In western France, the desertions and resulting brigandage took on political overtones as émigrés, Chouans, and priests began to organize and lead the rebels. The former provinces of Brittany, Normandy, and Anjou were all infested with royalists and draft dodgers, and the army had to use thirteen demibrigades and a cavalry regiment, a total of 55,500 troops, to keep order.[19] In other departments, the situation was not as serious, but neverthless the minister of war felt that the situation was of sufficient gravity to report widespread desertion everywhere. Of the first 100,000 conscripts called, only some 35,000 had arrived at the army bases by the end of the year.[20]

While the government was trying to strengthen the army, it also set about trying to divert Turkish and Russian troops from the main war areas by creating uprisings in their rear. On November 14, the Directory established a three-man commercial agency at Ancona. The agency's objective was to create insurrections in Albania, Epirus, and Morea, but lack of funds hampered the group from the start. The agency did manage to send agents to Montenegro and Greece, and even entered into correspondence with the Bishop of Scutari.[21] The results, however, were disappointing, and aside from some rather grandiose schemes, the committee accomplished little. The government also sent an agent to Russia to create a palace revolution, but he disappeared and was never heard from again.[22]

The final French effort to strengthen their position was diplomatic. The Directory hoped that by concluding a definitive peace with the Empire future hostilities could be confined to Italy where they had their strongest armies. Talleyrand had originally held great hopes for a diplomatic triumph at the Rastadt conference. His instructions of November 2, 1797, stated that France should use her influence to create a stable third power in Germany that would be able to take Austria in reverse if Vienna tried to extend her influence to Italy. To create this third power, he planned to back the secular princes, especially the Protestant ones, in their search for compensations for loss of territory in the Rhineland, by offering them the opportunity of grabbing the lands of the ecclesiastical princes. Talleyrand assumed that the princes, owing their gains to the Republic, would have to align themselves with France to preserve the new *status quo*.[23] Talleyrand also hoped to force the Congress to recognize the Rhine as the French frontier without offering any Italian territory as an indemnity to Austria. Austria and the ecclesiastical princes naturally opposed the French plans and worked to defeat them by employing delaying tactics. Vienna hoped to keep the issues open, for if events took an unfavorable turn for France, the Austrians intended to force the Directory to make concessions in order to obtain a quick settlement. Austria also continued to press the French for concessions in Italy in return for cooperation at Rastadt, a policy that was carried over to the Selz conference.[24]

In the first months of 1798, the French were in no mood to compromise, and in March, they forced the Congress to recognize the Rhine as the French frontier by threatening to break off the talks. But as the international situation grew more serious, the French felt compelled to modify their demands for the possession of various islands in the Rhine and for several forts on the right bank. On July 10 Talleyrand told his agents to show great moderation so as to avoid driving the princes into the arms of Russia and Austria, and, on July 19 the French gave up their claims to the disputed islands in the Rhine.[25] As the situation further deteriorated, Talleyrand, on September 9, informed the directors that since Austria was preparing for war it was necessary to settle the territorial *status quo* in Germany on its present basis.[26] In other words, the foreign minister abandoned his plan of creating a Germanic third power in return for obtaining a quick peace on the Rhine, and on September 14 he made even further concessions by giving up French claims to the right bank fortresses.[27]

On October 3 the French made another attempt to push through a final treaty by telling the imperial delegation that if it did not accept the Republic's concessions of the islands and forts and proceed to settle the issue of indemnities and secularizations, Paris would assume that the Empire wished to continue the war. This threat, however, had no effect, for the Austrians continued to delay the settlement. Talleyrand then decided to try a second ultimatum, and on December 6 the French delegates told the Congress that if they did not accept the French terms within six days, Paris would discontinue the negotiations. On December 12 the imperial delegation finally accepted the French demands, but Austria was still determined to hinder the final settlement by creating delays over the issues of indemnification and secularization.[28] Since these two questions were the main issues before the Congress, and the most complicated ones, the Austrians could easily prolong the discussions for many months by raising numerous minor questions over the varying claims. Thus despite Talleyrand's efforts, the Republic at the end of the year was still in a state of war with the Empire and had to keep many valuable units guarding the Rhine frontier.

In addition to the numerous diplomatic setbacks arising from the defeat of the eastern expedition there were also various military repercussions, none of which were to the benefit of the Republic. Nelson's triumph had left him with absolute control of the sea, and he was quick to make use of it. Leaving three frigates to blockade the Egyptian coast, he set off for Naples on August 19. While he was en route to Naples, the Maltese population had risen in rebellion against the French garrison. The French by their taxation policies and by their attacks on the religious beliefs of the Maltese had managed to antagonize the majority of the population. Inspired by the news of Abukir, the growing resentment finally erupted into open rebellion on September 2. By September 8, Nelson had learned of the revolt, and four days later he requested the Portuguese to undertake the blockade of Valetta. A Portuguese squadron arrived on September 19, and on September 23 a British squadron, which was returning to England with the French ships captured at Abukir, joined them. On September 25, the allied commanders demanded the surrender of Valetta, but Vaubois refused. The English then supplied the Maltese with arms and munitions and continued their homeward voyage, leaving the Portuguese to continue the blockade. The rebels, led by their priests, quickly forced the French to take refuge in Valetta. The blockade, strengthened by the arrival of English ships on October 6, was unbreakable, and it rendered Malta useless as a naval base for the Republic.[29]

To extend their control of the Mediterranean even further, the British next decided to strike against the Spanish at Minorca. Three regiments under the command of Sir Charles Stuart landed on the island on November 6. The main forts, Mahon at the east and Ciudaella at the west end of the island, were separated by rough terrain with only one connecting pass between them, and Stuart made this pass his first objective. A six hundred-man advance guard seized the pass on November 8, and on November 9 the rest of Stuart's troops moved forward, splitting the defending force in two. Mahon surrendered without a fight, and by November 13 about three thousand English troops were in front of Ciudaella. By drawing up his force so as to give an exaggerated impression of its strength, Stuart bluffed the thirty-six hundred-man garrison into surrendering.[30] By November 15 the British had obtained with only minor losses a base in the western Mediterranean from which they could raid the Spanish coast and force Madrid to tie down many ships and troops in passive defense. Minorca also made an excellent base from which naval units could aid in the blockade of Spain, southern France, Italy, Malta, and Egypt.

Meanwhile, Nelson, having arranged for the blockade of Malta, had continued his voyage to Naples, where he arrived on September 22. News of his victory had preceded him, and he received a spectacular welcome. King Ferdinand reviewed the British fleet, and Queen Marie Caroline granted Nelson a private audience at which the Admiral suddenly transformed himself into a diplomat and urged her to attack the French. Nelson's efforts were seconded by Hamilton, the British ambassador, and by his wife, who was a personal confidante of the queen. They easily convinced the queen, but Ferdinand, though hating the French and having ambitions of his own in Italy, was thoroughly afraid of the Republic's army.[31] For the moment, he resisted the pressure for war, although in the past months he had been making preparations for just such an eventuality.

The French occupation of Rome in January had alarmed Ferdinand, because he regarded the Papal States as a buffer between his kingdom and the French. He had also entertained hopes of seizing some papal territory for himself. The activities of the Toulon fleet had also alarmed him, because he feared that Naples was one of its objectives. To protect his kingdom, he had allowed Nelson's fleet to obtain supplies and make repairs in his supposedly neutral ports.[32] In the summer of 1798 a revolt erupted in the Roman Republic, and Alexandre Macdonald, a divisional commander in the French army of Rome, noted that the local priests were leading the rebels, who were mainly peasants. He then discovered that the court of Naples had taken an interest in the rebellion and that Neapolitan officers were organizing and leading some of the rebel bands.[33] In August intelligence reports indicated that Naples was rapidly expanding its army, and on August 4 one of Macdonald's subordinates reported large concentrations of Neapolitan troops on the Roman frontier. Three days later, Macdonald told his commander in chief that he had sent a proclamation to Ferdinand, informing the monarch that he had defeated the rebels and that there existed no pretext for his sending troops into the Roman Republic to restore order.[34]

Evidently frightened by this proclamation, the court of Naples took no further action until Nelson's arrival. The queen then asked the Austrians to aid Naples in an attack on the French, but Vienna was not yet ready for war. The Austrians wished to wait until the Russians arrived before acting, and although they did send General Mack to command Ferdinand's army, they specifically told the king not to attack prematurely and that if he did, he could expect no help. From England as well came similar advice, for Grenville told Hamilton to urge the court of Naples to be cautious.[35] Hamilton, however, did nothing of the kind, and under the combined pressure of the queen, the Hamiltons, and Nelson, the king agreed to expand his army to fifty thousand men and invade the Roman Republic. Hamilton told Grenville on November 19 that he and Nelson had convinced the king to attack the Roman Republic by promising British naval support in the landing of five thousand men behind the French lines at Leghorn. By November 24, sixty-two infantry battalions and thirty-two squadrons of cavalry were ready to march.[36]

Since the start of September, the French had been watching Neapolitan preparations with growing alarm. Numerous reports indicated the growth of the Neapolitan army and its concentration near the frontier of the Roman Republic.[37] To further increase their problems, the French learned that the Kingdom of Sardinia was also making warlike preparations. If Sardinia entered the war in conjunction with Naples, it could seriously endanger the French position in Italy. Sardinian Piedmont stood directly across the shortest line of communications between France and the Italian republics, and a Sardinian attack would not only cut these communications but also would enable the Sardinians to attack the French and Cisalpine armies from the rear. As Naples was arming for war, reports reached Milan and Paris that Sardinia was concentrating troops around Turin, where the French maintained a garrison, that priests and royal agents were spreading anti-French propaganda throughout the countryside, and that assassinations of individual French soldiers were becoming a daily occurrence.[38] On November 7 Joubert, the commander of the army of Italy, told the war minister that the Sardinian army had armed twenty-six thousand peasants, and on November 11 he requested pemission to occupy Piedmont in case of war with Naples. The Sardinians for their part were quite confident of their strength, and on November 11 and again on November 16 demanded that the French evacuate the Turin citadel.[39]

To meet this double threat, the Directory decided to strengthen its forces in Italy at the expense of the Rhine Army. It sent seven demibrigades to Italy. They arrived on November 19 bringing the army of Italy's strength up to 129,360 infantry, 16,785 cavalry, and 6,286 engineers and artillerymen. The army of Rome, however, was still very weak. Under Championnet's command since the middle of October, it consisted of only 15,000 men plus 5,000 Polish and Roman troops.[40] Joubert was unable to spare any more men for he had to guard against potential attacks from both the Sardinians and the Austrians. Thus if the French were in a fairly strong position in north and central Italy, they were very weak in the south.

While the French were becoming increasingly concerned with the threatening situation in Italy, the Austrians seized the opportunity to move into eastern Switzerland and gain an excellent advance base for future operations. When the French had invaded Switzerland the previous March, at least one of their motives was the desire to use Switzerland as a defensive bastion for the Republic's undefended frontier.[41] The Protestant cantons had generally favored the creation of a Helvetian Republic, but the Catholic areas resisted, and the French had to use military force to compel them to accept the Helvetian Constitution. A few months later, when the Swiss republicans demanded an oath of loyalty to the new constitution, the Catholic cantons, this time aided by Austrian agents, refused and once more took up arms. Three demibrigades moved into the cantons, and after much bitter fighting, the French again defeated the Catholics.[42] Having failed to keep Switzerland out of French and republican hands, the Austrians took no further action until the diplomatic situation offered them an excellent opportunity to move into the Grisons, the easternmost region of Switzerland.

The French had not occupied the Grisons, and the local assembly had on July 29 refused to join the Helvetian Republic. On August 9 the French sent troops to the Grisons frontier, but on August 10 the Directory ordered the French commander not to invade because the government did not want to alarm the German princes with whom they were negotiating at Rastadt.[43] The Austrians, meanwhile, had decided to take advantage of French concern with the situation in the Near East, Italy, and Germany by moving into Grisons themselves, and at the end of December, Paris learned that Austrian agents were active in the region and that a large Austrian force was encamped on the frontier.[44] Inside the Grisons, a pro-Austrian faction took control, and on October 7 it crushed a French-inspired popular revolt. Ten days later the Grisons signed a convention with Austria, and on the night of October 18 to 19, Austrian troops moved into the area.[45]

The Directory felt that it was too weak to take any counter-action. The situation in Italy was rapidly deteriorating; the Austrians already had twelve thousand men in the Grisons and by November would have twenty thousand men there. They also had about one hundred thousand men in Germany and another one hundred thousand in Italy, and the minister of war told the Directory that it would be folly to demand an explanation from the Austrians before the French armies had completed their reorganization.[46] Not wishing to run the risk of still another power entering the war before they were fully prepared, the directors did nothing, and allowed the Austrians to complete their bloodless conquest of the Grisons and turn it into an excellent bastion from which to launch attacks into Switzerland and northern Italy. The one benefit that the Directory gained by its inaction was that it was able to face the Neapolitan attack without a simultaneous involvement with the Austrians.

The Neapolitan offensive was not long in coming, and on November 23 Mack's forces began to move on Rome. General Mack's army moved in five columns spread across the peninsula with most of the troops concentrated in the two columns moving on Rome. Since the French were heavily outnumbered, they had little choice but to fall back, and on November 27 Championnet ordered Macdonald to evacuate Rome.[47] In the center of the peninsula, however, the Ninety-seventh demibrigade attacked and defeated the two central Neapolitan columns. The French were equally successful on the Adriatic coast, where Cassabianca's division suddenly attacked and routed the twelve battalions and eight squadrons whose mission was to take Ancona, but these victories did not prevent Mack from entering Rome in the first days of December.[48]

On December 4 Mack directed thirteen battalions to take the town of Nepi just to the north of Rome and expose the French right flank. Such a move would force the French to retreat and enable Mack's troops to move into Tuscany and link up with the division that Nelson had recently landed at Leghorn. The attack was almost successful, but the opportune arrival of a Polish battalion that struck at Mack's flank turned the victory into a rout. The Neapolitans fled, leaving two thousand prisoners behind.[49] On December 5 the French also turned back a second attack, but since they had concentrated most of their troops on their right, other Neapolitan units were able to push to Otricoli, on the French left. There were no troops at Otricoli except some wounded whom the Neapolitans set about slaughtering, but Macdonald rapidly organized a counterattack and drove them out of the town.[50] As a result of this victory, the French had definitely checked Mack's offensive, and Championnet began to prepare a counterattack.

As the army of Rome was engaged in halting Mack's offensive, the army of Italy prepared to act against the threat of a Sardinian offensive against their rear. On November 24 Joubert learned that the Sardinians were raising new troops for their army, and three days later he learned that these troops were moving to Turin.[51] The Sardinians were either preparing to enter the war or, by threatening to do so, force the French to abandon their bases in Piedmont. On December 3 Joubert told the commander of the Turin citadel that the army of Italy was going to move, and two days later the French entered Piedmont.[52] Joubert informed the population that he would protect their religion and incorporate the Sardinian army into the army of Italy, and that he had invaded Piedmont only to forestall a Sardinian attack. There was no opposition from the Sardinian army, and on December 6 the king, realizing that resistance would be futile, issued a proclamation directing his subjects to obey the French. The king left for Sardinia on December 9, and two days later the French established a provisional government.[53] By their rapid movement, the French had scored their only major success of the year, for they had relieved themselves of the danger of an attack from the rear if a major war erupted in Italy.

As the army of Italy was conquering Piedmont, the army of Rome began its offensive against Naples. On December 8 the Sixty-fourth and Ninety-seventh demibrigades reentered Rieti, while further south Macdonald's division recrossed the Tiber. By December 12 Macdonald was able to report that the enemy was in full retreat toward Rome, and this retreat gradually became a rout. At Vienna, the British ambassador noted, "The Neapolitan troops have begged to be excused everywhere. They have fled and deserted uniformly."[54] The French reentered Rome on December 16, and on Christmas Day began to move south. At the same time, troops from the army of Italy entered Tuscany to attack the

Neapolitan division at Leghorn. The Directory, however, soon suspended this advance, because it discovered that the enemy troops in Tuscany did not represent a serious threat, and the French did not wish to antagonize the Austrians further by making more conquests in Italy.[55]

The Neapolitans had meanwhile continued to retreat, and by New Year's Day of 1799 were at Capua. The French followed, and on January 11 took Gaetta. Mack then asked for an armistice and agreed to surrender the fortified camps at Naples. He resigned his post and fled to the French lines, fearing that the population of Naples would blame him for the defeat and capitulation.[56] On January 14 Championnet ordered his army to push on to Naples, and within a week the French were in the outskirts of the city. The royal family had already fled to Sicily on December 11, leaving a vicar-general in charge of the mainland. The vicar-general was willing to surrender the city to the French, but the *lazzaroni,* the populace, armed themselves and prepared to resist. When Championnet's troops tried to enter the city, they put up furious resistance. It took the French, aided by a prorepublican minority, who seized several of the city's key forts, three days of bitter street fighting, in which one thousand French and three thousand *lazzaroni* perished, to pacify Naples. On January 23 the French organized a provisional government, and on January 25, without the Directory's approval, Championnet proclaimed the establishment of a Neapolitan Republic and began to levy heavy taxes on the already bitter and hostile population.[57]

The French had apparently won a great victory, but this victory was illusory. The Catholic population refused to accept the new regime, and in the countryside, bands of peasants led by their priests took up arms. The resistance soon became so serious that Joubert had to send reinforcements to Naples, and although the French took Naples with fewer than thirty thousand troops, it required over forty thousand men to maintain even the most precarious control over the area. By February, only large mobile columns could move about outside the immediate vicinity of the city with any degree of security.[58] On February 7 Cardinal Ruffo, who had been appointed vicar-general by Ferdinand, landed on the mainland and began to organize the various rebel bands into the Christian Army of the Holy Faith. With Ruffo's ability to weld royalists, bandits, and fanatics into a unified army, the French hold on Naples became even more tenuous.[59]

To make matters worse, Championnet and Faipoult, the government army commissioner, came into conflict when the commissioner objected to the general's taxation policy, which was little more than a system of authorized plundering. Championnet arrested Faipoult, and the Directory in turn relieved Championnet of command and put Macdonald in his place.[60] In addition to the administrative confusion caused by these events, this was hardly an edifying example to be placed before the army and the nation on the eve of war.

The conquest of Naples had thus drawn a huge force into southern Italy, where in case of an Austrian attack on the Adige it would be unable to aid the army of Italy. The army of Italy, which would bear the full weight of any Austrian attack, had to divert vital troops to the south to maintain control of an area that was, in fact, a strategic liability to the Directory. The conquest of Naples was, therefore, the last in a long series of errors, starting with the original decision to invade Egypt. The disastrous results of the eastern venture as a whole were clearly enunciated by Reubell, who later declared:

> It is incontestably the violation of Ottoman territory by the expedition to Egypt, which is the principal cause of the dangers of the country because it has led the Turks into a new coalition; and the Austrio-Russians, free in consequence of all incertitude in regards to this power, have sent against us superior forces, and can continue to send them up to their last man.[61]

NOTES

1. Historical Manuscripts Commission, *Report on the Manuscripts of J. B. Fortescue, Esq., Preserved at Dropmore*, 4: 92–93.

2. Paul Montarlot and Léonce Pingaud, eds., *Le Congrès de Rastadt (11 juin 1798–28 avril 1799) correspondance et documents*, 1: 199.

3. Leopold Neumann, ed., *Recueil des traités et conventions conclus par l'Autriche avec les puissances étrangères depuis 1763 jusqu'à nos jours*, 1: 593–96.

4. Frédéric Masson, *Les diplomates de la Révolution*, pp. 188–91, 205, 210–11. The Constitution of the Year III forbade an ex-Director to leave French territory for two years after the end of his term of office.

5. Archives nationales, AF III, carton 59 (hereafter, AN).

6. Ibid.

7. Ibid.

8. Ibid.; and A. R. von Vivenot, ed., *Vertrauliche Briefe des Freiherrn von Thugut*, 2: 115.

9. *Manuscripts of Fortescue*, 4: 190.

10. Ibid., pp. 378–79.

11. Fedor Martens, ed., *Recueil des traités et conventions conclus par la russie avec les puissances étrangères*, 9: 418–24.

12. Ministère de la Guerre État-Major de l'Armée, Archives historiques, Correspondance, Armée d'Italie, 1798, carton B355 (hereafter, Min. de la Guerre, AH).

13. Min. de la Guerre, AH, Correspondance, Armées de Mayence et d'Helvétie, 1798–99, carton B265.

14. Patrice Mahon, *Études sur les armées du Directoire*, p. 120.

15. AN, AF III*, carton 13.

16. Ibid.

17. Ibid.

18. Min. de la Guerre, AH, Correspondance du général Jourdan, 1798–99, carton B2 *260.

19. AN, AF III, carton 150A.

20. Ibid. Desertion from the draft need not be attributed entirely to royalism or disaffection with the Republic. Much of it was simply a dislike of military service, because as late as 1907, thirty-six percent of the French army reservists failed to report for duty when called. See A. T. Horne, *Price of Glory: Verdun 1916* (London: 1962), p. 9.

21. AN, AF III*, carton 13; Michel A. B. Mangourit, *Défense d'Ancone et des départments romains, Le Toronto, Le Musone, et Le Metauro par le général Monnier aux années VII et VIII*, 1: 21–22; and Spyridon Pappas, "Un point d'histoire ignoré, l'agence de commerce français d'Ancône (1799)." *Revue d'études historiques*, vol. 68.

22. Raymond Guyot, *Le Directoire et la paix de l'Europe*, p. 876.

23. Georges Pallain, ed., *Le ministère de Talleyrand sous le Directoire*, pp. 174–82.

24. Ibid., pp. 207–8.

25. *Congress at Rastadt Official Correspondence from the Original Papers*, pp. 174, 313. The frontier was to follow the *thallweg*, i.e., the deepest navigation channel of the river.

26. Pallain, *Talleyrand*, p. 378.

27. *Congress at Rastadt*, pp. 424–25.

28. Ibid., pp. 463–74, 479–80, 652–53.

29. William Hardman, *A History of Malta*, pp. 78, 106–10.

30. John W. Fortescue, *A History of the British Army*, 4, pt. 2: 616–19.

31. Harold Acton, *The Bourbons of Naples (1734–1825)*, pp. 303–6.

32. André Bonnefons, *Marie Caroline reine des Deux-Siciles (1768–1814)*, p. 151; and *Manuscripts of Fortescue*, 4: 237–38.

33. Min. de la Guerre, AH, carton B355.

34. Ibid. Naples had in fact increased the size of its army by about 15,000 men.

35. Vivenot, *Vertrauliche Brief*, p. 124, and J. Holland Rose, *Napoleonic Studies*, p. 353.

36. Min. de la Guerre, AH, Précis historique de la campagne de l'armée napolitaine par le général Mack, Mémoires historiques, no. 453 (hereafter, **MH**).

37. Min. de la Guerre, AH, cartons B355, B356.

38. Ibid.

39. Min. de la Guerre, AH, carton B356 bis.

40. Ibid. Unlike the Cisalpine army, the Roman army was badly organized and very weak.

41. Even the British admitted that the need to defend their eastern frontiers was the basic motive for the French occupation of Switzerland. See the chronicle section of *The Annual Register or a View of the History, Politics, and Literature for the Year 1798*, p. 37.

42. Min. de la Guerre, AH, Correspondance, Armées de Mainz et d'Helvétie, septembre 1798, carton B266.

43. AN, AF III*, carton 18.

44. Min. de la Guerre, AH, carton B266.

45. Min. de la Guerre, AH, Correspondance, Armées de Mainz et d'Helvétie, september 1798, B267.

46. Ibid.; and Min. de la Guerre, AH, carton B268.

47. Min. de la Guerre, AH, MH, no. 453.

48. Ibid.

49. Ibid.

50. Ibid.

51. Min. de la Guerre, AH, carton B356 bis.

52. Min. de la Guerre, AH, carton B357.

53. Ibid.

54. Countess Minto, ed., *Life and Letters of Sir Gilbert Elliot First Earl of Minto from 1751 to 1806*, 3: 49.

55. Min. de la Guerre, AH, carton B357, and MH, no. 453. The Neapolitan troops in Tuscany were evacuated by the British on January 4, 1799. See Mahon, *Armées du Directoire*, p. 481.

56. Min. de la Guerre, AH, Correspondance, Armées d'Italie et de Rome, janvier 1799, carton B358, and MH, no. 453.

57. Min. de la Guerre, AH, carton B358; and Acton, *The Bourbons,* pp. 323, 325–26, 329–32.

58. Min. de la Guerre, AH, Correspondance, Armées d'Italie et de Rome, février 1799, carton B358 bis; and AN, AF III, carton 150B.

59. Acton, *The Bourbons,* pp. 341–42; and Jacques Godechot, *La contre-révolution doctrine et action 1789–1804,* p. 353.

60. See Min. de la Guerre, AH, carton B358 bis. Championnet was ordered back to France to face a court martial.

61. Bernard Nabonne, ed., *La diplomatie du Directoire et Bonaparte d'après les papiers inédits de Reubell,* p. 164.

10

The Coming of War

The Directory realized that hostilities would begin as soon as the Russian corps reached Austria. From the end of 1798, reports from diplomatic officials in Germany and Austria indicated that the Russians were nearing the Rhine. On October 4 Talleyrand informed the directors that Vienna was talking openly about the imminent arrival of the Russians, and that the Austrians were concentrating troops and getting them ready for action.[1] On December 27 the minister of foreign relations told the government that his agents estimated the Russian corps to consist of 23,928 men and that the Austrian army comprised 324,000 men: 125,000 in Italy, 81,000 in South Germany, 61,000 in Bohemia, 56,000 in Austria, and 17,000 in Moravia.[2] By January 17, 1799, reports placed the Russians in Moravia with 45,000 more troops on their way to reinforce the first echelon. Other reports stated that Condé's *émigré* corps was also preparing for a campaign on the Rhine.[3] The Directory, therefore, had no choice but to draw up plans for the inevitable conflict.

In contrast to the campaigns of 1792 to 1797 when the government had to devise strategy while fighting raged, the Directory in 1799 had the time to elaborate a detailed plan. In formulating military plans, the Directory typically acted in conjunction with the minister of war and his staff. It also called upon the Military Bureau for advice and suggestions, but it usually did this in technical rather than strategic matters. Generals also submitted suggestions either to the government or to the war minister. In practice, the Directory would usually set forth its general wishes in regard to the strategic objectives, and the minister of war would draw up a detailed operational plan. The Directory would then review the plan making changes where it saw fit, and finally the war minister would send the completed plan in the form of operational orders to the field commanders.[4] The government generally gave field commanders a wide range of tactical initiative, although the Directory, acting through the agency of the War Ministry, could and sometimes did issue specific tactical instructions. Following these general lines of conduct, the government set about devising its instructions for the campaign of 1799.

On December 3, 1798, the Directory received a preliminary war plan from Louis Milet-Mureau, an engineer officer serving in the Military Bureau. Milet-Mureau suggested a series of offensive operations against the Austrians and Russians. One army would cross the Rhine and advance into Swabia. A second army would capture Philippsburg on the Rhine, and a third force would push to the headwaters of the Danube River by way of the Inn valley. At the same time, the French forces in Italy would occupy Tuscany and invade Venetia.[5] This plan had many obvious weaknesses. It failed to provide for a uniform system of field command and left five offensive operations uncoordinated and without a final goal. It also failed to specify which if any of the projected attacks was the most vital and would as a consequence receive the heaviest concentration of troops. Milet-Mureau's suggestion did, however, indicate that the Directory intended to wage a war of defensive political aims by means of offensive military operations.

There were many reasons why the Directory chose to fight an offensive campaign. In the first place, France could not strike directly at either England or Russia. If the French wished to disrupt the Coalition, they would have to attack the Austrians in the hope that, as in 1797, they could force Vienna to sue for a separate peace. If the French could also defeat the Russian corps, the czar would be unable to continue the fight in western Europe because England did not have an army large enough to support him, and with Austria out of the war, the Russians would have no major continental ally.

A second reason for desiring an offensive campaign was because

of the structure of the French army. Ever since 1793, French tactics had been based upon the concept of rapid, hard-hitting attacks. From a response to circumstances, the idea of the tactical offensive had evolved into a military doctrine. Even when fighting a defensive battle or when outnumbered, the typical French reaction was to launch audacious counterattacks. In 1799, then, it was not surprising that general officers thought in terms of tactical offensives even though the national objectives were, in political and strategic terms, defensive.

A second aspect of the army's organization added to the necessity of an offensive concept. The new citizen armies were many times larger than their royal predecessors, and could not supply themselves through the old system of fixed magazines. In addition, the greater mobility of the new armies made it impossible to rely on fixed bases. To remedy their difficult logistic situation, the French armies began to live off the countryside by requisitioning or by simply taking whatever they needed. Although somewhat modified after 1798, this method of obtaining supplies was still in general use in 1799, and it was obviously better from the point of view of national economic interests to have the army live off the enemy's country rather than one's own.

A final reason why the Directory wished to wage an offensive war was that it feared internal royalist revolts. The Vendée was still restive, the Chouans in Brittany still active, and it would take very little allied effort to rekindle the flames of a serious revolt. In many other departments there was much royalist activity, especially in Lyons, the area around Toulouse, and in the Gironde. In these areas, a secret royalist organization was busily engaged in organizing an army.[6] If an allied army could enter French territory, these royalists would take the field, and many who were sick of the constant wars would probably join the enemies of the Republic and support a restoration simply to attain peace. To avoid such an uprising, the Directory had to keep the fighting away from French soil at all costs. Thus the strategic situation, the nature of their army, and fear of internal revolt all influenced the Directory and its advisors to plan an offensive operation for the forthcoming campaign.

After several weeks of further discussion among the directors, the Military Bureau, and the minister of war, the government on January 30, 1799, issued to the field commanders a final battle plan entitled "Instructions on the Destination and General Movements of the Armies when Hostilities Resume."[7] Five active armies—the armies of Observation, Mainz, Helvetia, Italy, and Rome—were to participate in the campaign. The Observation army was to guard the Rhine and cover the Mainz army's left flank. The Mainz army commander was to exercise control over the Observation army's strategic movements. The army of Mainz would operate in Swabia and Bavaria. It would enter Swabia by way of the Rhine cities of Kehl and Hunnigue and push forward through the Black Mountains until it reached the source of the Danube River. Once at the Danube this army would change its designation to the army of the Danube, and from the Danube, it would advance to the Leck and Inn rivers in order to gain control of the Bavarian passes into the Tyrol. The directors assigned the army of Helvetia a double task. Its left wing was to capture the Grisons and Tyrol while the right wing gained control of the Valtelline and drove on to Botzen and

Brixen. The left wing was then to push to the valley of the Inn and follow the river to its source. After this it was to capture Innsbruck. The government gave the commander of the Danube army control over the army of Helvetia for strategic movements. The army of Italy was also to carry out several tasks. It was to cross the Adige River, seize Verona, and then push on to the Piave River. A detached corps was to move north to Brixen and Botzen to cover the right flank of the army of Helvetia. Other units were to protect Piedmont, Liguria, and the Cisalpine Republic, and to occupy Tuscany. The army of Rome, which was to become the army of Naples once it had conquered this area, was to continue to hold southern Italy and was subordinated to the commander of the army of Italy. The government gave troops stationed in the Batavian Republic and the units in the interior of France primarily defensive roles. Units in Batavia were to cooperate with the Dutch in defending their Republic and by so doing secure the northern frontier of France. Units in the interior of France were to continue to pursue royalists, bandits, and deserters and act as cadres for new battalions.[8]

The French war plan contained many of the serious shortcomings of Milet-Mureau's original suggestion. Due to the diversity of objectives, the Directory had failed to designate which goal was of major importance. It would have been wiser to concentrate the bulk of the troops on a single front where they could obtain decisive results rather than scattering them and risking defeat in detail. Furthermore, the Directory failed to state clearly the ultimate military objectives of the campaign, and the instructions stopped short after ordering the conquest of Venice, the Grisons, and the Tyrol. Doubtless the Directory felt that if their armies could attain control of these objectives, Austria would sue for peace, but in the eventuality that Austria still continued to fight there were no further plans. This particular shortcoming would not be too difficult to overcome, but the idea of launching several simultaneous attacks without a major area of concentration remained a dangerous weakness.

Numerical inferiority was the second serious shortcoming of the Directory's plan. In fact, the field armies were even weaker than the government had thought. The Directory planned to assign 46,-000 men to the Danube army, 30,000 to the Helvetian army,

40,000 to the army of Naples, 90,000 to the army of Italy, 48,000 to the army of Observation, 15,000 to the army of Batavia, and 112,000 to the army of the Interior.[9] These estimates were, however, highly optimistic, for although the army of Helvetia reported in December that it had 37,673 effectives, the Danube army noted that it had only 26,000 men. The army of Italy was also under strength and reported that it had a strength of only 57,857 men, a figure that was even further reduced by the fact that only 46,369 of them were available for action on the Adige.[10] Final estimates for the size of the active armies including recent conscripts indicated that the army of the Danube consisted of 39,347 men, several thousand of whom were in garrisons, thereby reducing combat strength to about 25,000. The army of Observation numbered only 28,394 men, and the Helvetian army after sending reinforcements to Italy had but 26,339 troops. The army of Italy managed to increase its size to 70,059, but it stationed 37,640 of these soldiers in various garrisons or depots. The army of Naples was comprised of about 32,000 troops. In addition, the army of England, which guarded the coasts and provinces of western France, consisted of 42,285 men, and a further 94,264 troops were in garrisons throughout the interior of France. Finally, the government kept 18,990 men in depots ready to reinforce the active armies. The French could place a total of 351,678 troops in the field and could expect a gradual increase in numbers as conscripts were trained and sent to the fighting fronts, but the government retained a large percentage of its men in the interior and scattered the rest over many fronts. Moreover, the front line troops had to face an estimated 324,000 Austrians, 70,000 Russians, and an unknown number (but probably well over 10,000) of British troops.[11]

A final step in the war preparations was the appointment of the various army commanders. On February 21 the Directory nominated Schérer, then serving as war minister, to command the armies of Italy and Naples. He was to exercise direct tactical command over the army of Italy and control the grand movements of the army of Naples, which the government placed under Macdonald's command. Five days later Milet-Mureau replaced Schérer as minister of war. On March 2 General Jourdan received overall command of the armies of the Danube, Observation, and

Helvetia. He was personally to lead the Danube army in battle while Masséna was to command the army of Helvetia and Bernadotte the army of Observation. Brune was to continue to command the French troops in Batavia, a position that he had held since October.[12]

Meanwhile, Pitt was determined not only to reduce France within its former limits as they subsisted before the Revolution, but also to destroy the Republic and restore the monarchy. He had become convinced that the Republic was such a great danger to the social and political *status quo* that England could not allow it to survive.[13]

The Irish rebellion, continuing republican sentiment in Ireland, the apparent danger of subversive societies in England, and industrial unrest in northern England that could easily become tinged with republicanism all influenced Pitt in the belief that, in order to end these social threats as well as the threat to the balance of continental power, the allies had to destroy the center of revolutionary ideology.

Pitt also had several other important reasons for desiring a restoration. First of all, if he were to call for aid from French royalists, he would have to promise them a restored monarchy. Further, the French Constitution of the Year III had declared Belgium to be an integral part of France, and the Directory had later incorporated the Rhineland and Piedmont into the Republic. No republican government would accept the loss of these areas as a basis for peace, and only a weakened monarchy would do so. Furthermore, a restored monarch would be weaker than the Directory and dependent on the powers who put him back upon his throne. Consequently, England would benefit by the decline of her foremost continental rival. Also, a weak monarchy would be unable to hinder British plans for the disposition of reconquered territories, because although the British planned to force France to surrender her conquests, they were far from planning a return to the territorial *status quo* of 1789. In fact, Pitt had specific plans for the disposition of the Low Countries, an area in which England had long-standing strategic and commercial interests.

Once the Coalition had forced the French from Holland, the British planned to restore the House of Orange, but they did not intend to return Belgium to Austria. Rather, the English planned to unite Belgium and Holland into a single kingdom under the rule of the former Dutch stadtholder.[14] Having united Belgium and Holland under a friendly ruler, Grenville then planned to secure England's domination of the area by creating an offensive and defensive alliance that would bind the stadtholder to British policy. He also planned to force the stadtholder to renounce his rights of neutral commerce when England was at war, thereby securing Britain's commercial domination of the area.[15] The British planned to compensate Austria for the loss of Belgium by giving Vienna expanded holdings in Italy. The Austrians, however, objected to the idea of the unification of the Low Countries, and their objections forced the British to contemplate active participation in an invasion of Holland in order to obtain actual possession of the Low Countries, which would enable them to negotiate with the Austrians from a position of strength. Also, such an invasion would contribute to the defeat of France by turning the northern end of the Rhine barrier and opening Belgium to invasion.[16]

To obtain troops for a continental campaign, England had already opened negotiations with Russia and had signed a provisional treaty with the czar calling for a combined English, Russian, and Prussian attack on the Batavian Republic. To obtain Prussia's agreement, the English continued their negotiations with Berlin, which they had started at the end of 1797. English diplomatic agents, however, failed to convince the Prussian king to abandon his neutrality, and Grenville next sent his brother to Berlin to convince Haugwitz to join the Coalition. At the same time, another envoy continued his efforts at the Prussian court and tried to get the duke of Brunswick to use his influence on Frederick William III and convince the monarch to enter the war against France. The Russians also undertook negotiations with Prussia.

These efforts, however, all failed, and although England and Russia continued well into the summer of 1799 to try to draw Prussia into an alliance, Berlin refused. The British were unable to shake Frederick William's belief in the benefits of the neutrality that enabled Prussia to dominate northern Germany, nor were they able to overcome Prussia's suspicions of Austrian ambitions.[17] The Russians went even further in their efforts to draw Prussia into the Coalition, and in September, 1798, the czar concentrated sixty thousand troops in Poland in order to threaten Prussia if Haugwitz continued to refuse to join the projected alliance.[18] Haugwitz, however, was not taken in by this maneuver and gave only vague answers to the Russian offers and threats. The king meanwhile told his ambassador in Paris that Prussia would never depart from its system of neutrality and would fight only if France invaded Prussian territory. Later, Haugwitz did have second thoughts and began to suggest that Prussia force France from Holland by threatening to join the Coalition, but for the moment, the king firmly refused to sacrifice his precious neutrality to fight what he regarded as Austria's war.[19] As a consequence of the Prussian refusal to join the Coalition, the English and Russians had to revise their original treaty.

The English did not complete a new convention with the czar until June 22, 1799. The two powers dropped the idea of a Russo-Prussian invasion of Batavia and brushed aside a Swedish offer of eight thousand troops because of the expense.[20] Instead the British agreed to transport seventeen battalions of Russian infantry, two companies of artillery, a company of pioneers, and a hussar squadron, a total of 17,593 men, from Reval to England. From there, along with 13,000 British troops, the combined force would mount a seaborne invasion of Holland. In return for the use of the Russian battalions, Pitt's government agreed to pay the czar an initial sum of £88,000 plus £44,000 per month as long as the troops were on active service against the French. In addition, the Russians agreed to supply six ships of the line, five frigates, and two transport vessels in return for which England was to pay £48,927 plus £19,642 per month.[21] The czar also agreed to employ the 45,000 men originally assigned to cooperate with the Prussians against the French. Since both Russian and English generals would serve in the forthcoming operation, the British decided to place in supreme command one whose rank would be exalted enough to satisfy the Russians on questions of precedence. For this purpose, Pitt chose King George III's brother, the duke of York, to command the expedition.[22]

While England and Russia were settling these questions, the British were also seeking to find the men and money for the projected invasion. The Cabinet's first step was to disengage itself from the costly campaign against Toussaint L'Ouverture in the West Indies. By 1797, Toussaint's forces had killed thirty-five thousand and wounded about forty thousand English troops.[23] Throughout 1797, the British were unable to make any progress against Toussaint's well-disciplined and fanatical troops, and in February, 1798, Toussaint launched an offensive of his own and by the end of April had recaptured Port-au-Prince.[24]

With a casualty list approaching fifty thousand killed and fifty thousand wounded and with renewed fighting in Europe becoming more and more probable, the British decided to cut their losses and abandon the island. By so doing, they hoped to obtain veteran troops for action in Europe, use reserves, originally destined for the West Indies, to support these veterans, and use the money designated for the West Indian campaign to subsidize their continental allies. The government, therefore, directed Lieutenant-colonel Maitland to open negotiations with Toussaint, and on October 3, in return for a promise by Toussaint to remain neutral for the duration of the European war, the British evacuated all of Saint-Domingue.[25] Maitland next went to America, where he reached an agreement with the United States. The two powers agreed to cooperate to prevent the spread of subversive principles among the slaves of the southern United States and the British possessions in the Caribbean. Finally, Maitland signed a second convention with Toussaint on June 13, 1799, in which Toussaint agreed to refrain from attacking either the British West Indian colonies or the southern United States. In return, Toussaint obtained a commercial agreement with both nations.[26]

The French national agent in Saint-Domingue tried to counter British policy by backing Rigaud, a Mulatto general, who was willing to carry on the war against the British by creating slave rebellions in their colonies. The French hoped to keep British troops occupied in the West Indies, thereby preventing Pitt from sending them to the Continent. Toussaint, however, was not willing to become an instrument of French global strategy. His primary concern was for the security of his own island, and upon learning of Rigaud's negotiations with the French, he forced the Directory's agent to leave the country. In a final attempt to keep the war in the Indies alive, the agent before his departure freed

Rigaud from his oath of loyalty to Toussaint.[27] Rigaud wanted to obtain the Directory's support in his efforts to displace Toussaint as the *de facto* ruler of Saint-Domingue, and therefore followed French policy by directing one of his officers to organize a slave revolt in Jamaica. The British uncovered and destroyed it before it could do any damage, but Rigaud's actions convinced Toussaint that he had to crush his rival before the latter ruined the peace settlement.[28] Consequently in June, 1799, Toussaint once again plunged his island into war, and with the support of the American navy eventually emerged triumphant.[29] Thus British policy in the Caribbean had been successful, because by retreating from Saint-Domingue and making peace with Toussaint, the British had gained security for their West Indian colonies and also freed men and money for use in continental campaigns.

On July 12 Parliament took another step designed to increase the number of men available for action in Europe. The government reduced the size of the militia and permitted militiamen to join regular line regiments in return for a bounty amounting at times to as much as ten pounds. In this way, the government brought regiments that had been seriously reduced in strength owing to losses sustained in the West Indian campaign back to their normal strength of seven hundred men per battalion. In addition, the British brought some seventy-three hundred regulars back from Ireland, thereby raising the strength of the regular army in England to fifty-two thousand men.[30] As the troops destined for the invasion concentrated around the embarkation ports of Margate, Ramsgate, and Deal to await their final orders, their fighting condition was quite good. The admixture of militiamen had its drawbacks, because the new men were for the most part inexperienced and undisciplined, but their morale was high, and the Cabinet could reasonably expect that the regulars would be able to turn the raw militia into competent soldiers.[31]

The invasion force was to sail in two echelons. Sir Ralph Abercromby, a veteran officer who had served in Europe, the Indies, and Ireland, was to command the first group, consisting of two guard and two line brigades, a total of ten thousand men. The duke of York was to follow with the second echelon, consisting of the remainder of the British force and the Russian battalions.[32]

To assist the invasion, the English were also at work to obtain support from the Orange party within the Batavian Republic. In fact, the British relied heavily on a pro-Orange uprising, and Dundas informed Grenville that, "unless the Dutch cooperate with us cordially and *actively*, I do not believe it possible to do as much by force of arms as we flatter ourselves."[33] Members of the Orange party in England were optimistic about the possibility of an insurrection, and the prince of Orange even went so far as to present a plan of internal rebellion that required no foreign aid. The prince's son, who was in Germany, constantly sent secret agents into Holland to contact sympathizers, and in Berlin, Thomas Grenville opened secret correspondence with an officer of the Batavian navy who promised that the fleet would desert and join the allies.[34] There were also rumors that high-ranking officials in the Batavian army were ready to desert, and for a while members of the deposed Federalist party plus certain members of the Batavian Directory were in contact with the prince of Orange. The French semiofficial journal the *Moniteur* accused these two groups of corresponding with London for the purpose of arranging a restoration, but the refusal of the prince to promise any reforms of the old government coupled with sharp warnings from the French put a stop to these negotiations. The British, however, remained quite hopeful of a favorable reception by the Dutch people when they landed.[35]

While the British were evolving their plans for the invasion of Holland, the Cabinet was also formulating an overall military strategy for the destruction of the French Republic. The strategy developed was more straightforward than the French plan but harder to execute successfully. The crucial part of the operation was to turn the Rhine River barrier. To do this, the Anglo-Russian force, after invading Holland and restoring the stadtholder, would push south into Belgium and go on from there toward the pre-1792 French frontier. Meanwhile, the Austrians and Russians would drive the French out of Italy and secure the line of the Alps. Finally, a third offensive operation in Switzerland would turn the Rhine barrier from the south, and in the following spring, the Austrians and Russians in Switzerland would move toward Lyons, where they would proclaim the restoration of the Bourbon monarchy, while on the northern front the British and Russians would plunge deep into northern France. At the same time, the British fleet would harass the French coasts to assist royalist outbreaks in the Vendée, Brittany, and Normandy where the royalists were organized and awaiting the signal to rise.[36] The allies and royalists would then advance on Paris, overthrow the Republic, and dictate their peace.

The Austrians accepted the English strategic war plan, at least for the present, and placed the bulk of their forces consisting of 64,200 infantry and 12,000 cavalry behind the Adige River in Italy. An additional 18,000 men served in the garrisons of Verona, Venice, and Legnano, and Vienna placed General Kray in command of the Austrian army in Italy.[37] The Russians had temporarily halted the march of their corps because of a dispute with the Austrians over the scale of rations that Austrian commissaries would give to the Russian troops, but on October 17 the Austrians agreed to furnish the corps with the Russian rather than the Austrian scale of rations, and by October 25 the 24,000 Russians had entered Austrian Galicia.[38] The Russians would be ready to enter combat by April, and Vienna agreed that Marshal Suvorov would lead the combined Austro-Russian forces. General Rosenberg would command the Russian corps, and General Melas would replace Kray in command of the Austrian troops in Italy. General Belegarde with 45,000 Austrians held the Tyrol; and 25,000 Austrians under Hotze occupied the Grisons. In Germany, the Archduke Charles commanded an army of 80,000 men, and his major task was to prevent a French drive into southern Germany. He was also to drive any French troops on the right bank of the Rhine back across that river, a move that would expose the left flank of French troops operating in Switzerland.[39] Basically, Charles was to give support to the main area of operations in Italy.

The Austrians agreed to conduct their major campaign in Italy for political as well as military reasons. For years, Thugut had wanted to extend Austrian control in Italy and was in fact less concerned with destroying the Republic than with wresting Tuscany, Milan, the Papal legations, and Piedmont from it. Earlier he had tried to accomplish this end by diplomatic means, and only when France had refused concessions did he begin to seek a military alternative. In fact, the British ambassador at Vienna felt that Thugut would still sign a peace treaty with France if the Directory would comply with his desires for new Italian provinces.[40] Thus Thugut agreed with the British concept of strategy more in the hope of gaining allies to aid him in his Italian ventures than because of any desire to restore the Bourbon monarchy. With Russian help, he planned to conquer Italy, but since the forces in the peninsula would be mainly Austrian, he felt that it would be fairly easy to retain political control of the area after the war. Thugut was also confident that England would support many if not all of Austria's demands for concessions in Italy in return for the sacrifice of Hapsburg claims to Belgium, but such a policy would come into direct conflict with the plans of Czar Paul I.

The czar agreed wholeheartedly with the English military plans. He had three reasons for his support of Pitt's policy, the first being that he hated republican ideology and was for the moment the self-proclaimed champion of legitimacy. The second reason lay in Russia's strategic interests. In fighting the French, the czar had already gained many advantages in the eastern Mediterranean. His troops were in the Ionian Islands, and the Ottoman Empire was in effect under his tutelage. The elimination of France as a competing force in the area could not help but strengthen his position. Finally, the czar did not want Austria to gain new accretions of territory that would strengthen the Hapsburg domains and enable Vienna to counter Russian influence in the Balkans. If the allies restored the old governments in Italy, Switzerland, and France, Austria would not gain new strength. A restored French monarchy would side with England and Russia in demanding the restoration of the legitimate governments in Italy and Switzerland, because a royalist France would naturally support the principles of legitimacy, and Louis XVIII, like Czar Paul, would also be opposed to any extension of Austrian power. Furthermore, the restored governments would be weak and divided, and Russia would be left as the most powerful state in the Mediterranean and the Balkans.[41]

Nevertheless, despite this latent conflict of war aims, at the start of 1799 the Coalition was a fairly powerful one. Its armies outnumbered those of the French, and for the moment the allies were agreed on a strategic plan. As Sorel noted, "this coalition, the second in the historical series was better woven and infinitely more redoubtable than the one of 1792–1793."[42]

As the Russian columns continued to move through Austrian territory toward their battle positions, the Directory realized that it would soon have to take action. By January 2 the directors had already protested to the Imperial Delegation at Rastadt against the march of the Russian corps, but the emperor told the French delegates that the movements of the Russian troops were no concern of the Congress. On January 31 the French deputation informed the Congress that they would undertake no further negotiations until they received a satisfactory reply to their protest of January 2. On the same day, the French informed Francis II that unless they received assurances within fifteen days that the advance of the Russians had ceased, they would have no choice but to regard the Russians' movements as acts of hostility.[43]

Realizing that its demands would probably fail to influence Austrian policy, the Directory continued to prepare for war. It granted money for the construction of a telegraph line from Paris to Italy and took the important imperial fortress of Ehrenbreitstein on the Rhine, and Kosciusko prepared a report on the nature of the Russian army for the French field officers.[44] The Directory's ultimatum had meanwhile expired without a reply. Paris was still reluctant to open hostilities, but since the Russians and Austrians had failed to stop their war preparations, the Directory felt compelled to take preliminary measures to insure that when the campaigns opened they would do so on favorable terms.

On February 20 the Directory stated in a public announcement that the emperor had refused to answer questions concerning the march of the Russian corps and that Austrian troops had crossed the 1797 armistice line in Germany. The declaration then went on to state that, as a result of these warlike acts, the French would have to take measures for their own security, but if the Russians returned home, and if the Austrians withdrew to their old positions, the powers could still avoid war.[45] On March 2 the government directed the army of Mainz to cross the Rhine and to

advance to the Black Mountains. Jourdan, who had been plead-
ing with the government since the end of January to make such
a move, led his army across the river on the morning on March
2.[46] On the same day, the Directory ordered Masséna to move
into the Grisons and to send troops to Schaffhausen to protect
Jourdan's right flank. On March 3, Paris told Schérer to keep
in close touch with Masséna and Jourdan, coordinate his movements with theirs, and prepare to occupy Tuscany.[47]

To this show of force the Austrians made no reply except to
speed up their preparations, and the Directory came to feel that
it had no choice but to declare war. On March 12 the directors
asked the Legislative Corps for a declaration of war on Austria
and Tuscany. The councils complied, and on March 13, 1799,
the campaign to decide the fate of the Republic began.

NOTES

1. Archives nationales, AF III, carton 59 (hereafter, AN).

2. Ibid.

3. Ministère de la Guerre, État-Major de l'Armée, Archives historiques,
Correspondance, Armées de Mainz et d'Helvétie, janvier 1799, carton
B269 (hereafter, Min. de la Guerre, AH).

4. George Duruy, ed., *Mémoires de Barras*, 3: 87.

5. Min. de la Guerre, AH, Milet de Mureau, Louis Marie Antoine, carton
BonYid322; and AN, AF III, carton 152A.

6. Abbé Joseph Lacouture, *Le mouvement royaliste dans le sud-ouest
(1797–1800)*, pp. 110–11.

7. Min. de la Guerre, AH, carton B269.

8. Ibid.

9. Ibid.

10. Min. de la Guerre, AH, Correspondance, Armées de Mainz et d'Helvétie, février 1799, carton B270; Min. de la Guerre, AH, Situations, Armées
de Mainz et d'Helvétie, 1798, carton B2339; and Min. de la Guerre, AH,
Situations, Armées d'Italie et de Naples, 1792–1801, carton B3381.

11. AN, AF III, carton 59; Min. de la Guerre, AH, carton B3381; and
Min. de la Guerre, AH, Ordres de bataille des armées en campagne, 1792–
1815, carton XP3.

12. AN, AF III, carton 13; and AN, AF III, carton 14.

13. See William Cobbett, ed., *The Parliamentary History of England from the Earliest Period to the Year 1803*, 34: 1168; and Reginald Coupland, ed., *The War Speeches of William Pitt the Younger*, pp. 244–45. See also *The Speeches of the Right Honourable William Pitt in the House of Commons* (London: 1806) , 3: 415, 418–24.

14. Historical Manuscripts Commission, *Report on the Manuscripts of J. B. Fortescue, Esq., Preserved at Dropmore*, 5: 423.

15. Ibid.

16. H. T. Colenbrander, ed., *Gedenkstukken des Algemeene Geschiedenis van Nederland van 1795 tot 1840*, 2: 979; *Manuscripts of Fortescue*, 5: 109.

17. Henri Weil, ed., *Le général Stamford d'après sa correspondance inédite (1793–1806)*, p. 217.

18. Ibid., p. 141.

19. Paul Bailleu, ed., *Preussen und Frankreich von 1795 bis 1807 Diplomatische Correspondenzen*, 1: 239, 270–72, 285–87, 302–3.

20. *Manuscripts of Fortescue*, 5: 109.

21. *The Annual Register or a View of the History, Politics and Literature for the Year 1799*, pp. 213–15.

22. John W. Fortescue, *A History of the British Army*, 4, pt. 2: 665.

23. Ibid., pt. 1, p. 496. Most of those wounded had to be discharged from the army as unfit for service.

24. Charles Moran, *Black Triumvirate*, p. 60.

25. Fortescue, *History of the British Army*, 4, pt. 2: 560, 563.

26. Moran, *Black Triumvirate*, pp. 66–67.

27. Jacques Léger, *Haiti, Her History and Her Detractors*, pp. 94–95.

28. R. C. Dallas, *The History of the Maroons*, pp. 308–12.

29. Moran, *Black Triumvirate*, pp. 68–69. Adams wished to aid Toussaint for two reasons. First, he wished to support Toussaint, who had promised not to spread subversive propaganda among slaves in the United States, and second, he wished to strike a blow at France, with whom America had been engaged in an undeclared naval war since 1797. Since Toussaint was following his own rather than the Directory's policy, Adams decided to help him against the Directory-supported Rigaud.

30. Fortescue, *History of the British Army*, 4, pt. 2: 939; John Surtees, *Twenty-five Years in the Rifle Brigade*, p. 3. In the British army, the regiment was a depot unit, not a combat formation. A regiment could consist of any number of battalions. Battalions of various regiments were placed together in brigades for combat. The brigade corresponded to the French demibrigade or the Russian regiment in strength.

31. Sir John Moore, *Diary*, p. 339; and Surtees, *Rifle Brigade*, p. 5.

32. James Dunfermline, ed., *Lieutenant-General Ralph Abercromby* (Edinburgh: 1861) , p. 179; and Fortescue, *History of the British Army*, 4, 2: 654.

33. *Manuscripts of Fortescue,* 5: 215.

34. Colenbrander, *Gedenkstukken,* p. 930; and *Manuscripts of Fortescue,* 5: 16, 92.

35. Colenbrander, *Gedenkstukken,* 2: 1976.

36. William Wickham, ed., *The Correspondence of the Right Honorable William Wickham for the Year 1794,* 2: 97.

37. Min. de la Guerre, AH, Campagne de l'armée autrichienne-russe en Italie en 1799, MH, no. 438.

38. A. R. von Vivenot, ed., *Vertrauliche Briefe des Freiherrin von Thugut,* 2: 128; and Peter I. Bartenev, ed., *Papers of Mikhail Larionovich Vorontsov and Other Members of the Family,* 18: 173–74.

39. Min. de la Guerre, AH, Correspondance, Armée de Mainz devenue Armé du Danube et d'Helvetie, mars 1799, carton B²71.

40. Countess Minto, ed., *Life and Letters of Sir Gilbert Elliot First Earl of Minto from 1751 to 1806* (London, 1874), 3: 93–94.

41. Bartenev, *Papers of Vorontsov,* 8: 237–39.

42. Albert Sorel, *L'Europe et la Révolution française,* 5: 401.

43. *Annual Register,* pp. 262–64.

44. AN, AF III, carton 17.

45. Min. de la Guerre, AH, carton 13²70.

46. Ibid.; AN, AF III, carton 23; and Min. de la Guerre, AH, Correspondance de Général Jourdan avec le Directoire et le Ministère de la Guerre (5 nivose à 27 ventose an VIII–29 décembre–17 mars 1799) carton B2* 262.

47. Min. de la Guerre, AH, Correspondance, Armées d'Italie et de Naples, mars 1799, carton B³59.

11

The Republic in Danger

Throughout the first week of March, the five divisions of Jourdan's army advanced steadily through Swabia, and by March 8 they reached the western foothills of the Black Mountains.[1] There they learned of the declaration of war and received instructions to attack immediately. The minister of war told Jourdan that, although outnumbered, the audacity and experience of his troops was sufficient to bring victory.[2] Despite his great numerical inferiority, Jourdan on March 13 and 14 issued his orders directing the army of the Danube to begin its advance through the mountains. His only faint hope for victory was to strike at the Austrians before they could complete their concentration.[3]

The Austrians, however, had also been advancing. Moving westward from the Leck River with seventy-eight thousand men, large advance units had occupied Ulm on March 12. On March 21, Austrian troops pushed three demibrigades of the French avant garde out of the small town of Ostrach. Jourdan then sent a fourth demibrigade to reinforce the avant garde, but these additional troops were unable to stem the retreat. The Austrians continued to advance and even cut off and surrounded a brigade. To extract this unit, Jourdan ordered another division to the rescue. The French pushed forward, cut their way through to the surrounded force, and freed it. The unit then covered the retreat of the rest of the avant garde, but this withdrawal in turn exposed the flank of troops located near Ostrach. To avoid encirclement they joined the general retreat.[4]

Although they had inflicted over twenty-nine hundred casualties on the Austrians, the French had lost twenty-five hundred men of their own and had discovered that the archduke's army, far from being scattered, was ready to advance. Jourdan had thus failed to carry out his plan of defeating the Austrians in detail, and any hope of victory on the German front was doomed. The Danube army, therefore, had no choice but to pull back, and on March 22 the French army began to evacuate the Black Mountains. Two days later, after several vicious rearguard actions, the French stabilized their line, basing it on positions west of Pfullendorff and Stockach on the right and on Emmingen on the left.[5]

Undaunted by his first setback, still hoping for victory, and fearful of exposing the left flank of Masséna's army, Jourdan decided to attack again despite the Austrian numerical advantage of more than two to one. He issued orders on the night of March 24 for the division on the left to advance east from Emmingen toward Moeskirch. To the right, the avant garde and the reserve division were to move forward. After breaking the archduke's line Jourdan planned to detach a column southward in order to cut the avenue of retreat of Austrian units centered on Aach. He also directed the division in his center to move eastward on the main road to Stockach, the archduke's principal position.

On the French right a division was to support the central advance.[6] The attack was to begin on March 25.

The next morning troops on the left pushed forward with Jourdan personally directing the most advanced units. At first the attack went according to plan. Two demibrigades plus three cavalry regiments, a total of 3,400 men, forced 11,800 Austrians to retreat. Five battalions then cut south through the Grey Forest, but at this point the Austrians first dislocated and then shattered Jourdan's offensive. Under the impact of the first French attacks, the commander of the Austrian right wing had fallen back and appealed to the archduke for help. Charles quickly rushed twelve battalions to the threatened part of his line and went there himself to reform his shattered troops. The French defeated the first three battalions of reinforcements, but six Hungarian battalions and twelve cavalry squadrons turned the tide.

After pushing covering troops aside, they advanced through the forest, threatening to cut the French forces in two.[7] Jourdan ordered his cavalry to counterattack, but the Austrians broke the attack and forced the horsemen to scatter. To avoid being surrounded, the French had no choice but to retreat. At 4:00 P.M. the French left began to pull back, forcing the center to follow suit.[8]

Further south the French had no better success. One division managed to take Aach, but sixteen Austrian battalions stopped it on the outskirts of Stockach. The Austrians also halted Jourdan's right after bitter fighting. The battle was vicious, with the French suffering thirty-six hundred casualties and the Austrians fifty-nine hundred, but the French had again failed to win, and faced by overwhelming numbers, they had to pull back to the Rhine.[9]

The defeat at Stockach also had the result of dislocating Masséna's offensive in Switzerland, because with Jourdan's army in full flight, the army of Helvetia had to face not only Austrian attacks from the Grisons but also thrusts from Swabia against its left and rear.[10]

Masséna opened his campaign with great success. On March 7 he took Chur, the capital of the Grisons, along with three thousand prisoners, and by March 13 a division operating on the Upper Rhine had taken Engadine. Masséna next began his drive into the Tyrol, and on March 26 the French captured Martinsbruck, the key to the province.[11]

Jourdan's defeat, however, radically altered the Helvetian army's situation. After Jourdan's initial check on March 21, Masséna had informed the Directory that he would have to pull back his forward elements to avoid encirclement. After the Battle of Stockach, Masséna felt it necessary to withdraw even further in order to protect Constance and hold it against an attack by the archduke's victorious army. To add to his many problems, the directors reorganized the command structure of the French center and left wings, a move that extended Masséna's authority but did not increase the total number of troops available to him. On March 28 Jourdan asked the government to allow him to come to Paris to explain the reasons for his defeat. The Directory granted his request on April 9. Paris then relieved him from command, and appointed Masséna as commander of the armies of the Danube and Helvetia. On April 21 the government merged the two armies into one force and eight days later gave it the title of army of the Danube.[12] Masséna then had under his command a total of 79,436 men organized into nine infantry and two cavalry divisions. Covering a line extending from Kehl on the Rhine to the Grisons, this force faced a total of 115,000 Austrians: 30,000 in the Tyrol, 28,000 in Voralberg, 40,000 around Constance, and the rest in South Germany.[13]

Masséna's first task was to restore order on the left of his line. To do this, he decided to stand on the defensive, and informed the directors on April 10 that he could not for the moment undertake further offensive operations. Next he strengthened the fortresses on the French side of the Rhine, placed Alsace in a state of readiness to resist invasion, and instituted a policy of carrying out numerous raids across the Rhine to pin down as many Austrians as possible. He also garrisoned the Rhine town of Schaffhausen on the Swiss-German frontier to prevent the archduke from sending reinforcements to Switzerland or Italy.[14]

The Austrians for their part continued to maintain pressure along Masséna's whole front. On April 20 Masséna ordered his troops in central Switzerland to prepare to fall back behind the Thur River and from there to positions covering Zurich. Two days later the Austrians forced the French troops guarding the Valtelline, a major line of communication between Switzerland and Italy, to abandon their positions, and Masséna countered by burning the Rhine bridge at Schaffhausen. This move, however, did not materially improve the French position, and on April 30 Masséna told the Directory that despite his efforts his army was still disorganized and unable to carry out offensive operations. In addition to these problems, the general also told Paris that the army lacked supplies, and that the promised aid from the Republic of Helvetia in the form of six demibrigades had not yet arrived.[15]

The situation did not improve in May, because the Austrians continued to keep up their pressure on the Danube army, and on May 5 Masséna painted a gloomy picture of his situation for the directors. In the Grisons, some ten thousand peasants, led by priests and encouraged by the Austrians, seriously hampered communications and supply lines. Although the Rhine Valley from Steig to Chur was still in French hands, Masséna said that the Austrian numerical superiority plus the exposed position of his army's flanks would probably force him to continue his retreat.[16] On May 6 the Directory aggravated this situation even further by ordering Masséna to send fifteen thousand men to the hard-pressed army of Italy, with the result that two days later Masséna felt it necessary to ask the Directory to allow him to evacuate all of the Grisons and set up a shorter and stronger line. On May 13 the Directory, feeling that the situation in Italy was serious enough to warrant sacrifices in Switzerland, gave him permission to withdraw from the Grisons, the Valtelline, and the Italian-Swiss cantons.[17]

By May 20 Masséna had completed his retreat, and his army was in position in front of Zurich. The Austrians lost little time in attacking, but on May 26 the French beat back their probing attacks against posts along the Thur River to the city's east. The next day the French held off renewed attacks while Masséna prepared other positions behind the Glatz River nearer Zurich. Before the Austrians could attack again, he withdrew his army to these positions. Meanwhile, in the Valais, the French defeated six thousand rebels on May 29 and again on May 31, and re-pulsed renewed Austrian assaults around Schwyz and Wassen, while on the Rhine the situation also improved slightly as the French broke up an Austrian attack across the river near Coblenz on May 23–24, inflicting five hundred casualties on the assault troops.[18] For the moment, Masséna had managed to stabilize his front, but the archduke was already bringing in reinforcements from Germany and was determined to force the French lines covering Zurich.

On June 3 he struck at the French positions around the city. After a day of bitter fighting, the Austrians finally abandoned the battlefield, but on June 4 they renewed their advance. The key to the battle was the Zurichberg, a height that dominated the roads around Zurich as well as the bridges over the Limmat River, which flowed through the city. Exceptionally heavy fighting raged around this mountain as the Austrians tried again and again to capture and hold the summit only to be driven back each time by reckless French bayonet attacks. Having failed to break the

French lines or to secure a foothold on the Zurichberg, and having lost over three thousand men, the archduke called off the battle at dusk. The French, however, were also worn out, for their method of constant local attacks did nothing to hold down casualties or lessen troop fatigue. Fearing that the Austrians would renew their assault next morning, Masséna decided to abandon Zurich and retreat to a stronger position. The new line to the west of the city ran from Basel along the left bank of the Rhine to the chain of the Albis Mountains, which overlooked the Limmat, and from there to Lake Zug.[19]

Thus Masséna had for the moment definitely halted the Austrian drive and stabilized his front, but in order to do so he had relinquished much valuable territory. His position, however, soon improved as one of his divisions began to counterattack toward the St. Gothard pass. In addition, the minister of war had told Masséna on June 3 that he was sending him twelve infantry battalions and ten cavalry squadrons, and the first of these troops began to arrive a week later. To ease his command problems, the Directory created a new army, the army of the Rhine, on June 13 and gave it the responsibility of holding the Rhine barrier from Düsseldorf to the Swiss frontier, thereby enabling Masséna to concentrate all of his energies on the Swiss campaign. Thus despite the continuing lack of supplies, Masséna's position had improved to such a degree that by the middle of June he was able to launch a local counteroffensive at Alstetten.[20]

Throughout July, the lines around Zurich remained quiet, although in the Canton of Schwyz, east of Lucerne, a 10,000-man division continued to battle the Austrians. The army continued to suffer from a lack of supplies, and the situation eventually grew so serious that Masséna finally fired the army contractors who were supposed to do the army's foraging. Nevertheless, the only really disturbing military factor was the approach of a Russian corps of 27,300 men under the command of General Rimski Korsakov. The allies decided that this unit would serve in Switzerland, and by August 2 the first elements arrived at Zurich.[21]

To strengthen his position in case the new allied dispositions led to further attacks and to gain good terrain from which to launch a counteroffensive, Masséna decided to retake the St.

Gothard pass. He ordered a division to carry out this task, and to retake the town of Schwyz. He also ordered a second division to the north to drive east in the direction of Lake Zurich, and to cover these two attacks, Masséna ordered two other divisions to make probing thrusts around Zurich.[22]

On August 14 the French pushed the Austrians out of Grimsel, one of the key towns guarding the St. Gothard pass. The second division also pushed forward, but it encountered unexpectedly heavy resistance from eight Austrian battalions commanded by General Hotze and had to retreat. This setback, however, failed to stop the main offensive, and by August 18 the French had retaken the whole of the St. Gothard pass while other units moved on Glaris.[23] To counter the French attacks, the archduke decided to attack their positions along the Aar River. The Austrian engineers, however, failed to examine the ground carefully, and when they tried to throw a bridge across the Aar on the night of August 16, they discovered that their bridging material was insufficient. Masséna rushed two companies of Zurich riflemen to the scene, and the snipers rapidly picked off the Austrian sappers who were still trying to complete the bridge on the morning of August 17. At midmorning French light artillery batteries arrived and opened fire, making the Austrians' task completely hopeless, and soon after, Masséna agreed to a cease-fire to allow the Austrians to withdraw their pontoons.[24]

The next day the archduke's army began to pull out of its lines and march to Germany. He left two Austrian corps, those of Hotze and Jellachich, totaling about forty thousand men, to support Korsakov, who had just arrived with the new Russian corps. This movement offered Masséna a chance to catch the Allies off guard as they were switching positions, and the war minister also favored an attack to help the hard-pressed army of Italy. Masséna, therefore, threw a division across the Limmat on August 29, but this attack failed because of harassing fire by an allied flotilla that dominated Lake Zurich. A second effort the next day also failed, but to the south, French troops finally captured Glaris, thereby compensating for the defeat on the Limmat.[25]

Thus by the end of August, Masséna had vastly improved his position. Reinforcements had begun to reach his army in May, and by July 1 over 18,000 men had arrived in Switzerland. By the end of August the army of the Danube comprised 88,667 men.[26] Although the Allies had forced him to sacrifice some valuable territory, Masséna had regained some very important parts of it, and his positions were well sited and strong. The army of the Danube, though still on the defensive, had recovered from its earlier defeats and would soon be able to attack. It would, however, be the only French army able to do so, for on other fronts the situation was little short of disastrous.

Like the other French armies, Schérer's forces were preparing for action in the first days of March, and on March 3 the Directory told him that Jourdan and Masséna were already on the move and that he should prepare to act in close cooperation with them. Paris also directed him to occupy Tuscany as soon as he received word of the official declaration of war.[27] On March 6, Schérer assigned troops to act in the Valtelline to protect Masséna's right flank, while in Naples, Macdonald continued his campaign against the royalist irregulars led by Cardinal Ruffo. He was, however, unable to stop Ruffo from gaining control of Calabria and Bari. Menwhile, Schérer received news of the outbreak of war. Four days later he told Paris that he would advance as soon as possible, but it was not until March 24 that he issued his plans for crossing the Adige River and attacking Verona.[28]

One of the reasons for this delay was the fear of a popular uprising. The policy of creating sister republics had already turned the Italian aristocrats against the French, and French hostility, or at least indifference, to the Catholic Church, combined with the policy of forcing the satellites to disgorge huge amounts of money for the benefit of the Republic, had alienated the priests, peasants, and portions of the middle class. Finally, the creation of numerous weak republics dependent on France turned those Italians who favored a unitary republic against the Directory. On January 17 the French civil commissioner in Piedmont reported that the unitary party there was willing to fight the French to create a united Italian republic, and less than a month later he and a colleague told Paris that the "anarchists" were in league with Austria to destroy French influence in Italy. On the same day, the commander of the French garrison at Turin reported that the "anarchists" had a well-organized system of secret committees engaged in preparing a revolt.[29] On January 25 Macdonald reported that royalist rebels were again active in the Roman Republic. Schérer was, therefore, reluctant to advance without first dealing with hostile elements who could hamper his lines of communication. The Directory, however, felt that he would have to accept the risk of rebellions in his rear, for it was far more vital that he move immediately to relieve the pressure on Jourdan's army of the Danube, which the Austrians had just defeated at Stockach.[30]

For his attack on the Adige River line, Schérer had at his disposal 55,000 men and planned to attack the Austrians on a line stretching from Lake Gardia in the north to Legnano in the south, thereby reproducing on a tactical level the Directory's strategic error of failing to concentrate superior forces at decisive points. On the French left, two divisions under Schérer's personal command were to attack the Austrian right wing around Pastrengo. A division flanking this attack on the left was to take Rivoli. In the center, Moreau, commanding two divisions, was to cross the Adige and take Verona, while another division on the French right was to capture Legnano. The Austrians also wanted to attack, but Vienna decided that until Suvorov arrived, Kray would remain on the defensive. He therefore placed 27,500 men around Verona and 29,000 around Legnano to meet any French attack. He then sent smaller detachments to Arcola and Pastrengo, while holding the rest of his force, 19,500 men, in reserve behind the Adige.[31]

On the morning of March 26 the French seized Rivoli while two divisions advanced on Pastrengo. The French took the town and the bridges across the Adige, but were unable to secure a foothold on the Austrian side of the river. In the center, Kray drove the republicans back from the outskirts of Verona and repulsed another division near Legnano. During the day, the Austrians lost seventy-one hundred men, but the French lost eight thousand, and their situation became critical.[32] The next day, Kray increased the garrison of Verona to thirty-five thousand men, while Schérer did little more than push a few battalions toward Pastrengo. On the same day, the French occupied Tuscany, meeting no resistance, but this success could not offset the fact that the Austrians had halted their offensive on the first day of hostilities. On March 28, Schérer tried to build a bridge across the Adige between Verona and Legnano, but after his engineers had completed the bridge, the Austrians launched a sudden counterattack, throwing the French back across the river.[33]

Although outnumbered, Schérer, like Jourdan, could devise no other course of action but renewed attacks, but Kray was also planning to cross the river and seize Mantua. His advance units crossed to the French side of the Adige on April 1 and drove the French out of Rivoli, taking eleven hundred prisoners in the process.[34] After this defeat, Schérer finally gave up his project of crossing the Adige, went over to the defense, and concentrated his troops so as to be able to strike at any Austrian units advancing from Verona.

On April 5 Schérer launched an attack designed to contain the Austrians around Verona. One division advanced and took Villafranca as the other four divisions also moved forward. The French forced the Austrians to fall back, but Kray's massed artillery batteries soon halted them. Kray then sent forward six infantry battalions and six cavalry squadrons that struck the disorganized French divisions and drove them back. In the center the French managed to push to the outskirts of Verona, but the collapse of Schérer's right forced the rest of the line to retreat hurriedly. Schérer lost 7,500 men, killed or wounded, and 3,231 prisoners as compared to the Austrian losses of 3,800 killed or wounded and 1,900 prisoners.[35]

As a result of this battle, Schérer felt it necessary to abandon the Adige front and retreat, and on April 6 he withdrew the army of Italy behind the Mincio River, leaving garrisons in Mantua and Peschiera to hold up the Austrian pursuit. He also informed the Directory that his losses were so serious that it had become necessary to call the army of Naples north to his assistance, although this meant the sacrifice of all of southern Italy, including Rome. The next day he offered his resignation, suggested that Moreau replace him, and on April 8 told Macdonald to be ready to evacuate Naples and move north.[36] Meanwhile the army of Italy continued to fall back until, by April 14, it had reached the left bank of the Adda River. On the same day, Suvorov arrived to take overall command of the Coalition's army in Italy. Melas now led the Austrian army, and the Russian corps of twenty-four thousand men had by April 18 concentrated at Verona and was ready to attack.[37]

In Aleksandr Suvorov, the sixty-nine-year-old Russian marshal, the French were to meet the most brilliant opponent they had ever faced, and it was not until Wellington landed in Portugal ten years later that the enemies of France were able to find as great a soldier to lead their armies. Personally Suvorov was quite eccentric. The British ambassador at Vienna described him as, "a little old shrivelled creature in a pair of red breeches and his shirt for all clothing. . . . He pretends or thinks at times that he had seen visions. . . . He is the most perfect Bedlamite that ever was allowed to be at large."[38] He was known to send dispatches in rhyme and was devout to the point of fanaticism. When he arrived in Vienna, he insisted that all the mirrors be removed from the palace in which he was quartered, and he refused to sleep in a bed, sleeping instead on straw, because Christ was born in a manger.[39] Yet despite these elements of Slavic whimsy, he was an experienced soldier, and during his long career he had developed a tactical system closely resembling that of the French.

His years of fighting nomadic tribes, Poles, whose forces had large elements of cavalry, and Turks, who were highly susceptible to hard-hitting attacks, had convinced Suvorov that speed and energy in all operations, use of the immediate attack without complicated maneuvers, and the bayonet charge were the true elements of victory. Suvorov insisted that the goal of any attack should be the swift and sudden annihilation of the enemy.[40] These tactics combined with his natural military genius were to make Suvorov a dangerous foe.

True to his doctrine, Suvorov planned to attack at once despite the fact that Vienna wanted him to confine his activities to the defense of the Adda until he captured Mantua. Suvorov, however, intended to clear the French out of the Lombard Plain and isolate the army of Naples before it could move north. He enjoyed a considerable numerical superiority over the French, because the Austrian field army had grown to eighty-six thousand men, while the Russians had twenty-four thousand with another ten thousand reinforcements on the way. The French forces, on the other hand, were reduced to about thirty thousand active troops. Disobeying his orders from Vienna, Suvorov began his offensive on April 19 by driving on Brescia with eleven thousand Russians and twenty-nine thousand Austrians, while leaving Kray with twenty-three thousand men to besiege Mantua and Peschiera.[41]

Suvorov's drive went forward rapidly. On April 21 Brescia, with a garrison of 11,200 men, surrendered to the Russians without firing a shot, and the next day the Austrians entered Cremona. As a result of these rapid allied attacks, Schérer on April 24 fell back across the Adda hoping to hold the right bank until reinforcements arrived from the south, but Suvorov was determined to give the French no respite and prepared to continue his offensive with the capture of Milan as his immediate objective.

On the night of April 26 the Allies threw a series of bridges across the Adda, and the next morning they began to attack Lecco and Trezzo. Counterattacks were of no avail, because Suvorov sent up fifteen thousand reserves, who forced the French to break off their attack. Suvorov next forced the army of Italy to abandon Cassano, and at the same time other allied troops entered Lodi. Moreau, who had been instructed to replace Schérer on April 21, did not get these orders until he was in the midst of the battle. He proceeded to take command and tried to rally his forces for a stand in front of Milan but he was so heavily outnumbered that he felt it necessary to continue the hasty retreat. The Allies had meanwhile surrounded a division at Lecco, and Moreau's first task was to rescue this unit. He ordered two divisions to counterattack, but they were able to release only part of the encircled unit, and three thousand prisoners remained in Suvorov's hands. Finding it impossible to stem the allied advance, Moreau on April 28 abandoned Milan, leaving two thousand men to hold the citadel, and fell back behind the Po River into Piedmont, where he planned to concentrate his troops around Alexandria. Melas meanwhile entered Milan, disarmed the National Guards, and instituted an Austrian military government.[42]

In the first days of May, Suvorov continued his offensive without a pause, his objects being to capture Turin and to push the French back to the Alps. He also wished to prevent the army of Italy from linking up with Macdonald's army of Naples.

Starting on May 3 the Russians occupied Novarra and then moved on to Pavia while the Austrians crossed the Po River and advanced on Ferrara. The Allies were aided in their offensive by the peasants, who rose in their favor and began to ambush isolated French units, supply convoys, and couriers. On May 7 Peschiera's garrison of fifteen hundred men capitulated, and two days later the Austrians entered Tortona.[43]

On May 10 Moreau beat back an Austrian attempt to cross the Po, and on May 11 as the Austrians pushed into Novi, the French halted a larger Russian effort to cross the Po at Bassignana. On May 15 Moreau launched a small counteroffensive against the Austrians at Marengo, but Suvorov sent four Russian battalions forward, and they forced him to relinquish the town. This defeat forced Moreau to resume his retreat. He abandoned the line of the Po, and on May 18 he moved the bulk of his army to Turin, leaving a three thousand-man garrison in Alexandria. The allies crossed the Po the next day and advanced on Turin. The advance proceeded methodically, aided by the peasantry who continued to attack small French units and seriously hampered Moreau's communications.[44]

Meanwhile the Allies also besieged Milan, and on May 24 the French garrison capitulated. The attackers immediately marched to reinforce Kray, whose forces attacking Mantua then amounted to thirty-one battalions and sixteen squadrons. On the same day, the French garrison of Ferrara surrendered, and two days later an Austrian seaborne assault launched from Venice took Ravenna.[45] While the Allies were reducing these isolated French garrisons, Suvorov continued his advance on Piedmont. On May 27, Austrian troops assaulted Turin, which Moreau's rearguards held in order to cover the army of Italy's retreat to the Genoa River. The Austrians quickly seized the town and the arsenal, which contained three hundred cannon, and also cut off the rearguard troops in the citadel. As Moreau continued his retreat into Liguria, where he hoped to hold positions in front of Genoa until Macdonald came to his assistance, Suvorov was taking steps to face this new French threat. He united the bulk of his forces between Alexandria and Tortona so that he could prevent the French armies from linking up by striking at one of them before the other could move. Since Moreau's army had been severely weakened by the losses sustained in the previous months and comprised only 21,184 actives and 13,508 garrison troops, it was Macdonald's 36,686 men who posed the main threat to the security of the allied forces, which by June numbered over 100,000 men.[46]

After the initial defeats in April, Schérer had suggested that he bring Macdonald's army north, and on April 27 he wrote to Macdonald telling him that the appearance of the army of Naples in the north was absolutely vital. Meanwhile, Paris was examining Schérer's suggestion, and on April 18 Milet-Mureau recommended that Macdonald abandon southern Italy and move north, because if he could defeat Suvorov it would be easy to reoccupy the south. The Directory agreed, and on May 4 it took the decision to abandon southern Italy by ordering Moreau to instruct Macdonald to leave Naples, proceed to Liguria and join the army of Italy.[47] Expecting such orders, Macdonald had already recalled his mobile columns from the countryside around Naples and established garrisons at the fort of St. Elmo in Naples, and in Gaete and Capua. After receiving his orders, he set out from Naples on May 7, planning to join Moreau at Genoa.[48]

Abandoned by the French, the Republic of Naples collapsed. The republicans had managed to organize a twelve thousand-man army, but on June 13 Ruffo's troops, aided by five hundred Russians, who had landed at Brindisi in May, defeated them. The royalists then pushed rapidly toward Naples, slaughtering suspected republicans on the way, and by June 15 Ruffo held the city with the French and republicans retaining only the forts of St. Elmo and St. Angelo. Wishing to avoid further bloodshed, Cardinal Ruffo proceeded to negotiate with the French commander, and on June 22 the French, Ruffo, and the commander of the British fleet blockading the forts signed an armistice agreement. According to this convention, the Allies allowed French soldiers and any Neapolitan citizen who wished to join them to go to Toulon in return for the surrender of the forts.[49]

Nelson, however, undid Ruffo's moderate settlement. When he reached Naples on June 24, he strongly disapproved of the armistice terms and insisted upon the arrest of Neapolitan republicans. Ruffo refused to transmit these new conditions to the French and told Nelson that his army would not violate the armistice. On June 25 the king and queen learned of Ruffo's terms and re-

jected them. They gave Nelson full powers and told him to
proceed with the arrests of the Neapolitan rebels. On June 29
he suspended the armistice and sent English marines to arrest
republicans who had left the forts and had taken up residence
in the city while awaiting transportation to France. English
marines seized a Neapolitan officer who had organized the republican navy. They took him aboard Nelson's flagship and
executed him after a drumhead courtmartial by Neapolitan officers acting under Nelson's direction.[50] Ruffo continued to oppose
such vicious behavior, but the king backed Nelson and even gave
him authority to arrest Ruffo if the cardinal resisted royal policy.
Repression in Naples continued unabated until by the end of
August there were over eight thousand persons in prison awaiting
judgment by a special tribunal.[51]

As the Neapolitan republic crumbled, Macdonald was moving
north, and by May 19 the army of Naples was in Florence. Macdonald was, however, beginning to have doubts about joining
Moreau at Genoa. To reach Genoa, he would have to march
through Liguria, thereby exposing his right flank to attacks from
Suvorov's army, and even if he did reach Genoa safely, the Coalition would still have possession of the Cisalpine Republic and
most of Piedmont. As early as May 15 Macdonald told his chief
of staff that he was thinking of taking another route. Moreau
was thinking along similar lines, and on May 16 he suggested
that Macdonald, rather than marching northwest to Liguria, move
northeast toward Modena. On May 19 Macdonald wrote to
Moreau, saying that marching to Genoa posed too many problems
and that he preferred to move by way of Modena and Parma while
Moreau advanced to meet him at Parma.[52] On May 27 Macdonald issued orders to his four divisional commanders to march
on Modena.[53]

Conventional military doctrine would indicate that the outnumbered French should have united their forces into a single
army rather than launch separate offensives. In this case, however, the advantages of separate attacks seemed to justify the
risks. Macdonald and Moreau both realized that by moving toward Genoa they would expose the right flank of the army of
Naples. They also realized that until the two forces were united

Suvorov would in any case be able to strike at one of them separately. Since there was no way to avoid this risk, the French generals decided upon a two-pronged attack in order to threaten simultaneously Suvorov's left and front and attain the advantage of surprise. Both generals had come to favor a dual attack at about the same time. Macdonald was the first to contemplate changing the original plan and Moreau the first to suggest Modena as the new objective. Macdonald elaborated this suggestion into a completed plan of operations, and the minister of war also approved the change of plans.[54]

Macdonald led his 29,360-man force out of Florence on June 4, and on June 5 he made contact with advance units of Moreau's army. Moreau informed Macdonald on June 8 that he would assign two divisions to support his attack, and as supreme commander in Italy he also told Macdonald that he approved of all the plans and dispositions of the army of Naples.[55] On June 12 Macdonald gave orders to advance on Modena and Reggio, and the next day the French took Modena after killing fifteen hundred Austrians and capturing three thousand. A division entered Reggio on June 14, and French troops entered Parma on June 15. The French then pursued the Austrians across the Trebbia River and by June 17 were approaching the Tidone. Moreau, however, had failed to advance with the bulk of his army, and his inaction was to be disastrous. The peasants had cut communications between the two armies by killing the couriers, and fearing to act without detailed information, Moreau did nothing. By his inaction, he thereby left the army of Naples without support to face Suvorov, who had quickly responded to the French move.[56]

Upon receiving news of the French advance, Suvorov set out for the Tidone on June 15 with thirty-two infantry battalions, fifteen cavalry squadrons, and four regiments of cossacks. On the Tidone, Macdonald was preparing to attack, and on June 17 he sent two divisions forward against the Austrians. At first the attack was successful, but Suvorov arrived on the field and immediately threw his cavalry and cossacks against Macdonald's Polish volunteer division. He then sent four Russian battalions against the Poles while Austrian troops attacked a French division. After vicious fighting, he gradually forced the French to retreat back across the Tidone. At night both sides concentrated their forces for the next day's battle.

The battle of June 18 was very bitter, but Suvorov's numerical superiority ultimately decided the issue. Suvorov stopped the French from crossing the Tidone and pushed them back to the Trebbia, but Macdonald stopped the Allies from crossing the river and splitting his army in half. Nightfall put an end to the fighting, but both Macdonald and Suvorov planned to resume the conflict the next morning.[57] Macdonald was the first to attack on June 19, sending two divisions across the Trebbia. On the other flank, the Poles pushed forward, but Russian counterattacks forced them back across the river. Another division also crossed the Trebbia but ran out of ammunition and withdrew. The French right, however, pushed steadily forward until Suvorov halted them with heavy artillery fire. An Austrian cavalry charge then hit the leading French brigade, which was already weakened by the artillery, and completely shattered it. The defeat of this brigade in turn forced the neighboring units to retreat, and soon the whole division was in flight. The retreat exposed other units, and they too had to fall back.[58]

By sundown, Macdonald had inflicted twelve thousand casualties on the enemy, but his own losses of eight thousand were very serious considering his smaller numbers. He concluded that he was too weak to resume the battle, and on the evening of June 19 he began to retreat toward Genoa. The retreat was a difficult one marked by numerous rearguard actions in which both sides lost heavily. The army of Naples did manage to escape complete destruction, and on July 12, it arrived at Genoa with seventeen thousand men.[59]

Throughout these crucial days, Moreau had remained inactive. He did, it is true, carry out a minor offensive around Novi, but this attack failed to influence events on the Trebbia. It was in fact Moreau's inaction as much as any other single factor that caused Macdonald's defeat, because it allowed Suvorov to concentrate overwhelming numbers against the army of Naples. Even if he had lacked precise information as to Macdonald's movements, Moreau had agreed to Macdonald's original plan and should not have altered it without at least trying to inform his fellow commander.

After the battles of the Trebbia, the French army was too weak to launch offensives. It had no choice but to confine itself to the passive defense of those portions of Piedmont and Liguria that it still held. Thus in a few months time the allies had wrested control of most of Italy from the French, and the Directory would have to take truly desperate measures if it wished to reverse this disastrous strategic situation.

As the defeats in Italy caused ever-increasing alarm in Paris, the Directory decided upon a daring naval counterstroke. Originally, the directors had planned to have the Atlantic fleet resupply Bonaparte's isolated units, and for this purpose they had named Admiral Bruix on March 14 to command the Brest fleet. His command comprised twenty-four ships of the line, ten frigates, and seven supply vessels. France also put pressure on Madrid to order its eighteen ships of the line stationed at Cadiz to join Bruix.[60] On April 26 the French ships left Brest, eluding Birdport's blockade squadron, and the British, instead of sending reinforcements to their naval force at Cadiz, rushed ships to Ireland, fearing renewed invasion attempts. By May 4 Bruix was at Cadiz, where he hoped to engage the smaller British squadron, but the next morning a storm dispersed the British. Unable to find his opponent and being pushed onward by the storm, Bruix had to proceed through the Strait of Gibraltar into the Mediterranean. The storm, however, damaged some of his ships, and he had to enter Toulon for repairs. It was at Toulon on May 20 that the directors gave him new orders. They instructed him to assist Macdonald's army on its march north, but six days later they again changed their plans. This time the directors ordered him to proceed to Egypt with his and the Spanish fleet. He was to drive off the British blockaders, reembark the army of the East, and transport it to Italy.[61] This bold plan might well have succeeded had it not been for the unwillingness of the Spanish to cooperate.

Bruix left Toulon on June 8 and arrived at the Spanish naval base of Cartagena on June 22, but the Spanish admiral refused to leave port. Madrid felt that even the combined French and

Spanish fleets were no match for the sixty ships of the line that the British could deploy in the Mediterranean. Secondly, Spain was not at war with Turkey, Naples, or Russia and did not want to get involved with them. Madrid wished to avoid hostilities in the Mediterranean in order to protect their long-standing dynastic claim to Parma. Also, the Spanish feared that the Turks would encourage the Algerian pirates to raid their coasts.[62]

The Spanish commander, therefore, persistently refused to join Bruix, and although the French put continuous pressure on the court at Madrid, they could accomplish nothing. Bruix felt that the French fleet was too weak to act alone, and on July 16, with a combined Franco-Spanish fleet numbering sixty-five ships of the line, he returned to the Atlantic. He reached Brest on August 9, and the French thereby lost an excellent chance to influence the strategic position in the Mediterranean and Italy.[63]

In Italy there was little action during the month of July as both sides prepared for major operations in August. As a result of the Prairial Coup, which eliminated two moderate directors and replaced them with more radical types, Bernadotte, a favorite general of the left, became minister of war on July 1. On July 4 the government relieved Moreau of command and sent him to command a new army on the Rhine, which it had not yet constituted, and selected Joubert to replace him in the command of the army of Italy. Finally, the government gave Championnet command of a new force, the army of the Alps, which was to number about thirty thousand men and operate under Joubert's general direction.[64]

Reinforcements for the Italian front arrived steadily throughout June and July; 8,200 recruits reached Italy in June, and another 3,000 in July. This rather meager total is explained by the fact that the conscription system was still obtaining only about fifty percent of those drafted. Nevertheless, the army of Italy did recover some of its strength due mainly to the arrival of the troops taken from Masséna. In August, Joubert had a total strength of 61,975 men, 59,222 of whom were actives; the others were in garrisons or depots. Of the active troops, however, some 19,000 were besieged in various cities throughout north Italy, and Joubert, therefore, had at his immediate disposal only 40,623 men.[65]

For this army, the post-Prairial Directory decided on a new offensive, and on July 10 told Joubert that his mission was to attack as soon as possible, recapture the right bank of the Po, and reestablish communications with the Danube army.[66] It is well known that Sieyès, who was planning to reverse the results of Prairial, planned to use Joubert as his sword and encouraged him to win a rapid victory so that he could return to Paris covered with glory and could gain popular support for the projected coup. Military motives, however, also help to explain the reasons why the Directory wanted a renewed offensive. It was not within the scope of French military thinking to remain on the defensive for long periods, and to avoid growing war-weariness among the population, Paris felt that a victory was necessary. In addition, Joubert learned of the arrival of Korsakov's corps in Switzerland and wanted to strike before these new troops reached the front. The war minister also encouraged him to attack, telling him to strike while the enemy still had troops tied down in siege operations.[67]

On the allied side, Suvorov received 8,200 Russian troops as reinforcements, bringing his total forces to 32,269 Russians, 143,640 Austrians, and 7,448 Piedmontese. Of these, Suvorov could unite 68,000 men in an active field army while the rest remained in garrisons or carried on various sieges. Despite his excellent position, Vienna, nevertheless, decided that he was to suspend all operations until the fall of Mantua, Alexandria, and Tortona.[68] Such a decision is hard to explain on military grounds alone, because Suvorov had more than enough men to carry out the various sieges and to undertake simultaneous offensive operations. Vienna was, however, less interested in attacking the French than in gaining control of northern Italy. As the allied armies had moved forward, the Austrians, instead of restoring the ancient governments as the czar wished, governed the conquered areas as newly won territories. Since the Austrian troops were conducting the sieges of Mantua, Alexandria, and Tortona, Vienna hoped that their successful conclusion would further confirm their control over the newly conquered regions.[69] Suvorov objected but obeyed. He prosecuted the sieges, and on July 21 Alexandria surrendered. Mantua capitulated on July 27, but before Suvorov could take Tortona,

Joubert forced an active campaign upon the unwilling Austrians. On August 12 Joubert issued orders for the advance of his army, and on August 13 the army of Italy set out for Novi.

Joubert, however, had waited too long before advancing, and by the time he had advanced the Allies had completed many of their sieges and had reinforced their field forces. Unaware of this critical development, he ordered his left wing, two divisions, to move on Acqui. The right wing, also of two divisions, pushed to Novi, but on the night of August 14 he learned that Kray had captured Mantua and with twenty-two thousand men had joined Suvorov's field army. Faced with these overwhelming numbers, Joubert decided to withdraw, but before he could act, Suvorov attacked.[70]

On the morning of August 15 Kray struck at the French left, but he was unable to dislodge the republicans. Joubert, however, went to the threatened part of his line and was killed by a stray bullet. Moreau, who had not yet left for his new post, once again found himself in command of the army of Italy. Meanwhile, Russian troops had attacked Novi, but the French threw them back three times and then began a counterattack. At this point, eight thousand Austrians attacked Moreau's right flank, and the Russians mounted a fourth frontal assault. After a desperate fight, the republicans fell back and the Russians surged into Novi. With his right wing in retreat, Moreau ordered a general withdrawal, but one division got tangled up in the narrow streets of Pasturana due to the congestion caused by artillery pieces, ammunition carts, and baggage wagons all trying to move at once. Austrian troops, after scaling a neighboring height, began to fire into the densely packed throngs, slaughtering hundreds. Confusion rapidly degenerated into panic as the troops, losing all discipline, raced for open country. The division lost all cohesion, and the Austrians captured four thousand men including two divisional generals. In the course of the afternoon, the French lost sixty-five hundred killed and wounded and more than four thousand prisoners, while Suvorov suffered a total of eight thousand casualties.[71] As a result of Suvorov's victory at Novi, the Allies had completely shattered the army of Italy, which could do little more than limp back to Genoa, where on August 29 it merged with Championnet's army. The next day Championnet reported that the army was far too disorganized to embark on further offensives. The directors could do nothing but accept this situation, and on September 1 they told Championnet that he was to defend the line running from Genoa to Geneva.[72]

As the French were retreating from Italy events in the north were also going badly. The French and Batavians had been expecting an invasion of Holland for some time, and in anticipation of such a move, Paris had convinced the Batavian Directory to place their troops under Brune's orders. With twenty thousand Batavian troops at his disposal, he placed one division between the Hague and the Texel and gave another the task of covering Frisia and Gronigen. The fifteen thousand French troops occupied Haarlem. On August 15, the French sighted the allied fleet, consisting of 130 ships including nineteen ships of the line off the Belgian coast, and on August 22 the fleet appeared off the Helder forts where Abercromby had decided to make his landing. He had chosen the Helder because the seizure of the Helder Point and the adjacent Texel Island would enable the British fleet to control the Zuider Zee and observe the Dutch fleet. Furthermore, the army would be in an advantageous position for a descent on Amsterdam.[73]

As the Allies were preparing to land, the Batavian Republic faced still another threat, because by April 30 Thomas Grenville was able to report from Berlin that Haugwitz had come to favor a Prussian invasion of Holland, and in May he noted that he was making progress in winning the king over to a war policy.[74]

The allied successes demonstrated to the Prussians that they could attack France, and made them desirous of gaining territorial advantages in Germany to offset the probable Austrian gains in Italy. The next day Haugwitz met Otto, the French chargé-d'affaires, and told him that although Prussia wished to remain neutral, the king was concerned about the fate of the Rhineland and Holland. Holland, Haugwitz insisted, should regain her ancient independence, and the French should consult with Berlin to accomplish this goal rather than see the Coalition do it by force. Otto demanded time to send these demands to Paris, and the directors, also playing for time, did not send an answer to Berlin until the end of August. They stated that they had already taken measures to defend Holland. Haugwitz then concluded that Prussia should either join the Coalition or continue talks with the French, using the threat of armed intervention as a bargaining point.[75] The king, however, still refused to contemplate entering the war. Renewed French disasters, however, might well stiffen the monarch's resolve. Moreover, this temporary diplomatic respite did not prevent the Allies from landing in Holland.

After their first appearance near the Dutch coast, the Allied fleet had to stand out to sea because of bad weather. On August 27 the British reappeared off the Helder, and only one division was there to dispute their landing. At 3:00 A.M., under cover of the fleet's guns, the British began their seaborne assault. The first wave landed amidst great confusion. The high surf swamped several boats, and those units that did get ashore were in a state of grave disarray. Fortunately for them, the ship's guns kept the Batavians pinned down behind a row of sand hills, and Abercromby was able to land the rest of his advance battalions. Recovering from their initial shock, the Dutch threw two demibrigades against the British right flank, forcing them to retreat to the cover of their ships' guns, but reinforcements, advancing under covering fire from the fleet, checked the Batavian advance. Later in the day, the Dutch attacked again, but by this time the English were ready and easily drove them back. By nightfall, the invaders were securely lodged on the Dutch Coast, and at a cost of only five hundred men had driven back the Batavian counterattacks, inflicting fourteen hundred casualties on them. That night the Batavians withdrew the eighteen hundred-man garrison from the Helder forts and began to retreat south, leaving the British in undisputed possession of the Helder entrenchments and the Texel Island.[76]

The next day the British navy in cooperation with an infantry brigade occupied the Helder forts, and Admiral Mitchell summoned the Batavian fleet, consisting of twelve ships of the line manned by 3,690 sailors, to surrender. The Dutch admiral, Story, declined, but his officers, many of them holdovers from the old navy and still loyal to the stadtholder, refused to fight. The crews drew the charges from their guns, threw the extra ammunition overboard, and hauled down their colors. On Au-

NORTH HOLLAND 1799

gust 30 the Batavian fleet raised the flag of the House of Orange and passed into the service of the Coalition. Only Story and a few loyal officers refused to serve the prince and became prisoners of war.[77] Although the Batavian army and civilian population remained loyal to the Dutch Republic, the Allies had gained a firm beachhead in Holland and captured the Dutch fleet. They were in a good position to launch their offensive toward Belgium and northern France.

To add to the Directory's problems, royalist revolts flared up in southwest and western France. By 1799 there were an estimated fifteen to twenty thousand royalists in southwestern France. Returned *émigrés* and refractory priests furnished the core of antirepublican strength, while devout Catholics and deserters made up the rank and file. The royalist leaders had organized combat units and by the spring of 1799 were awaiting news of the expected Allied invasion before rising. Toulouse was an island of republicanism in this royalist sea, but the authorities there had only a single cavalry squadron and the semitrained National Guard for protection, and in the whole southwestern area, there were fewer than four thousand regular troops.[78]

Fortunately for the Directory, the army intelligence managed to penetrate the royalist organization. An officer from the eleventh military district at Bayonne had arrested several royalists and uncovered elements of a conspiracy. He and his superiors then formed a secret committee to run down the implications of subversive activity, and the officer joined the counterrevolutionaries as a spy and *agent provocateur*. He entered the royalist organization in Pau and learned that the royalist headquarters was located at Lyon, and that in each province there was a royalist *chef de division*. Each group of nine provinces had an inspector general, and in each department a secret civil council stood ready to replace the republican authorities. The royalists had plans for numerous simultaneous uprisings not only in southwestern France, but also in the Vendée, Brittany, and Normandy. They were awaiting their final orders, which were issued by the pretender on August 2. The revolt was to begin in six days from the receipt of these orders, and its starting point was to be the department of the Haute Garonne. The capture of Toulouse was to be the signal for the general uprising.[79]

Fortunately for the Republic, the royalist organization suffered from a failing common to many underground units—bad communications. Instead of a simultaneous uprising throughout the Haute Garonne, the rebellion began prematurely around Toulouse. On the night of August 4 to 5, partisan bands around Toulouse went into action, and despite their failure to create simultaneous uprisings, their rebellion was initially quite effective. The revolt spread along an eighty-mile arc south of the city. The city administration, however, reacted quickly and called out its National Guard, while the departmental administration declared itself *en permanence* and called for fifteen hundred National Guard volunteers to form mobile columns. The royalists, meanwhile, concentrated the bulk of their forces at Pech David, a hill dominating Toulouse. They then launched an attack on the city on the night of August 7, but the republicans defeated them.

The next day eleven battalions of National Guards attacked and routed the rebels, killing about three hundred. The commander of the republican forces, General Aubugeois, then turned his forces about to meet a second attack coming from the west. On August 9 he defeated a force of five thousand royalists and pursued them to the town of Isle en Jourdain, which he captured after a bitter fight in which the republicans killed four hundred rebels and took eight hundred prisoners. Aubugeois then pursued the remnants into the department of Gers.[80]

As Aubugeois saved Toulouse, revolt spread elsewhere. On August 6 rebellion flared up in the Aude department, and on August 7 royalist agents in the Ariege distributed an appeal from Suvorov urging the French people to rise and join the Allies. In Gers, counterrevolutionaries ambushed a National Guard detachment and took control of a number of towns. Fighting also erupted in Tarn. The fighting in these areas was often very confused, because it was carried out by small columns and bands, each acting on its own. Meanwhile, the main republican force under Aubugeois began to move on the new royalist headquarters located at Muret, but finding that the position was too strong, Aubugeois returned to Toulouse to await reinforcements.[81]

General Commes, the commander of the tenth military district, who had already taken precautions to guard the Spanish frontier, organized a new drive. He first mobilized columns in the Pyrenees department and then went to Toulouse to take command of operations there. On August 11 he organized four large columns to clear the rebels out of the rest of Gers, Tarn, and Garonne. He personally took command of a fifth column that was to attack Muret, and a sixth column of fifteen hundred men from the Pyrenees region attacked the town from the rear. Commes's advance forced the royalists to abandon Muret, and on August 20 his column caught and attacked them at Montrejeau. At the same time, the sixth column also attacked, and the republicans forced their foes to break and flee, losing out of a total force of four thousand about two thousand killed and one thousand prisoners. The remnants made for the Spanish frontier, but other isolated royalist units continued their resistance. Mobile columns had to operate throughout the rest of the year to keep order in the southwest.[82]

Revolt had also erupted in the west. In July army units defeated a force of eight hundred royalists in the Vendée, but other rebel bands continued to ambush government troops. In Brittany Chouan bands already active in 1798 continued their raids, while royalists forces in the Vendée grew to fifteen thousand.[83] Unlike their compatriots in the southwest, the guerrillas in the west did not attempt to form an army. Instead they operated in small bands. They continued their raids and assassinations throughout the summer, and further allied success, especially in Holland, might well have encouraged further uprisings on a massive scale.

Finally, in April, a royalist agent at Hamburg reported to the pretender that he had entered into contact with Barras's secretary, who had assured him that Barras would, in return for money and a guarantee of personal security, organize a royalist uprising in Paris. Louis XVIII agreed to give the agent at Hamburg 1,500,000 francs to bribe Barras and pay for the coup, which was to take place within six months.[84] Later Barras revealed to the Directory the fact that the royalists had contacted him, but his revelation may have been the result of the fear of discovery and the consequent desire to reveal the plot before somebody accused him of treason. Another view is that the whole idea of a coup was a fabrication on the part of Louis's agent to obtain money for himself, but in any case the very idea that a director, even one as venal and corrupt as Barras, could be bribed to betray the Republic indicates the depth to which the fortunes of France had sunk by August, 1799.

NOTES

1. Ministère de la Guerre État-Major de l'Armée, Archives historiques, Armée de Mainz devenue Armée du Danube et d'Helvétie, mars 1799, carton B271 (hereafter, Min. de la Guerre, AH).

2. Min. de la Guerre, AH, Correspondance du Ministère de la Guerre avec les armées du Danube, d'Helvétie, d'Observation, d'Orient de l'Ouest, de Batavie et du Rhin du 12 ventose en VII and 13 fructidor an VIII, carton B2* 171*.

3. Min. de la Guerre, AH, carton B271.

4. Ibid.

5. Ibid.

6. Ibid.

7. Édouard Gachot, *Les Campagnes de 1799: Jourdan en Allemagne et Brune en Hollande*, pp. 114–16.

8. Min. de la Guerre, AH, carton B271.

9. Gachot, *Campagnes de 1799*, pp. 106–9; and Min. de la Guerre, AH, carton B271.

10. Min. de la Guerre, AH, Rapports du ministre de la guerre au Directoire exécutif, 12 ventose an 7–3 vendemaire an 8, carton B12*37.

11. Min. de la Guerre, AH, carton 7 B271; and Général Philebert, ed., *Le général Lecourbe d'aprés ses archives, sa correspondance et d'autres documents*, p. 221.

12. Min. de la Guerre, AH, carton B271.

13. Général J. B. F. Koch, ed., *Mémoires de Masséna rédigés d'après les documents qu'il a laissés*, 3: 158–60.

14. Min. de la Guerre, AH, Correspondance, Armées du Danube et d'Helvétie, avril 1799, carton B272.

15. Ibid.

16. Min. de la Guerre, AH, Correspondance, Armée du Danube, mai 1799, carton B273.

17. Ibid., and Min. de la Guerre, AH, carton B2* 171*.

18. Min. de la Guerre, AH, Correspondance, Armée du Danube juin 1799, carton B274.

19. Ibid.; and *London Gazette. Bulletins of the Campaign 1799*, pp. 107–10.

20. Min. de la Guerre, AH, carton B274.

21. Min. de la Guerre, AH, Correspondance, Armées du Rhin et du Danube, juillet 1799, carton B275; Min. de la Guerre, AH, Correspondance, Armées du Rhin Danube, août 1799, carton B276; and Min. de la Guerre, AH, Ordres de bataille des armées en campagne, 1792–1815, carton XP3.

22. Min. de la Guerre, AH, carton B276.

23. Ibid.

24. Ibid., B276 and XP3.

25. Min. de la Guerre, AH, carton B276.

26. AN, AF III, carton 151B; AN, AF III, carton 151A; and Min. de la Guerre, AH, Situations, Armées du Danube et du Rhin, 18 août–23 octobre 1799, carton B2342.

27. Min. de la Guerre, AH, Correspondance, Armées d'Italie et de Naples, mars 1799, carton B359.

28. Ibid.

29. Giorgio Vaccarino, ed., *I Patrioti "Anarchistes" E L'Idea dell Unit à*

Italiana (1796–1799) , pp. 227, 232, 234–35.

30. Min. de la Guerre, AH, carton B12*37.

31. Min. de la Guerre, AH, Campagne de l'armée autrichienne-russe en Italie en 1799, Mémoires historiques, no. 438 (hereafter, MH) .

32. Ibid.

33. Ibid.

34. Min. de la Guerre, AH, Correspondance, Armées d'Italie et de Naples, avril 1799, carton B360; and Min. de la Guerre, AH, MH, no. 438.

35. Ibid.; and Min. de la Guerre, AH, MH, no. 438.

36. Min. de la Guerre, AH, carton B360.

37. Ibid.; and Min. de la Guerre, AH, MH, no. 438.

38. Countess Minto, ed., *Life and Letters of Sir Gilbert Elliot First Earl of Minto from 1751 to 1806*, 3: 107–8.

39. K. Osipov, *Alexander Suvorov*, pp. 134–35.

40. Ibid., pp. 113–14.

41. William Wickham, ed., *The Correspondence of the Right Honorable William Wickham from the Year 1794*, 2: 207; and Min. de la Guerre, AH, MH, no. 438.

42. Min. de la Guerre, AH, MH, no. 438; and Min. de la Guerre, AH, carton B360.

43. Min. de la Guerre, AH, Le général Grouchy, Précis des opérations de l'Armée d'Italie depuis l'Affaire de l'Adda jusqu'à la bataille de Novi, MH, no. 443.

44. Min. de la Guerre, AH, Correspondance, Armées d'Italie et de Naples, mai 1799, carton B361.

45. Min. de la Guerre, AH, MH, nos. 443, 438. Units from the Sardinian army that had been incorporated into the army of Italy when Joubert had occupied the kingdom also deserted *en masse* to the allies.

46. Ibid., Min. de la Guerre, MH, no. 438.

47. AN, AF III*, carton 19; and Min. de la Guerre, AH, carton B1237.

48. Maréchal A. Macdonald, *Souvenirs du Maréchal Macdonald*, p. 76.

49. Herman Hueffer, "Fin de la République napolitaine," *Revue historique* 73: 248, 252–58; George P. Naish, ed., *Nelson's Letters to His Wife and Other Documents*, pp. 507–8; and Jacques Godechot, *La contre-révolution doctrine et action 1789–1804*, p. 355.

50. Hueffer, "Fin de la République," 74: 34–35; and Naish, *Nelson's Letters*, p. 507.

51. Naish, *Nelson's Letters*, pp. 509–10; and Hueffer, "Fin de la République," pp. 36–37.

52. Min. de la Guerre, AH, Correspondance, Armées d'Italie et de Naples, mai 1799, carton B361.

53. Ibid.

54. Min. de la Guerre, AH, Correspondance, Armées d'Italie et de Naples, juin 1799, carton B362.

55. Ibid., and Min. de la Guerre, AH, Correspondance de Macdonald, Armée de Naples, mai–octobre 1799, Carton B3* 322*.

56. Min. de la Guerre, AH, cartons B362, B3* 322. See also Min. de la Guerre, AH, MH, no. 443.

57. Min. de la Guerre, AH, carton B3* 322*.

58. Ibid., and Min. de la Guerre, AH, carton B362.

59. Min. de la Guerre, AH, carton B3* 322*.

60. Georges Douin, *La Campagne de Bruix en Méditerranée mars–août 1799*, pp. 42–43, 55, 59; and Alfred Boulay de la Meurthe, *Le Directoire et l'expédition d'Égypt*, p. 96.

61. Christopher Lloyd, ed., *The Keith Papers* (London: 1950), 2: 30–31; Boulay de la Meurthe, *Le Directoire*, pp. 114–15, 119; and *Clément de la Jonquière, L'expédition d'Égypte 1798–1801*, 5: 167.

62. Douin, *Campagne de Bruix*, pp. 156–57, 189.

63. Ibid., p. 220; and Boulay de la Meurthe, *Le Directoire*, pp. 154–55.

64. AN, AF III*, carton 16; and AN, AF III, carton 151A.

65. AN, AF III, carton 13; AN, AF III, carton 151B; and Min. de la Guerre, AH, Situations, Armées d'Italie et de Naples, 1792–1801, carton B3381.

66. Min. de la Guerre, AH, Correspondance particulière du Général Moreau, 1791–1803, carton B298; and Min. de la Guerre, AH, carton B363.

67. Min. de la Guerre, AH, Correspondance, Armées d'Italie et de Naples, août 1799, carton B364.

68. Min. de la Guerre, AH, MH, no. 438.

69. Wickham, *Correspondence*, p. 111; and Peter I. Bartenev, ed., *Papers of Mikhail Larionovich Vorontsov and Other Members of the Family*, 10: 69.

70. Min. de la Guerre, AH, MH, no. 443.

71. Ibid.

72. Min. de la Guerre, AH, carton B364.

73. H. T. Colenbrander, ed., *Gedenkstukken des Algemeene Geschiedenis van Nederland van 1795 tot 1840*, 1: 61; James Dunfermline, ed., *Lieutenant-General Ralph Abercromby*, p. 156; and AN, AF III, carton 23.

74. Historical Manuscripts Commission, *Report on the Manuscripts of J. B. Fortesque, Esq., preserved at Dropmore*, 5: 34–35, 50, 65, 67.

75. Paul Bailleu, ed., *Preussen und Frankreich von 1795 bis 1807 Diplomatische Correspondenzen*, 1: 319–20, 331–32.

76. Sir John Moore, *Diary*, pp. 341–42; Henry Bunbury, *Narratives of Some Passages in the Great War with France from 1799 to 1810*, p. 3; Min. de la Guerre, AH, Correspondance, Armée de Batavie, juillet–septembre 1799, carton B192; and *History of the Campaign of 1799 in Holland*, p. 56.

77. Colenbrander, *Gedenkstukken,* p. 223; and C. D. Yonge, *The History of the British Navy,* 2: 147.

78. Abbé Joseph Lacouture, *Le mouvement royaliste dans le sud-ouest (1797–1800)* (Paris: 1932), pt. 1, chap 2; Bertrand Lavigne, *Histoire de l'insurrection royaliste de l'an VII,* pp. 16, 21; and Godechot, *La Contre-révolution,* pp. 363–64.

79. Lacouture, *Le mouvement royaliste,* pp. 65–67, 71–73.

80. Min. de la Guerre, AH, Correspondance, République Directoire, 11 au 20 août 1799, carton B13105.

81. Ibid., and Lavigne, *L'insurrection royaliste,* pp. 197, 236.

82. Min. de la Guerre, AH, Correspondance, République Directoire, 21 au 31 août 1799, carton B13106.

83. P. V. J. de Bourniseaux, *Histoire des guerres de la Vendée et des Chouans,* 2: 392–93, 401, 403.

84. *Manuscripts of Fortescue,* 5: 23–24, 28; letters of the royalist agent.

12
Zurich

The Austrian decision to violate the strategic plan for the invasion of France, a plan to which both England and Russia adhered, gave the Directory its long-sought opportunity to launch an effective counterblow at the forces of the Second Coalition.[1] According to the original Anglo-Russian plan, Suvorov, after defeating the French in Italy, was to lead his Russian corps into Switzerland. His troops would join Korsakov near Zurich to form a single Russian army under Suvorov's command. This force plus Condé's *émigrés*, a total of some sixty thousand men, would in the spring of 1800 move west, turn the Rhine barrier, and then drive across the unfortified Franco-Swiss frontier. At the same time, the Austrian troops in Switzerland were to move into southern Germany and, from there, cover Korsakov's right flank until Suvorov arrived. When Suvorov began his final drive into France, the Austrians were to continue to protect the Russian right by attacking Basel and Belfort.[2] Thus the presence of the Austrian army on Korsakov's right flank was essential to the success of the Allied strategy. Moreover, it was especially vital that the archduke protect Korsakov while Suvorov was in transit between Italy and Switzerland, because during this period the French would outnumber the Russians at Zurich, and only the presence of the Hapsburg army in close support of Korsakov could prevent Masséna from attacking.

Thugut, however, was devising a diplomatic scheme that was ultimately to imperil the whole of the Coalition's strategy. The basis of the Austrian minister's new plan was his desire to expand the Hapsburg domains. At the start of the war, his main objective had been to make new acquisitions in Italy, if necessary by sacrificing Belgium to England or even by concluding a separate peace with Frence. The Allied triumphs in Italy had, however, enabled Thugut to drop plans of negotiating with the Republic. Instead he set out to make sure that Austria would retain political control of the Allied conquests in Italy. As the Allied armies advanced, the Austrian authorities, instead of restoring the old monarchs to their thrones, proceeded to rule the captured territories as prizes of war, and the Russians, who desired a restoration of the prewar *status quo,* began to protest. On May 30 the Russian ambassador at London told Grenville that the czar expected the Allies to return Piedmont and the Papal States to their rightful rulers instead of allowing them to pass permanently into Austrian hands, and on August 2 Suvorov went so far as to ask the king of Sardinia to return to Piedmont.[3] The Austrians were able to prevent the king from returning, and on August 23 Suvorov complained directly to the czar about the course of Austrian policy.[4] As a result of this growing Russian opposition to his plans, Thugut became anxious to get them out of Italy. The British strategy presented him with a perfect opportunity to accomplish this objective, and on July 31 he told the British that he agreed with their general war plan.[5] By this astute move, he not only got the Russians out of Italy but also gained a free hand for Austrian ambitions in the peninsula. At the same time, he had placed the burden of the difficult Swiss campaign on the Russian army. This striking diplomatic success, however, encouraged Thugut to undertake still another coup against his own allies; a coup that was to involve a betrayal of both the English and the Russians. With Italy firmly in Austrian hands, Thugut decided to employ the archduke's army to regain control of Belgium and carry out the long-contemplated Bavarian exchange, despite the fact that such a move would leave Korsakov isolated and exposed in Switzerland.

As early as the middle of July, Thugut, much to the dismay of the English, had turned his attention to the question of the future disposition of the Low Countries. On July 16 Grenville, in a letter to his brother, noted that the Austrians were becoming interested in the Netherlands. They were, according to this report, thinking of attacking Mainz, which lay far to the north of Korsakov's army, in order to gain control of the left bank of the Rhine, and then pushing on into Belgium.[6] Grenville realized that such a move would dislocate his whole strategy by exposing Korsakov's army to a French reposte. He grew even more alarmed when other officials told him that if the Austrians decided to attack Mainz, fronts other than Switzerland would also suffer. On July 24 General Abercromby warned him that an Austrian attack on Mainz would enable the French to send reinforcements to Holland and perhaps defeat the Allied expedition.[7] The British envoy at Vienna also noted that an Austrian attack on Mainz would endanger the campaigns in both Switzerland and Holland. The Austrian objective, he added, was to cross the Rhine, enter the Low Countries from the east, and restore Hapsburg rule in Belgium. In such an eventuality, the English and Russian forces would be reduced to the role of flank guards for the Austrian offensive.[8]

Grenville tried to convince Thugut to modify his plans first by making political concessions to Vienna and then by warning the Austrians of the military dangers involved in a unilateral alteration of the Coalition's strategy. He first contemplated offering Vienna the assurance that no peace would be concluded that did not restore the Austrian Netherlands to them, if in return they would drop the project of attacking Mainz.[9] As a result, Grenville had to abandon his plan of unifying Belgium and Holland. As early as July 27 he had told Dundas that to obtain the cooperation of the archduke's army England would have to agree to return Belgium to Austria, but that he hoped to make a special arrangement with the Austrians to safeguard England's vital interests in the area.[10] Pitt also agreed with this policy. On August 2 he told Grenville that England should guarantee the restoration of Belgium to Austria in the hope that this political sacrifice would persuade Vienna to continue to adhere to the British military plans.[11] On the military level, Grenville instructed his envoy to tell Thugut that the Mainz operation would never produce a restoration in France, and three days later he told his ambassador that an Austrian attack on Mainz would make operations in Switzerland virtually impossible.[12]

Thugut, however, remained impervious to both concessions and military arguments, for he was determined to gain control of the Low Countries as well as northern Italy without having to agree to any limitation of Austrian authority in either area. Despite a renewed promise made on August 23 to protect Korsakov's flank until Suvorov arrived, Thugut ordered the archduke to move north. Charles had no choice but to comply, and by September 6 he was attacking the French army of the Rhine around the fortress of Philippsburg and driving it back to the left bank of the river. On September 18, his forces entered Mannheim, the first step in the plan to invade the Rhineland.[13] Meanwhile, on August 17 Suvorov received his first instructions to go to Switzerland, but the necessity of pursuing the French after Novi enabled him temporarily to ignore this order. On August 28 he protested to Vienna against the decision to send him to Switzerland, but learning that the archduke had already started to move into Germany, he had no choice but to go to the aid of Korsakov. He drew up his plans for the march to Zurich on September 8, intending to move by way of the St. Gothard pass.[14]

The British at this point continued their attempts to stave off disaster by offering Vienna new compensations, but these efforts all failed. On September 10 Pitt suggested to Grenville that England offer to compensate Austria in Italy in return for allowing Holland to take the Austrian Netherlands after the war. Three days later Pitt stated his willingness to back Austria's claim to Piedmont against the objections of the czar, but Thugut remained unmoved. Since Vienna was in actual occupation of northern Italy, he felt no need of British diplomatic support in retaining these conquests. Pitt had no other leverage, and Thugut was therefore able to ignore his overtures. Thus by the middle of September, Pitt came to the conclusion that he could not trust Austria and that England would have to consider carrying on the war with only Russia as an ally.[15]

The original British plan had excellent possibilities. The Franco-Swiss frontier was unfortified, and if a Russian army, supported by the Austrians on their immediate right, could have broken Masséna's force, an invasion of France was well within the realm of probability. Moving Suvorov out of Italy was also sound military strategy. The Allies had crushed the French armies in Italy. They posed no serious military threat, and there were more than enough Austrian troops in Italy to deal with the remnants of the French forces. To organize a large homogeneous force under the command of the Coalition's best general and to place this force on a strategically vital front was a logical military prelude for the most important offensive of the war.

Moving the archduke's army north was also a sound idea, because it would force the French to divert troops to the Rhine instead of sending them to reinforce Masséna's army. The cardinal error, then, was not moving Suvorov out of Italy nor the archduke out of Switzerland. Rather, the major Allied blunder was the Austrian decision to attack Mainz instead of Basel and Belfort. By moving on Mainz, the archduke's army marched too far north to support Korsakov if the French attacked in Switzerland, and even if the French remained on the defensive and the two Russian corps joined forces safely they would not be strong enough to attack Masséna with more than a fair chance of success. To make matters worse, the Austrians did not wait for Suvorov's arrival in Switzerland before moving toward Mainz. Thus while the Austrians were moving on Mainz and Suvorov was moving into Switzerland, Korsakov's army had to face a French force superior in numbers. If the French were alert, they could attack and smash this isolated corps before the other Allied armies could bring sufficient pressure to bear on other fronts to force the French to recall troops from Switzerland. Once victorious in Switzerland, the French could then threaten the flanks of one or both Allied armies and completely dislocate their offensive. Thus as a result of their desire to regain control of the Low Countries, the Austrians had presented the Directory and Masséna with a unique opportunity to attack one of the Allied armies on very favorable terms and thereby rescue a seemingly desperate situation.

The Directory and its advisors realized that Switzerland was the vital front in the autumn of 1799. In an analysis of the general military situation presented on August 14, Bernadotte told the directors that the enemy was going to try to turn the line of the Rhine near Mannheim, envelop Mainz, and push into

Belgium, where they expected the population to rise in their favor. To counter such a move, Bernadotte rejected the idea of acting on the Rhine in order to force the enemy back along the Neckar River, because such a policy would weaken the defense of Switzerland and expose eastern France to attack. As an alternative, he suggested an attack on the Allied forces in Switzerland that, if successful, would split the Allied armies and threaten the enemy in both Italy and Germany from the rear.[16] Thus long before the Austrian blunder had become apparent, the French realized the strategic importance of the Swiss battle zone.

In recognition of the vital importance of the Swiss front, the Directory had steadily reinforced Masséna's army throughout the summer, and by September it numbered 88,768 men, including 4,934 Helvetian troops. Masséna reorganized the army of the Danube into eight combat divisions, a reserve division, and a division of the interior. He had also revised his command system since the first Battle of Zurich in June and had appointed the able and energetic Oudinot as his chief of staff. Thurreau commanded the 9,100 men of the First Division in the Valais, and Lecourbe's Second Division of 13,500 men held the area around the St. Gothard pass. Soult's 9,950-man Third Division was on the Linth River, and the 9,100 men of Mortier's Fourth Division faced Zurich. Lorge's Fifth Division of 9,000 troops, and Menard's Sixth Division with 10,600 men held the line of the Limmat River. Klein commanded the 5,460 men of the Seventh Division, which Masséna had placed behind Lorge and Menard, and the 7,950 men of Chabran's Eighth Division held the line of the Rhine as it flowed in an east-west direction through Switzerland. The Division of the Interior had 3,400 men and devoted its efforts mainly to guarding the army's communications line with France and hunting down royalist partisan bands. The Reserve Division was 4,680 men strong, and the artillery comprised 1,050 troops.[17] Facing this force was Korsakov's 27,350-man Russian corps. It held a line stretching from Zurich to the Limmat River and from there to the Rhine. An Austrian force of 21,800 men under Hotze manned positions along a line stretching from Lake Zurich along the Linth River to Dissentis in the Grisons. To the south, Suvorov with 30,400 men was moving toward Switzerland.[18]

The directors and the war minister were quick to realize the import of the archduke's departure from Switzerland, which Masséna reported on September 1, and they urged their field commander to attack as soon as possible. On September 5 the minister of war told Masséna that "the result of this campaign and perhaps the destiny of the Republic rests on your force and on your courage."[19] The minister went on to point out that of all the active armies only Masséna's force was fit to resume the offensive, and a successful attack would not only relieve the pressure on the Italian front but also force the Anglo-Russian army out of the Batavian Republic. The Directory, he added, wanted the army to take advantage of the momentarily favorable military position and attack as soon as possible.[20] Masséna for his part realized the opportunity presented him, and by September 12 he was busily preparing for an offensive.[21] Replacements, rations, and ammunition flowed steadily to the front until by the third week in September the army was ready to strike.

From September 22 to 24 Masséna issued his final orders for the forthcoming offensive. His front resembled a large U placed on its side with the closed end facing east. The bottom or southern portion of the U ran from the St. Gothard pass to the Lake of the Four Cantons and from there to the Linth River. The closed portion of the U ran along the Linth to the southern part of Lake Zurich, and from there along the southern part of the lake to a point just south of Zurich. After circling to the west of Zurich, the line then followed the northwest course of the Limmat River past the confluence of this river with the Reuss and Aar rivers until it joined the Rhine. The northern part of the U followed the Rhine as it flowed in a westerly direction through Switzerland. Masséna's objective was not just to force Korsakov to retreat but rather to annihilate his corps as a fighting force. His tactical plan was to convince the Russians that he was going to strike north across the Rhine, while in fact he prepared a series of strokes in the vicinity of Zurich[22]

Masséna ordered Chabran and Menard to make diversionary attacks along the Rhine while the main assault force, fourteen thousand men drawn from Menard's, Lorge's, Klein's, and Mortier's divisions, struck across the Limmat at Dietikon, a mere seven miles from Zurich. The main force was to seize the Fahr plateau, thereby splitting the Russian front, and then send brigades to the left and right. Units moving left were to contain Russian units along the Rhine, while the troops advancing to the right were to threaten the northwest approaches of Zurich. While the main attack moved out, another division was to move against the western face of Zurich and still another unit was to strike at the city from the south. As the pincers snapped shut around Zurich, Soult was to break out on the central front. His objective was twofold: to defeat Hotze's Austrians and to prevent them from reinforcing Korsakov.[23]

On the night of September 24 engineers secretly brought forward boats and bridging material. Artillery pieces, their wheels muffled with rags, rolled silently forward. On September 25 at daybreak cannons along the Rhine began to bombard the Russian advance posts, and infantry units made obvious preparations to ford the river. The Russians shifted their reserve units to meet this thrust, and only then did Masséna send in his main attack.[24]

Along the Limmat, field artillery guns spoke. Engineers raced forward and launched their assault boats. Grenadiers and skirmishers from the Tenth Light Brigade and Thirty-seventh Demibrigade landed on the enemy's side of the river and raced for the Fahr plateau. Sappers threw a pontoon bridge across the river, while the forward infantry elements seized the plateau. The Russians threw a brigade against Masséna's bridgehead, but French sharpshooters cut it to pieces. As the Russians recoiled, French reinforcements began to cross the pontoons. By 9:00 A.M. Lorge's entire division had crossed the Limmat, and Masséna's army had split the Russian front in half.[25]

With hardly a pause, Lorge sent two demibrigades to his left, while two others led by Oudinot moved toward Zurich. Oudinot's immediate objective was the Zurichberg, a large hill that dominated the city's northern approaches. As Oudinot's men closed in on the Zurichberg, Mortier threw his entire division against the western approaches of the city. Shaken by the suddenness of the attack, the Russians abandoned their forward positions and retired hastily behind the city walls. Korsakov, however, recovered his nerve, sent up two fresh battalions, and ordered a counterattack. Storming out of Zurich, the Russians blunted the French drive and pushed them back at the point of the bayonet. Colonel Humbert, having been exchanged after his capture in Ireland, now seized his chance to strike a critical blow against the enemies of the Republic. Leading a battalion of grenadiers, he plunged headlong into the advancing Russians. For a few moments the foes remained locked in mortal combat, but it was the Russians who finally broke and went reeling back toward Zurich. In desperation Korsakov threw his cavalry reserve into action. French field artillery batteries galloped up, unlimbered, and firing cannister at near point-blank range shattered the Russian horsemen into a welter of screaming men and animals. The gunners then manhandled their cannon into positions from which they could support Oudinot's attack.[26]

As the fighting raged in front of Zurich, Oudinot led the men from the Tenth light brigade and the Thirty-seventh, Fifty-seventh, Second and 102d half-brigades, a Swiss unit, and a cavalry regiment toward the suburbs of Zurich and the Zurichberg. Realizing the full extent of the French threat, Korsakov launched a violent counterattack in a desperate effort to keep open his only escape route. As the Russians poured out of Zurich the French field guns opened fire. Tearing huge gaps in the Russian lines, the gunners succeeded in bringing the enemy to a virtual standstill. Masséna's men then closed in. They engaged the shaken Russians in vicious no-quarter combat and drove them back to the very foot of the Zurichberg.[27]

At noon a silence fell over the carnage. Neither the French nor the Russians, both stunned by their losses and the bitterness of the fighting, had the strength to resume combat. The generals, however, soon rallied their men. In front of Zurich, Mortier's sharpshooters began to enter the western suburbs. To the north, French infantry moved up the Zurichberg. Russian bayonet charges rolled them off the slopes. Oudinot then sent men around the Russian right. Having committed his last reserves, Korsakov was unable to check this new threat and had to abandon control of the mountain. He pulled his troops back into the northern suburbs and ordered them to fortify the houses for a last-ditch stand. The French pursued. The Russians poured a withering fire into the republican assault columns, which recoiled, leaving the streets carpeted with their dead. Renewed attacks made no headway, but shortly after dark, Oudinot pushed combat patrols to the top of the Zurichberg. During the night he strengthened his hold on the mountain, a move that spelled doom for the Russian army.[28]

As fighting raged before Zurich, Soult's division was also on the move. Prior to the general assault, Soult had created a special commando unit to seize a foothold on the Austrian side of the Linth river.[29] On the night of September 24 the commandos plunged into the icy Linth and reached the Austrian bank undetected. Moving with murderous silence, the commandos sabered the Austrian sentries, captured several artillery emplacements, and slipped a cable back to their own side of the river. Soult then rushed fresh troops to the Austrian bank, and by 5:00 A.M. September 25, twelve hundred infantrymen were probing into the Austrian lines. Hotze, the Hapsburg commander, received word of the French attack and dashed off into the foggy morning to rally his troops. Racing through the mist, he inadvertently blundered into Soult's leading elements. French fusiliers cut him down. Hotze's demise made effective resistance impossible. As Soult's engineers threw a pontoon bridge across the Linth, Austrian officers mounted a series of ill-coordinated company- and battalion-strength counterattacks. These the French easily repulsed, and then plunged deep into the Austrian positions. By early evening Soult's brigades had penetrated the Austrian main line of resistance, unhinged the center of the Allied front, and made it impossible for the Austrians to detach units to assist Korsakov's embattled regiments at Zurich.[30]

During the night Korsakov rejected Masséna's offer to arrange a peaceful evacuation of the city.[31] He then called a war council that resolved to break out of the French trap and escape northward into Germany. Korsakov detailed five battalions and a cavalry regiment to hold the French in the western suburbs. Four battalions were to retake the Zurichberg, and six more were to hold the city itself while the rest of the corps with its supply and artillery elements dashed north.[32]

In the early morning hours of September 26, Russian infantry stormed out of Zurich, raced up the mountain slopes, and bayoneted the surprised Frenchmen off the peak. Swarming into the suburbs, Russian troopers in bitter hand-to-hand fighting cleared the narrow streets and houses of French sharpshooters. The main column then moved out, but Masséna quickly recovered his balance and initiative and threw in a series of violent and effective attacks. His horse artillery galloped forward, unlimbered, and pounded the city. Packed into the narrow streets hundreds of Russians perished helplessly under the hail of shot and shell. Meanwhile on the Zurichberg, Oudinot reorganized his command and lunged back up the slopes. Snipers decimated the Russians, and storming columns smashed through the weakened lines. Oudinot's battalions regained the peak and then raced for the city gates where Korsakov's picked grenadiers prepared for a last desperate stand. Under a withering blast of musketry the Russians held their ground and died where they stood. Clambering over the bodies of their slaughtered foes, the French burst into the northern section of Zurich. There they found the rearguard battalions and most of the main column, delayed by Masséna's artillery barrage, still bottled up in the streets. Unable to deploy, the Russians could do nothing to prevent the French from pouring volley after volley into their helpless lines at point-blank range. The French mowed down rank after rank of green-clad Russian infantry, while bolting horses dragged guns and wagons into the mass of dead and dying men, adding further horror to the slaughter. Additional French units broke through the south central gates, and their muskets added to the growing carnage. When the smoke finally drifted off at the end of the day, over 2,000 Russian corpses littered Zurich's streets. Over 5,000 men including 142 officers remained as Masséna's prisoners, while the remnants of Korsakov's column, no longer a coherent fighting force, fled painfully along the roads to Germany.[33]

To the south Soult's men were also moving. After a brief clash, French infantrymen entered Wassen. Other brigades moved forward, driving the disorganized Austrians before them. Having lost some five thousand men in two days' fighting, the Austrians abandoned further efforts to hold their positions and began a general retreat to the Rhine. Soult pushed out patrols until one of them linked up with units from Lecourbe's division, which had been pushing a small Austrian column to the east.[34]

Having shattered the Allied front in Switzerland Masséna immediately prepared to pursue Korsakov's remnants and simultaneously crush Suvorov's force that had for the past several weeks been pushing north in a vain effort to aid his comrade-in-arms.[35]

On October 2 Masséna announced to the Directory that he intended to clear all the foes of the Republic out of Switzerland.[36] He dispatched two infantry divisions and his cavalry reserve northward. On October 8 French formations swarmed into Constance, driving Condé's *émigré* force from the town and threatening the rear of the Austrian army on the Rhine.[37] At the same time Masséna swung the bulk of his army south into the Alps with orders to destroy Suvorov.

Suvorov had meanwhile begun his march into Switzerland. On September 24 his advance guard had reached the St. Gothard pass and slashed its way through the French defenders at a cost of two thousand men.[38] The French had then retreated to the Devil's Bridge, an immensely strong position on the Reuss River. A tunnel-like path, five feet wide, flanked by solid rock on one side and a seventy-five foot drop on the other, led to the bridge. Lecourbe placed a cannon on the path, and Suvorov had no choice but to fling his grenadiers straight into its murderous fire. The path was soon choked with the bodies of the dead and dying. The rocks below were also strewn with corpses, but the Russian soldiers continued to clamber over their comrades' bodies and advance. Running low on ammunition the French cannoneers finally pulled back across the bridge. Again Suvorov threw his men forward, and again hundreds perished in a vain attempt to force the French position. Suvorov then sent a picked force of grenadiers and Cossacks down the slopes into the Reuss valley. This attack group managed to pick its way through the snow and threaten the French flank. Lecourbe realized that he could no longer delay the Russians. Satisfied that he had inflicted severe punishment on Suvorov, he withdrew north to await reinforcements from Masséna.[39]

By September 28, leading elements of Soult's division after several days of forced marches joined Lecourbe's force near the southern end of the Lake of the Four Cantons. Soult's men arrived just in time. They helped Lecourbe's tired and battered units beat back Suvorov's advance guard and scotched all further Russian efforts to march toward Zurich.[40] At this juncture Suvorov learned of Korsakov's defeat. He realized that Masséna would soon turn on him. Consequently, he decided to lead his command in a desperate march to the northeast in order to reach Germany before the French could trap him in the snow-filled Alpine passes and cut him to ribbons.

On September 29 Suvorov posted a rearguard at the mouth of the Klonthal pass and, mounted on a small sturdy Cossack pony, led the rest of his corps toward Glaris. The French in turn closed in on both ends of the column. At the pass French skirmishers and Cossacks fought in waist-deep snow. Both sides suffered heavy casualties, but the Russians held. The main force meanwhile entered Glaris on October 1 and then continued to march to the northeast. A Helvetian demibrigade threw itself in the path of the Russian line of march but soon recoiled with heavy losses. French units arrived to support their allies and dug in along the Linth River, a river that Suvorov had to traverse if he were to escape from Switzerland. The Russian general quickly threw a regiment across the river. A wild French bayonet charge threw it back. Suvorov sent in another attack. Again French and Helvetian rushing columns hurled it back. Fighting resumed the next day. Six times the Russians pushed across the river. Six times French sharpshooters decimated the assault lines, and six times French columns slashed forward to drive back their desperate foes. Suvorov lost some two thousand men and failed to break across the Linth.[41]

Unable to escape to the northeast, the Russian leader decided to march due east into the Grisons. He recalled his rear guard, abandoned his artillery and wounded, and led his tired corps forward on October 5.[42] For a week the Russians staggered eastward over incredibly rugged terrain. Plodding knee-deep through snow drifts, exhausted men dropped out of line never to rise again. Blizzards obliterated trails, horses and soldiers disappeared into crevices, and only their leader's iron will kept the Russians staggering on to safety. Suvorov's corps, worn out and verging on a shambles with its thinning lines stretching for miles, finally reached Germany. Behind them more than five thousand men lay dead or remained as French prisoners, and if the corps escaped total destruction, it was, nevertheless, unfit for further combat.[43]

The Directory and Masséna had thus worked together to achieve a resounding tactical and strategic victory. The Directory had realized that an offensive by the army of the Danube was their only hope of avoiding an invasion of France. Accordingly they had reinforced Masséna's units and ordered him to attack. When they grasped the significance of the Austrian attack on the Rhine, the cardinal error of the whole campaign, they became even more insistent on a counteroffensive, and Masséna was quick to comply. The Directory allowed him much tactical freedom, and if it is to their credit that they saw the opportunity offered them and ordered a rapid attack, it is to Masséna's credit that the victory was so complete. His plan was a brilliant one, and it was well executed by his subordinates. The extent of Masséna's victory also changed the entire outlook of the war. Whereas in August, the Directory had been fearful of an invasion of France, the minister of war on October 11 was able to suggest the resumption of offensive operations.[44]

Masséna's triumph also led to the disintegration of the Coalition and influenced the tactical situation on the other fighting fronts. The czar, already annoyed at Austrian policy in Italy, was furious at what he believed to be Austrian responsibility for the defeat of his armies. On October 11 the Russian ambassador at London stated that Korsakov's defeat was the natural consequence of removing the archduke from Switzerland, and on October 15 the ambassador noted that the czar was ready to leave the Coalition.[45] Masséna's victory also had a direct effect on the archduke's operations against Mainz, because upon receiving news of the Battle of Zurich, Charles abandoned his preparations to cross the Rhine and on October 17 evacuated Mannheim.[46] Had he instead marched for Switzerland to aid Korsakov, he might have retrieved the situation for the Allies or at least minimized the scope of the Coalition's defeat. The rapidity of Masséna's moves, however, unnerved him and made him fearful for the security of his army's left flank. Anxious to avoid the same fate as befell Korsakov, he withdrew to the east, thus ending the threat to the Republic on the middle-Rhine front.

The French victory also forced Prussian policy to undergo a rapid shift. Encouraged by the Allied victories, Prussia had increased her insistance that the French evacuate Holland and the Rhineland and on September 13 had demanded that Prussian troops be allowed to occupy these areas.[47] The French had continued to play for time by offering to discuss the issues, but after the Battle of Zurich and the consequent retreat of the archduke, the Directory informed the Prussian ambassador that France refused to discuss the evacuation of the Rhineland or Holland, and on October 28 Haugwitz was forced to tell his king that Prussia could do nothing but return to its system of neutrality.[48] Finally, Masséna's victory enabled the government to send reinforcements to the Helder front, and Brune, who had been carrying out a holding action, was able to stabilize his lines and crush the invasion forces.

Unlike his fellow generals in Italy, Brune did not have to cope with civilian insurgents and could concentrate all his forces on the problem of repulsing the invasion. The civilians in Batavia rallied loyally behind their government after the Allies landed. The Batavian Directory mobilized the National Guard, and bankers made loans to the government. There was almost no pro-Orangist sentiment in Batavia, and when on September 3 the Prince of Orange and some of his followers crossed into Holland from Germany, the National Guard of Arnheim routed them.[49] Even civilians in areas occupied by the Allies remained pro-republican, and one British officer noted, "Whatever might have been the notions instilled into the British government with respect to the political feelings of the Dutch, certainly there had appeared in North Holland nothing to favor the idea that the people would assist us in restoring the House of Orange."[50] Doubtless indifference and fear of reprisals if the Allies lost were factors involved in the hostility of the civilians, but basic loyalty to the republican regime was the vital element. If the British and Russians were to win, it would have to be exclusively by force of arms.

At first, the Allies seemed quite capable of achieving this goal, and after driving back the Batavian counterattacks, Abercromby had pushed rapidly south until he reached the Zype Canal, where he halted to await the arrival of the duke of York. The area in which the campaign was to take place formed a narrow peninsula about thirty miles long bounded by the North Sea on the west and the Zuider Zee on the east. High sand dunes ran along the west coast, and between them and the Zuider Zee, the land extended into a marshy plain intersected by numerous dikes and inundations. Numerous towns lay scattered throughout the area:

Egmont was located on the west coast, and Bergen lay slightly to the north. Alkmaar, the largest town in the area, lay five kilometers south of Bergen and thirty-one kilometers north of Amsterdam. Ten kilometers south of Alkmaar was the small village of Kastrikum, and the port town of Hoorn faced the Zuider Zee. In such an area, any offensive would have to consist of a series of frontal attacks along parallel lines of causeways, and only limited flanking movements were possible. The defense could maintain itself by holding various canal lines and using the numerous villages as fortified strong points. There was little room for clever maneuvers, and vicious face-to-face infantry fighting was to decide the issue.

Brune wished to attack before Abercromby received reinforcements. He therefore ordered a Dutch division into the Helder area, and he also sent seven thousand French troops to the battle zone. By September 10 Brune was ready to attack the line of the Zype Canal. The strongly entrenched British, however, easily drove off Brune's troops. The French division lost over one thousand men. The Batavians also suffered heavy losses, and one division panicked and fled, not stopping until officers shot at least one soldier for desertion.[51] Having failed to dislodge the enemy, Brune had no choice but to go over to the defensive and try to contain the Allies within the confines of the peninsula until the onset of winter made it impossible for them to remain on their exposed beachhead in northern Holland.

Naturally the British and Russians had to follow the opposite course. With bad weather approaching, it became imperative for the Allies to break out into open country and seize enough territory on which to maintain themselves throughout the winter. Reinforcements for an offensive began to arrive, and from September 12 to 15, the second echelon of the expedition landed. It consisted of the Russians, led by the brave but not very brilliant General Hermann, the remainder of the British troops, and the duke of York, who took command of the Allied forces.[52] Since the duke had proven himself so inept in his first Flanders campaign, the government had decided to safeguard him against his own errors by subjecting his decisions to the approbation of a council of war consisting of Abercromby, Hermann, and other ranking officers. Such a device was at best a mixed blessing, for if a council could correct the duke's worst blunders, it could also lead to complications in the chain of command and to the creation of interallied hostility.[53] Criticism of this arrangement must, however, be modified by the fact that the campaign was to be conducted in an area so circumscribed as to greatly reduce the margin for serious error.

The duke and his council decided to attack as soon as possible. The council's plan consisted of sending the Russians, supported by an English brigade, to attack Bergen while three other British brigades attacked Brune's center. A third column of four brigades under Abercromby's personal command was to take Hoorn and from there advance on Alkmaar. A total of 35,300 Allied troops were to attack 21,900 republicans.[54]

Abercromby's column was the first to set forth on the night of September 18, because it had to cover thirty miles over roads knee-deep in mud. Demolitions by the French sappers, who destroyed bridges and felled trees across the column's route, further slowed Abercromby's men. Despite these hindrances, the British arrived at Hoorn at dawn on September 19. They took the city with little trouble since it was not held in strength, after which the troops halted to await the results of the Russian attack.[55] The Russians had meanwhile been moving on Bergen, where they forced the outnumbered Fifty-fourth demibrigade to evacuate the town. The Forty-second demibrigade had more success and threw back a Russian column that was attempting to circle around Bergen, and Brune began to prepare a counterattack.[56] He quickly gathered troops from the Forty-second, Forty-eighth and Forty-ninth demibrigades and threw them against the Russians, who were advancing down the road toward Alkmaar. A masked artillery battery on the Alkmaar road opened fire on the Russians and tore great gaps in their ranks. In the resulting confusion, a French brigade pushed forward and retook Bergen while the others hit the Russians in the flanks to complete the rout. In Bergen, the French captured hundreds of Russians, including General Hermann, and only the timely arrival of an English brigade arrested the headlong flight of the remaining Russian units. The defeat of the Russians in turn exposed the flank of

Abercromby's column, and it too had to retreat. Brune's counter-thrust had thus turned the tide of battle at a cost to the Allies of over three thousand men.[57]

Having failed to pierce Brune's center and right, the duke and his council decided to throw the main weight of their next assault against his left. Three brigades under Abercromby were to advance through the sand dunes, seize Egmont, and turn the French flank. The Russians were to support Abercromby's left flank, and a third column of three brigades was to threaten the Batavian position.[58] Abercromby began his advance on the morning of October 2, meeting heavy resistance from two French demi-brigades. Brune's light infantry made excellent use of the cover provided by the numerous sand hills to harass the flanks of the advancing British. This gave Brune time to pull two Batavian battalions from the line and send them to reinforce the threatened flank. Upon their arrival, they immediately rushed forward, and forced the British to retreat. The duke then sent a fresh brigade to reinforce Abercromby, and the British resumed their advance. By dusk they had recovered their original positions, but Egmont remained in French hands. The Russians had also attacked, but a French demibrigade offered ferocious resistance, beating off five attacks before giving up the positions in front of Bergen while continuing to hold the town. The Allies did, however, achieve a partial success during the day's fighting, for they had managed to cut the road linking Bergen and Egmont.[59]

With the road cut, Brune realized that, although he could still hold his present position, the shifting of reserves would become a difficult operation. To obtain a shorter and stronger position, he decided on the night of October 2 to evacuate Egmont, Bergen, and Alkmaar. His retreat took the tired Allied army completely by surprise, and they failed to pursue him. He established a new line across the peninsula with advanced posts in Kastrikum. Engineers blocked roads, set up batteries, and made inundations to protect the right flank. The arrival of reinforcements brought the number of active French troops to 15,150. With these additional men, Brune was able to organize his French units into two complete divisions with Vandamme as corps commander.[60] Thus for their efforts, the Allies had managed to secure a few towns and hamlets of no great strategic value, and Brune still confined them within the limits of the Helder peninsula. The French, on the other hand, were in a stronger position than ever. In addition, news of Masséna's successes, which reached Holland at the beginning of October, indicated to both sides that it was only a matter of time before the Directory would send even more reinforcements. The British and Russians were left with little choice. They had to act quickly if they were to break into open country.

The final battle, however, took place by accident. On October 6 the Allies started to probe the French advance positions. General Essen, the new Russian commander, intended to occupy Kastrikum as an advanced post, but his men encountered heavy resistance from the garrison. Essen then sent more troops forward, and at the same time, the French reinforcements reached the beleaguered force at Kastrikum. A bitter fight ensued, but the Russians forced the heavily outnumbered French to evacuate the town.[61]

Realizing the gravity of the situation, Brune proceeded to gather twenty-five hundred men from one of his divisions and threw them against the right flank of the Russian force. The attack halted the Russians and went on to push them out of Kastrikum. Essen's men fell back to Bergen, where a body of English troops rallied them, and the united force began to move back toward Kastrikum. Brune then placed himself at the head of a cavalry detachment and led a charge while his infantry also rushed forward. The ensuing battle surged back and forth for several hours with neither side gaining the upper hand, but it was the Allies who finally gave way. Leaving 1,118 dead and wounded and 900 prisoners behind, the Russians fell back to Bergen. The British also retired in disorder, having lost over 600 men, and by nightfall, it was obvious that Brune had inflicted a decisive defeat on the Allies.[62]

That night, the duke and his advisors decided to retreat back to the Zype. Their losses had been heavy, supplies were short, and heavy rainfall was making campaigning almost impossible. Defeat, disease, and mutual recriminations between Russian and English commanders further weakened the army's fighting capacity. News of Korsakov's defeat served only to make Allied morale even lower. The retreat began on October 7. French and Dutch patrols followed the Allies, but Brune contented himself with picking off stragglers rather than instituting a general engagement. His men took over 500 prisoners in this manner, and a patrol even captured the British camp followers, a factor which no doubt contributed to the further decline of Allied morale. In a spirit of Gallic gallantry no doubt coupled with the desire to increase the problems of the British quartermaster, Brune ordered the ladies returned unhandled.[63] By October 8, the Allies were back at the Zype Canal, having nothing to show for their arduous campaign but a long casualty list.

At this juncture, the duke had three possible courses of action to follow: try and hold the Helder until spring, attempt to evacuate his army under fire, or negotiate with the enemy. The first alternative was impossible, because the army was too weak and could not obtain reinforcements due to the bad weather, and the French would soon be able to strike with overwhelming numbers. The possibility of a fighting embarkation was also ruled out when the duke's engineer officers informed him that they could not fortify the Helder in such a way as to cover a withdrawal by sea.[64] To save his army from total annihilation, the duke was left with no choice but to accept the third alternative, and on October 15 the duke's aide-de-camp and Brune's chief of staff met at Alkmaar to begin negotiations for the allied capitulation.[65]

The Convention of Alkmaar, signed three days later, contained nine articles providing for the end of hostilities and the details of the Allied evacuation of the Helder. Brune allowed the British to retain the Batavian fleet but forced them to return the batteries seized at the Helder point plus eight thousand republican prisoners taken in other campaigns. The two sides exchanged hostages and observers, and the duke agreed to embark his army by the end of November.[66] Many people criticized Brune for negotiating with instead of destroying the Allied army, but he doubtless felt that further attacks, even if successful, would be very costly and that his men could be better employed in the Vendée, on the Rhine, or in Italy. The Batavian Directory was pleased to get the invaders out of Holland without further destruction of life or property, and the French directors, glad to get the Anglo-Russian force off of the Continent without the dubious benefit of a costly victory, made no complaint about Brune's policy. The British, on the other hand, were dismayed at the magnitude of their defeat, and Lord Buckingham wrote to Grenville that the duke of York had "signed a convention which I consider as the most disgraceful to the British character of any document I ever read."[67]

By hard fighting, Brune had won a most important campaign. He did not, it is true, display the brilliance of Masséna, but in default of this he had been thoroughly schooled in the principles of the French republican school of warfare and was not afraid to use them. His constant emphasis on offensive tactics and local attacks was typical of this style of fighting, as were his use of light infantry and rapid shifting of reserves. These ingrained principles enabled him to triumph over the duke's superior numbers, capitalize on the Allied failure to concentrate their attacks against one vital point, and take advantage of their failure to exercise greater tactical control over their forces.

As a result of this victory, Brune had eliminated the threats to the northern end of the Rhine barrier and the Belgian departments. The rebels in the Vendée, Brittany, and Normandy found themselves isolated, and although they could continue to harass the authorities, they could no longer pose a serious threat to the security of the government. Only in Italy and southern Germany did large enemy armies stand against the Republic, and the French would be able to concentrate almost all of their strength against them next spring.

At the end of October, 1799, the military situation of the Republic was very promising. Masséna had crushed the Russians in the field, and the czar, furious at what he considered to be virtual treason on the part of the Austrians, had left the Coalition. On October 22 he had told the emperor that, after seeing his troops abandoned and delivered to the enemy by his trusted ally, and after seeing Russian policy for the future of Europe abandoned and sacrificed to the ambitions of Austria, he had no choice but to occupy himself with Russia's exclusive interests and "to cease to make common cause with Your Imperial Majesty."[68] France had broken the Coalition, because with Russia out of the war, England had lost her only powerful continental ally. Austria had never signed a treaty with Britain, and the conflicting war aims of the two powers made it unlikely that they would be able to devise a joint campaign. In addition, the Republic had defeated one of the largest British armies ever to land in Europe. London would, therefore, be unable to influence the campaign of the following spring, and Vienna would have to fight alone in Germany and Italy.

France, it is true, had lost control of the Mediterranean, and for all practical purposes, the army of the East was lost to the Directory. France had also lost control of Naples, Rome, the Cisalpine Republic, and most of Piedmont, but the overall military situation made it possible to regain most of these areas by a renewed offensive. On October 28 the war minister was able to tell the Executive Directory that the Republic was superior to its enemies and could take advantage of its recent victories by sending Brune's army to combat the royalists in the west and by launching a major drive against the Austrians from Switzerland. Switzerland, he pointed out, was now a vast armed camp from which Masséna's army could attack one of three objectives: the Grisons, Swabia, or Lombardy. Lombardy, he said, was the best alternative, because the government had reinforced the army of Italy and had brought it up to a strength of sixty thousand men. It was ready to attack in cooperation with Masséna's forces. By moving into the northern Italian plain from Switzerland, Masséna's army could outflank the Austrians, and taken between two French armies, the Austrians would have no choice but to retreat.[69]

When in the spring of 1800 Bonaparte began his famous Marengo campaign, he found that his preliminary work had been done for him by the armies of the government that he had overthrown. He did not have to worry about the Russians in Italy and Switzerland, the British and Russians in Holland, or the royalists in France. He was also able to concentrate the bulk of his forces against the Austrians in Italy, an idea that originated during the last days of the Directory.

NOTES

1. Historical Manuscripts Commission, *Report on the Manuscripts of J. B. Fortescue, Esq., preserved at Dropmore*, 5: 144–45.

2. William Wickham, ed., *The Correspondence of the Right Honorable William Wickham for the Year 1794*, 2: 170.

3. *Manuscripts of Fortescue*, 5: 72; and A. R. von Vivenot, ed., *Vertlauliche Briefe des Freiherrin von Thugut*, 2: 179.

4. Vivenot, *Briefe des Thugut*, 2: 181.

5. *Manuscripts of Fortescue*, 5: 216.

6. Countess Minto, ed., *Life and Letters of Sir Gilbert Elliot First Earl of Minto from 1751 to 1806*, 3: 81.

7. *Manuscripts of Fortescue*, 5: 191.

8. Ibid., p. 241.

9. Ibid., pp. 148–49.

10. Ibid., pp. 198–99.

11. Ibid., p. 224.

12. Ibid., pp. 243, 256.

13. Wickham 2: 172; and Émile Bourdeau, *Campagnes modernes*, 1: 432.

14. Wickham, *Correspondence*, 2: 210–11.

15. *Manuscripts of Fortescue*, 5: 380, 396, 404.

16. Ministère de la Guerre État-major de l'Armée, Archives historiques, Rapports du ministre de la guerre au Directoire exécutif, 12 ventose an 7–3 vendemaire an 8, carton B12*37 (hereafter Min. de la Guerre, AH).

17. Min. de la Guerre, AH, Situations, Armées du Danube et du Rhin, 18 août–23 octobre, 1799, carton B2342.

18. Wickham, *Correspondence*, 2: 195; and Min. de la Guerre, AH, Ordres de bataille des armées en campagne, 1792–1815, carton XP3.

19. AN, AF III, carton 151A.

20. Ibid.

21. Min. de la Guerre, AH, Correspondance, Armées du Rhin et du Danube, septembre 1799, carton B277.

22. André Masséna, *Rapport fait par le général Masséna au Directoire Exécutif sur les operations du 3 au 18 vendemaire an 8* (Paris: 1799), p. 4.

23. Ibid., pp. 4–5; and Min. de la Guerre, AH, carton B277.

24. Masséna, *Rapport*, p. 4.

25. Ibid., p. 6.

26. Ibid., p. 7.

27. Ibid.

28. Ibid., p. 8.

29. Min. de la Guerre, AH, carton B277.

30. Ibid.; and Masséna, *Rapport*, p. 9.

31. Min. de la Guerre, AH, carton B277.

32. Masséna, *Rapport*, pp. 11–12.

33. Ibid., p. 13; and Min. de la Guerre, AH, carton B277.

34. Min. de la Guerre, AH, carton B277.

35. Ibid.

36. Min. de la Guerre, Correspondance, Armées du Rhin et du Danube, octobre 1799, carton B278.

37. Ibid.

38. Min. de la Guerre, AH, carton B277.

39. Ibid.

40. Ibid., and Min. de la Guerre, AH, carton B278.

41. Min. de la Guerre, AH, carton B278.

42. Ibid.

43. Ibid.; and Louis Hennequin, *Zurich Masséna en Suisse*, pp. 382–83.

44. Min. de la Guerre, AH, Rapports du Ministre de la guerre au Directoire Exécutif 6e jour Complementaire de l'an 7–11 brumaire an 9, carton B12*39.

45. *Manuscripts of Fortescue*, 5: 468; and Peter I. Bartenev, ed., *Papers of Mikhail Larionovich Vorontsov and Other Members of the Family*, 8: 252–53.

46. E. Bourdeau, *Campagnes modernes*, p. 432.

47. Paul Bailleu, ed., *Preussen und Frankreich von 1795 bis 1807 Diplomatische Correspondenzen*, 1: 337.

48. Ibid., pp. 342, 344.

49. Min. de la Guerre, AH, Correspondance, Armée de Batavie, juillet-septembre 1799, carton B192.

50. Henry Bunbury, *Narratives of Some Passages in the Great War with France from 1799 to 1810*, p. 10.

51. Min. de la Guerre, AH, carton B192.

52. Bunbury, *Narratives*, p. 14; and Edward Walsh, *Narrative of the Expedition to Holland*, pp. 49–51.

53. John W. Fortescue, *A History of the British Army*, 4, pt. 2: 666.

54. Ibid., p. 671; and Édouard Gachot, *Les Campagnes de 1799*, pp. 247–48.

55. John Surtees, *Twenty-five Years in the Rifle Brigade*, p. 10.

56. Min. de la Guerre, AH, carton B192.

57. Ibid.; and *Mémoires historiques sur la campagne du général en chef Brune en Batavie*, p. 38.

58. Fortescue, *History of the British Army*, 4, pt. 2: 682–84.

59. Min. de la Guerre, AH, Correspondance, Armée de Batavie, octobre-décembre 1799, carton B193.

60. Ibid.

61. Ibid.

62. Ibid.

63. Bunbury, *Narratives*, p. 33; and Walsh, *Expedition to Holland*, p. 89.

64. Whitworth Porter, *History of the Corps of Royal Engineers*, 1: 224.

65. Min. de la Guerre, AH, carton B193.

66. Ibid.

67. *Manuscripts of Fortescue*, 5: 500.

68. Hennequin, *Masséna en Suisse*, p. 437.

69. Min. de la Guerre, AH, carton B12*39.

Conclusion

In military terms strategy involves planning campaigns designed to compel an enemy to bow to the effective application of force. Strategy also deals with the mobilization of a state's human potential and economic resources. Military strategy, however, does not exist in a vacuum. Warfare is a means of fulfilling political and diplomatic objectives; it is not an end in itself. When devising strategic operations planners must, of course, produce a scheme that will lead to military victory, but military victory in turn must lead to the fulfillment of the state's broader objectives. The planners must also consider the economic consequences of war and the public's reaction to the existence and progress of the conflict. Victory in battle is rarely sufficient, and effective strategy must also strengthen the nation's international position and bolster the regime's domestic support.

Between 1792 and 1799 French leaders struggled to solve monumental problems: social and political upheaval, civil insurrection, and foreign wars. In contrast to nonrevolutionary states, where the impact of public opinion was minimal and civil-military relations were rarely a major issue, the First Republic had to deal with a restive and often active public and with powerful ambitious generals in addition to the traditional problems involved in strategic decision making.

The Constitutional Monarchy went to war without giving due consideration to military and diplomatic preparations. Political factions—the Brissotins, aristocrats, royalists, and military men seeking power—regarded a foreign war as an avenue to political domination at home. Consequently, the army was unprepared for combat, and the nation had no allies, no diplomatic objectives, and no strategic plan. France nearly suffered a catastrophic defeat, and popular reaction to the military reverses toppled many of those who sought domestic control by means of external hostilities.

The new Republic, torn by internal dissension was at first unable to devise an effective strategy. The new regime did win some victories in the fall of 1792 but then found itself confronted by the problems of dealing with its conquests and its ambitious generals, who had political schemes of their own. To control their acquisitions and their officers, the republican leaders first contemplated the creation of satellite republics in Belgium and the Rhineland. The Convention then discovered that satellite states might not be pro-French and that generals might obtain undue influence in the new states. Paris, therefore, decided to annex their recent conquests to protect prorepublican elements, reduce military influence, and enhance French power. The annexations, however, brought new powers into the war, and the Convention's inability to subdue the military led to new battlefield defeats. By the summer of 1793 France again faced the prospect of destruction.

With the advent of the Committee of Public Safety and the Terror, the Republic obtained a government able to handle the multiple issues involved in strategy and policy decisions. The Committee raised new armies, mobilized and directed the populace, and ruthlessly dominated its field commanders. The Committee also produced a military strategy that won popular support at home and also fulfilled French military and diplomatic objectives. The vigorous counteroffensives at the end of 1793 halted foreign invaders, crushed domestic insurrections, and satisfied the politically active citizens who were calling for a vigorous war effort. The offensive operations in the spring of 1794 continued to satisfy popular demands for attacks upon the Republic's enemies. The campaign also took advantage of divisions in the Coalition by concentrating against Austria and England, the Republic's most dedicated foes, while leaving open the possibility of concluding an early peace with Prussia.

The post-Thermidorian Convention did not have as firm a grip upon the nation as the Robespierrist Committee of Public Safety. Consequently, the economic situation deteriorated, the army's numerical strength declined, and field commanders gained an ever larger measure of independence from political authorities in Paris. A revival of royalism that called for peace, even at the price of surrendering most if not all of the Republic's territorial conquests, forced supporters of the Republic to advocate a victorious peace to prove to the public that their policies were beneficial to the nation. The army's decline and the growing independence of the generals, however, made it extremely difficult to achieve the victories necessary for the Republic's domestic survival. Poorly planned by Carnot, who with remarkable inflexibility tried to repeat the Belgian campaign strategy in Germany, and badly executed by the field commanders, one of whom probably sabotaged operations, the 1795 campaign ended in bitter defeat. To win popular support, royalists continued to call for a peace of renunciation, while republicans desperately continued their search for victory.

Coming to power at the end of 1795, the Directory faced problems similar to those of the post-Thermidorian Convention. The Directory lacked broad popular support and needed victory to rally the public behind the regime. Declining numbers of troops and growing political interference by generals continued to plague the government. The Directory, nevertheless, drew up a bold scheme for the 1796 campaign and planned attacks in Germany and Italy as well as a thrust at Ireland. The German campaign upon which the French rested their chief hopes for victory was badly conceived, because Carnot again called for a repetition of the campaigns of 1794 and 1795. Moreau's refusal to act decisively then eliminated any possibility of tactical initiative rescuing straegic ineptitude. While the invasion of Germany collapsed, Bonaparte surprised the world by his brilliant victories in Italy. He then used his newly won prestige to rescue the Directory from the royalists, who had amassed great popular support in the wake of the defeats in Germany. Finally, Bonaparte imposed his own peace terms upon the Hapsburgs and his own reluctant government, terms that drastically altered the Directory's policy of gaining the Rhineland and Belgium by sacrificing Italian conquests. The result of military interference was to encourage Vienna to seek revenge and involve the Republic in a region not vital to French strategic and diplomatic interests. The blows at

England, though failures in a restricted military sense, did convince Pitt to negotiate. Divisions within the French government, however, prevented the Directory from negotiating effectively. Thus at the end of 1797, France had driven Austria temporarily from the war and had to defeat England to secure final victory.

In 1798 the Directory declined to attempt an invasion of the British Isles and, suprisingly, refused to consider a new thrust at Ireland, where revolutionary sentiment was ready to explode into a full-scale insurrection. Instead the Directory and its military advisors chose to strike at British India by way of Egypt. Since the Royal Navy dominated the high seas, a French colonial venture exposed itself to crushing ripostes. Moreover, the extension of operations into the Levant was bound to antagonize other powers. The result of the expedition to Egypt was the Battle of the Nile and the formation of a Second Coalition.

In preparing to resist the new alliance, the Directory and the war ministry decided upon an offensive strategy to disrupt the Coalition, reassure the French public, and prevent defeatism and a consequent increase of royalist sentiment. The specific plan, however, was faulty. By calling for attacks on a broad front against superior numbers, the government made defeat inevitable. The opening months of the war were disastrous, and battered French armies had to retreat in Germany, Switzerland, Italy, and Holland, while royalist insurrections erupted inside France.

The Directory recognized its initial mistake and energetically launched land and naval counterblows. At first all failed, because although the strategic conception of each counterthrust was valid, errors in tactical execution led to their collapse. The Allies, however, did not maintain their unity, and when Austria altered and dislocated the Coalition's strategy, the Directory seized its opportunity to strike a decisive blow. Aided by excellent tactical initiative, the Directory won major victories in Switzerland and Holland, victories that not only altered the military balance but also ruptured the Coalition's diplomatic front. When Bonaparte seized power and destroyed the Republic, the Directory was in the midst of planning another offensive to complete its triumph. In 1800 it was Bonaparte who, following the defunct regime's strategic plan, drove into Italy and brought the war to a successful conclusion. He then proceeded to employ the armies and military techniques created by the Republic in an attempt to establish his own imperial hegemony in Europe.

The Republic never fully solved all of the problems involved in strategic decision making. In fact the related issues of civil-military relations and public opinion led directly to the Republic's demise. To retain popular support republicans had to win a victorious peace, but in their quest for victory they failed to control the generals, one of whom seized power for himself just as victory was in sight. Still, despite its final collapse, the Republic's accomplishments were impressive. Midst war and political turmoil France built the best army in Europe, withstood the assaults of the great powers, and made extensive conquests. France then defeated a second Coalition and in 1799 stood as the most powerful single nation in Europe. Had Bonaparte been satisfied with remaining first among equals rather than trying to reduce all of Europe to vassalage, he might today be remembered as a great soldier-statesman instead of as a romantic genius who led a triumphant nation to catastrophe.

Bibliography

Manuscript Sources

Archives des affaires étrangères

Correspondance politique. Vols. 363, 364, 586, 651, 668.
Mémoires et documents. Vols. 28, 321, 652, 655.

Archives nationales

AF II. Cartons 3, 9, 27, 77, 212, 214^A, 214^B, 281.
AF II.* Carton 24.
AF III. Cartons 13, 23, 56, 57, 59, 61, 69, 76, 149, 150^A, 150^B, 151^A,
 151^B, 152^A, 152^B, 331, 332, 333, 334.
AF III.* Cartons 1, 2, 13, 14, 16, 18, 19, 20, 202.
DP II. Cartons 4, 5.
F^9. Carton 48.
Archives de la Marine. Cartons BB^{4}129, 139.

Ministère de la Guerre État-Major de l'Armée, Archives historiques

CORRESPONDANCE
Armée de Batavie, 1799. Cartons B^{1}92, B^{1}93.
Armée du Danube, 1799. Cartons B^{2}73, B^{2}74, B^{2}75, B^{2}76.
Armée d'Italie, 1798. Cartons B^{3}55, B^{3}56, B^{3}56^{Bis}.
Armée de Mayence devenue Armée du Danube et d'Helvétie,
 1799. Cartons B^{2}71, B^{2}72.

Armée du Rhin et du Danube, 1799. Cartons B²75, B²76, B²77, B²78, B²79.

Armées d'Italie et de Naples, 1799. Cartons B³59, B³60, B³61, B³62, B³63, B³64.

Armées d'Italie et de Rome, 1799. Cartons B³57, B³58, B³58ᴮⁱˢ.

Armées de Mayence du Rhin et d'Helvétie, 1798–99. Cartons B²63, B²64, B²65, B²66, B²67, B²68, B²69, B²70.

Armées du Nord et des Ardennes, 1793. Cartons B¹18, B¹19, B¹20.

Armées du Nord et de Sambre et Meuse, 1794. Cartons B¹32, B¹33, B¹34.

Correspondance du général Jourdan, 1798–99. Cartons B²*260, B²262.

Correspondance de Macdonald, 1799. Carton B³*322*.

Correspondance du ministère de la guerre avec les armées d'Italie et de Naples, 1799. Carton B³*221*.

Correspondance du ministère de la guerre avec la Convention et le Comité de Salut Public, 1792–94. Carton B¹253.

Correspondance du ministre de la guerre avec les armées, 1799. Carton B²*171*.

Correspondance particulière du général Moreau, 1792–1803. Carton B²98.

Indes orientales, 1797–99. Carton B⁸1.

Rapports du ministre de la guerre au Directoire exécutif, 1799. Cartons B¹²*37, B¹²*39, B¹³105, B¹³106.

Armées de la République situations générales, 1791–1803. Cartons B¹244, B¹245, B²339, B²340, B²342, B⁶190, B³381.

Ordres de bataille des armées en campagne, 1792–1815. Cartons Xᴾ3, Xᴾ5, Xᴾ33, Xᴾ34, Xᴾ81.

Organization générale de l'armée, 1793. Carton Xˢ4.

Registre de l'État-Major général, 1793–94. Carton B¹110.

INVENTAIRE ANALYTIQUE DE LA CORRESPONDANCE MILITAIRE
Armées des Alpes et d'Italie, mai–juin, 1796.

Armées des Alpes et d'Italie, juillet–septembre, 1796.

Armées des Alpes et d'Italie, avril–juin, 1797.

Armées des Alpes et d'Italie, octobre–décembre, 1797.

Armées du Nord et des Ardennes, janvier-mars, 1794.

Armées du Nord et des Ardennes, avril–juin, 1794.

Armées du Nord et de Sambre-Meuse, octobre–décembre, 1795.

Armées du Rhin et de la Moselle, janvier–juin, 1795.

Armées du Rhin et de la Moselle, juillet–décembre, 1795.

MÉMOIRES HISTORIQUES

Armée d'Italie campagnes de l'an IV et de l'an V. No. 417.

Armée des Pyrénées orientales campagne de 1793. No. 474.

Armée du Rhin journal général des opérations 28 septembre 1792 jusqu'au 8 janvier 1794. No. 322.

Bataille des Pyramides le 3 Thermidor an 6 (27 juillet 1798) par le général Berthier. No. 908[1].

Bulletin des Opérations de l'Armée de Rhin et Moselle, 1796–97. No. 348.

Campagne de l'an 5 en Italie. No. 423.

Campagne de l'armée autrichienne-russe en Italie en 1799. No. 438.

Campagne des Armées du Nord, des Ardennes et de Sambre-Meuse (5 mai 1794–18 mars 1795). No. 293.

Campagne de 1796 sur la Rhin. No. 301.

Campagne de 1796 sur le Rhin. No. 302.

Campagne de 1796 sur le Rhin. No. 333.

Campagne de Syrie en VII. No. 908[1].

Exposé des opérations des Armées du Nord et de Sambre-Meuse, 1794–95. No. 280.

Journal de la campagne de l'an IV sous le Commandement du Général en Chef Jourdan. No. 287.

Journal historique de quelques opérations militaires de l'Armée d'Italie commandée par Bonaparte et l'an IV. No. 426.

Mémoires militaires du Maréchal Jourdan, campagne de 1793. No. 608[1].

Mémoires militaires du Maréchal Jourdan, campagne de 1794. No. 608[2].

Précis de la campagne de l'Armée de Sambre et Meuse pendant l'an 4. No. 298.

Précis historique de la campagne de l'Armée napolitaine par le général Mack. No. 453.

Précis historique sur le siège de Toulon en 1793. No. 400.

Précis des opérations de l'Armée d'Italie depuis l'affaire de l'Adda jusqu'à la bataille de Novi. No. 443.

Précis des opérations des Armées de Rhin et Moselle et de Sambre et Meuse pendant la Campagne de 1796. No. 342.

Rélation de la bataille de Fleurs livrée le 8 messidor an 2 (26 juin 1794). No. 274.

RAPPORTS

Rapport fait par le général Masséna au Directoire exécutif sur les opérations du 3 au 18 vendemaire an 8.

Rapport fait par le ministre de la guerre L. de Narbonne à l'Assemblée Nationale le 11 janvier 1792.

Published Documents, Letters, and Memoirs

Albrecht and Wilhelm, Archdukes, eds. *Ausgewählte Schriften des Erzherzogs Karl.* 4 vols. Vienna: 1893.

Angers, David d', ed. *Mémoires de Larevellière-Lépaux.* 3 vols. Paris: 1895.

The Annual Register or a View of the History, Politics and Literature for the Year 1798. London: 1800.

The Annual Register or a View of the History, Politics and Literature for the Year 1799. London: 1801.

Arneth, A. R. von. *Marie Antoinette, Joseph II, und Leopold II ihr Briefwechsel.* Leipzig: 1866.

The Asiatic Annual Register; or a View of the History of Hindustan and of the Politics, Commerce, and Literature of Asia for the Year 1799. London: 1800.

Aspinall, Arthur, ed. *The Later Correspondence of George III.* Vol. 2. Cambridge: Cambridge University Press, 1963.

Aulard, F. V. A., ed. *Recueil des actes du Comité de Salut Public avec la correspondance officielle des représentants en mission.* 28 vols. Paris: L'Institut d'histoire de la Révolution française, 1889–1951.

Bailleu, Paul, ed. *Preussen und Frankreich von 1795 bis 1807 Diplomatische Correspondenzen.* 2 vols. Leipzig: 1881.

Barrow, John, ed. *The Life and Correspondence of Admiral Sir William Sidney Smith.* 2 vols. London: 1848.

Bartenev, Peter I., ed. *Papers of Mikhail Larionovich Vorontsov* and *Other Members of the Family*. 38 vols. Moscow: 1876–80.

Beer, Adolf, ed. *Joseph II, Leopold II und Kaunitz*. Vienna: 1873.

Berthier, Louis Alexandre. *Relation des campagnes du général Bonaparte en Égypte et en Syrie*. Paris: 1800.

Bertrand, Henri, ed. *Campagnes d'Égypte et de Syrie 1798–1799, Mémoires pour servir à l'histoire de Napoléon dictées par lui-même à Sainte-Hélène*. 2 vols. Paris: 1847.

Bishop of Bath and Wells, ed. *The Journal and Correspondence of William, Lord Auckland*. 4 vols. London: 1862.

Bonaparte, Napoléon. *Correspondance inédite officielle et confidentielle de Napoléon Bonaparte*. 3 vols. Paris: 1819–20.

Bouloiseau, Marc, Lefebvre, Georges, and Soboul, Albert, eds. *Oeuvres de Maximilien Robespierre*. 9 vols. Paris: Presses Universitaires de France, 1953.

Bourrienne, L. A., ed. *Memoirs of Napoleon Bonaparte*. 5 vols. London.

Byrne, Miles. *Mémoires d'un exile irlandais de 1798*. 2 vols. Paris: 1864.

Charavany, Étienne. *Correspondance générale de Carnot*. 4 vols. Paris: Siège de Société de l'histoire de la Révolution, 1897–1908.

Clercq, Alexandre, ed. *Recueil des traités de la France*. 2 vols. Paris: 1864.

Cobbett, William, ed. *The Parliamentary History of England from the Earliest Period to the Year 1803*. 36 vols. London: 1818.

Colenbrander, H. T., ed. *Gedenkstukken des Algemeene Geschiedenis van Nederland van 1795 tot 1840*. 22 vols. The Hague: M. Nijhoff, 1907.

Conches, Feuillet de, ed. *Louis XVI, Marie Antoinette et Madame Elizabeth lettres et documents inédits*. 5 vols. Paris: 1864–69.

Congress at Rastadt Official Correspondence from the Original Papers. London: 1800.

Corbett, Julian, ed. *Private Papers of George, Second Earl Spencer, First Lord of the Admiralty 1794–1801*. 4 vols. London: Navy Records Society, 1914.

Coupland, Reginald, ed. *The War Speeches of William Pitt the Younger*. Oxford: Clarendon Press, 1916.

Debidour, Antonin. *Recueil des actes du Directoire exécutif*. 4 vols. Paris: Imprimerie nationale, 1910.

Desbrière, Edouard, ed. *1793–1805 projets et tentatives de débarquement aux Iles britanniques.* 4 vols. Paris: R. Chapelot, 1900.

Dunfermline, James, ed. *Lieutenant-General Ralph Abercromby.* Edinburgh: 1861.

Duruy, George, ed. *Mémoires de Barras.* 4 vols. Paris: 1896.

Galli, Henri, ed. *Journal d'un officier de l'armée d'Égypte, l'armée française en Égypte 1798–1801.* Paris: 1883.

Goltz, Friedrich von der, ed. *Militarisch Schriften von Scharnhorst.* Berlin: 1881.

Gordon, James. *History of the Rebellion in Ireland in the Year 1798.* Dublin: 1801.

Gurwood, John, Lieut-Col., ed. *The Dispatches of Field Marshal the Duke of Wellington during his various Campaigns.* 13 vols. London: 1837.

Historical Manuscripts Commission. *Report on the Manuscripts of J. B. Fortescue, Esq., Preserved at Dropmore.* 10 vols. London: H.M. Stationary Office, 1905.

History of the Campaign of 1799 in Holland. London: 1801.

Jonquière, Clément de la, ed. *L'expédition d'Égypte 1798–1801.* 5 vols. Paris: Section historique État-major de l'Armée, 1899–1907.

Kaye, John W., ed. *The Life and Correspondence of Major-General Sir John Malcolm. G.C.B.* 2 vols. London: 1856.

Koch, J. B. F., ed. *Mémoires de Masséna rédigés d'après les documents qu'il a laissés.* 7 vols. Paris: 1848–50.

Lloyd, Christopher, ed. *The Keith Papers.* 2 vols. London: Naval Records Society, 1950.

London Gazette. Bulletins of the Campaign of 1799. London: 1800.

Macdonald, Maréchal. *Souvenirs du Maréchal Macdonald.* Paris: 1892.

Mangourit, Michel A. B. *Défense d'Ancone et des départements romains, Le Toronto, Le Musone, et Le Metauro, par le général Monnier aux années VII et VIII.* 2 vols. Paris: 1802.

Martens, Fedor, ed. *Recueil des traités et conventions conclus par la Russie avec les puissances étrangères.* 13 vols. St. Petersburg: 1875–83.

Martens, Fedor, ed. *Recueil des traités et conventions de*

paix, de trêve, de neutralité, de commerce, de limites d'échange conclus par les puissances de l'Europe. 8 vols. Gottingen: 1817–35.

———. *Nouveau recueil de traités d'alliance, de paix, de trêve, de neutralité, de commerce, de limites, d'échange conclus par des puissances et états de l'Europe.* 16 vols. Gottingen: 1843–75.

Mémoires historiques sur la campagne du général en chef Brune en Batavie. Paris: 1801.

Michon, Georges, ed. *Correspondance de Maximilien et Augustin Robespierre.* 2 vols. Paris: Librairie Félix Alcan, 1926–41.

Minto, Countess, ed. *Life and Letters of Sir Gilbert Elliot First Earl of Minto from 1751 to 1806.* 3 vols. London: 1874.

Montarlot, Paul, and Pingaud, Léonce, eds. *Le Congrès de Rastatt (11 juin 1798–28 avril 1799) correspondance et documents.* 3 vols. Paris: A. Picard et fils, 1912.

Moore, Sir John. *Diary.* London: 1804.

Nabonne, Bernard, ed. *La diplomatie du Directoire et Bonaparte d'après les papiers inédits de Reubell.* Paris: La Nouvelle Édition, 1951.

Naish, George P., ed. *Nelson's Letters to His Wife and Other Documents.* London: Naval Records Society, 1958.

Neumann, Leopold, ed. *Recueil des traités et conventions conclus par l'Autriche avec les puissances étrangères depuis 1763 jusqu'à nos jours.* 32 vols. Leipzig: 1855.

Nicolas, Nicholas H., ed. *The Dispatches and Letters of Vice-Admiral Lord Viscount Nelson.* 6 vols. London: 1845.

Noradoughian, G., ed. *Recueil des actes internationaux de l'Empire ottoman.* 4 vols. Paris: Pichon, 1897.

Owen, S. J., ed. *A Selection from the Dispatches, Treaties, and Other Papers of the Marquess Wellesley, K.G. during his Government of India.* Oxford: 1877.

Pallain, Georges, ed. *Le ministère de Talleyrand sous le Directoire.* Paris: 1891.

Pearce, R. R., ed. *Memoirs and Correspondence of the Most Noble Richard Marquess Wellesley.* 3 vols. London: 1846.

Perroud, Claude, ed. *J.-P. Brissot Mémoires (1754–93)* 2 vols. Paris: A. Picard et fils, 1911.

Pettigrew, Thomas J., ed. *Memoirs of the Life of Vice-Admiral Lord Viscount Nelson K.B.* 2 vols. London: 1849.

Pitt, William. *The Speeches of the Right Honourable William Pitt in the House of Commons.* 4 vols. London: 1806.

Plon, Henri, and Dumaine, J., eds. *Correspondance de Napoléon Ier.* 32 vols. Paris: 1858–70.

Réimpression de l'Ancien Moniteur. 31 vols. Paris: 1847.

Report of Committee of Secrecy of the House of Commons. London: 1799.

Richmond, H. W., ed. *Private Papers of George, Second Earl Spencer, First Lord of the Admiralty 1794–1801.* 4 vols. London: Naval Records Society, 1924.

Ross, Charles, ed. *Correspondence of Charles, First Marquess of Cornwallis.* 3 vols. London: 1859.

Saint-Cyr, Gouvion. *Mémoires pour servir à l'histoire militaire sous le Directoire le Consulat et l'Empire.* 2 vols. Paris: 1831.

Soult, Nicholas. *Mémoires du Maréchal-Général Soult Duc de Dalmatie.* 3 vols. Paris: 1854.

Stewart, J. H. *A Documentary Survey of the French Revolution.* New York: Macmillan Co., 1951.

Vane, Charles, ed. *Memoirs and Correspondence of Viscount Castlereagh, Second Marquess of Londonderry.* 8 vols. London: 1848.

Vivenot, A. R. von, ed. *Quellen zur Geschichte der Deutschen Kaiserpolitik Oesterreichs.* 4 vols. Vienna: 1873–85.

———. *Vertrauliche Briefe des Freiherrn von Thugut.* 2 vols. Vienna: 1872.

Walsh, Edward. *Narrative of the Expedition to Holland.* London: 1800.

Walter, Gérard, ed. *Las Cases le Comte de, Le Mémorial de Sainte Hélène.* 2 vols. Paris: Gallimard, 1956–57.

Weil, Henri, ed. *Le général Stamford d'après sa correspondance inédite (1793–1806).* Paris: 1923.

Wellesley Papers. London: 1914.

Wellington, Duke of. *Supplementary Despatches and Memoranda of Field Marshal Arthur Duke of Wellington K.G. India 1797–1805, edited by his son.* London: 1858.

Wickham, William, ed. *The Correspondence of the Right Honorable William Wickham for the Year 1794.* 2 vols. London: 1870.

Wolfe Tone, W. T., ed. *Life of Theobold Wolfe Tone.* 2 vols. Washington: 1826.

Secondary Works

Acton, Harold. *The Bourbons of Naples (1734–1825).* London: Methuen, 1956.

Adams, E. D. *The Influence of Grenville on Pitt's Foreign Policy 1787–1798.* Washington: Carnegie Institution, 1904.

Aimond, Charles. *L'énigme de Varennes.* Paris: J. de Gigord, 1936.

Allix, Jacques. *Système d'artillerie de campagne.* Paris: 1827.

Augustin-Thierry, A. *Masséna.* Paris: Éditions Albin Michel, 1947.

Azoux, A. "La France et Muscate aux dix-huitième et dix-neuvième siècles." In *Revue d'histoire diplomatique* 24 (1910).

Ballot, Charles. *Les négociations de Lille (1797).* Paris: E. Cornély, 1910.

Beer, Adolf. *Die orientalische Politik Oesterreichs seit 1774.* Prague: 1883.

Biro, S. S. *The German Policy of Revolutionary France: A Study in French Diplomacy during the War of the First Coalition 1792–1797.* 2 vols. Cambridge: Harvard University Press, 1957.

Blácam, Aodh de. *The Life Story of Wolfe Tone.* (Dublin: Talbot Press Ltd., 1935.

Blok, Petrus. *A History of the People of the Netherlands.* New York: G. P. Putnam's Sons, 1912.

Bonnefons, Andre. *Marie Caroline reine des Deux-Sicilies (1768–1814).* Paris: Perrin et cie, 1905.

Boudon, Jacques. "Le service de l'artillerie du XVIe siècle à nos jours." *Revue d'Artillerie* vol. 98 (1926).

Boulay de la Meurthe, Alfred. *Le Directoire et l'expédition d'Égypte.* Paris: 1885.

Bourdeau, Émile. *Campagnes modernes.* 3 vols. Paris: H. Charles-Lavauzelle, 1912–21.

Bourgeois, Émile. *Manuel historique de politique étrangère, II, les révolutions (1798–1830).* Paris: Belin, 1913.

Bourniseaux, P. V. J. *Histoire des guerres de la Vendée et des Chouans.* 2 vols. Paris: 1819.

Brace, R. M. *Bordeaux and the Gironde, 1789–1794.* Ithaca: Cornell University Press, 1947.

———. "Bordeaux's Opposition to Dictatorship in 1793." *Journal of Modern History* vol. 14 (1942).

Brinton, Crane. *The Jacobins.* New York: Macmillan Co., 1930.

Brown, P. *The French Revolution in English History.* London: Lockwood and Sons, 1918.

Bunbury, Henry. *Narratives of Some Passages in the Great War with France from 1799 to 1810.* London: 1854.

Burgoyne, Sir John. *A Short History of the Naval and Military Operations in Egypt.* London: 1885.

Caron, Pierre. *La défense nationale de 1792 à 1795.* Paris: Hachette, 1912.

Chabert, Alexandre. *Essai sur les mouvements des revenues et de l'activité économique en France de 1789 à 1820.* Paris: Librairie de Médicis, 1949.

Chandler, D. G. *The Campaigns of Napoleon.* New York: Macmillan Co., 1966.

Charles-Roux, François. *L'Angleterre et l'expédition française en Égypte.* 2 vols. Cairo: Imprimerie de l'Institut français d'archéologie orientale pour la Société royale de géographie d'Égypte, 1925.

————. *Bonaparte, gouverneur d'Égypte.* Paris: Plon, 1936.

————. *Les origines de l'expédition française en Égypte.* Paris: Plon-Nourrit, 1910.

Chevalier, Louis. *Histoire de la marine française sous la première République.* Paris: 1886.

Chodzko, Leonard. *Histoire des légions polonaises en Italie.* 2 vols. Paris: 1829.

Chuquet, Arthur. *Dumouriez.* Paris: Hachette, 1914.

————. *Jemappes et la conquête de la Belgique (1792–1793).* Paris: L. Cerf, 1890.

————. *La première invasion prussienne (11 août–2 septembre 1792).* Paris: L. Cerf, 1888.

————. *Valmy.* Paris: L. Cerf, 1887.

Clapham, J. H. *The Causes of the War of 1792.* Cambridge: 1899.

Clough, Shepard. *France, a History of National Economics 1789–1939.* New York: C. Scribner's Sons, 1939.

Clowes, William. *The Royal Navy.* 7 vols. London: 1899.

Colin, Jean. *L'éducation militaire de Napoléon.* Paris: R. Chapelot et Cᵉ, 1900.

————. *Études sur la campagne de 1796–97 en Italie.* Paris: 1898.

————. *La tactique et la discipline dans les armées de la Révolution.* Paris: R. Chapelot et Cᵉ, 1902.

Cooper, Duff. *Talleyrand*. London: J. Cape, 1952.

Coutanceau, M. H. M. *La campagne de 1794 à l'armée du Nord*. 4 vols. Paris: R. Chapelot et Cᵉ, 1903–8.

Curtis, E. N. *Saint-Just*. New York: Columbia University Press, 1935.

Dallas, R. C. *The History of the Maroons*. London: 1803.

Dard, Émile. *Le Comte de Narbonne*. Paris: Plon, 1943.

Daudet, Ernest. *Les émigrés et la Second Coalition*. Paris: 1886.

Dejoint, Georges. *La politique économique du Directoire*. Paris: M. Rivière, 1951.

Deschampes, Jules. *Les colonies pendant la Révolution: La Constituante et la réforme coloniale*. Paris: 1898.

———. *Les Iles britanniques et la Révolution française*. Paris.

Dodge, T. A. *Napoleon*. 4 vols. Boston: Houghton Mifflin and Co., 1904.

Douin, Georges. *La Campagne de Bruix en Méditerranée mars-août 1799*. Paris: Société d'éditions géographiques, maritimes, et coloniales, 1923.

———. *La flotte de Bonaparte sur les côtes d'Égypte*. Paris: Imprimerie de l'Institut français d'archéologie orientale pour la Société royale de géographie d'Égypte, 1922.

Droz, Jacques. *L'Allemagne et la Révolution française*. Paris: Presses Universitaires de France, 1949.

Duceré, Édouard. *L'Armée des Pyrénées occidentales*. Bayonne: 1882.

Dugan, James. *The Great Mutiny*. London: Deutsch, 1966.

Dunfermline, James. *Lieutenant-General Ralph Abercromby*. Edinburgh: 1861.

Elgood, P. G. *Bonaparte's Adventure in Egypt*. London: Oxford University Press, 1931.

Ellery, Eloise. *Brissot*. New York: Houghton Mifflin and Co., 1915.

Falkiner, C. L. *Studies in Irish History and Biography*. London: Longmans, Green and Co., 1902.

Ferrero, Guglielmo. *The Gamble Bonaparte in Italy 1796–1797*. London: Walker and Co., 1961.

Ferry, Edmund. *La France en Afrique*. Paris: A. Colin, 1905.

Ferval, Joseph. *Campagne de la Révolution française dans les Pyrénées orientales*. 2 vols. Paris: 1861.

Fisher, Herbert. *Napoleon*. London: Williams and Norgate, 1913.

Flammermont, Jules. *Négociations secrètes de Louis XVI et du baron Breteuil décembre 1791–juillet 1792*. Paris: 1885.

Fortescue, John. *A History of the British Army*. 13 vols. London: Macmillan and Co., 1910–35.

Froude, J. A. *The English in Ireland in the Eighteenth Century*. 3 vols. London: 1874.

Fugier, André. *Histoire des relations internationales*, vol. 4, *La Révolution française et l'Empire napoléonien*. Paris: Librairie Hachette, 1954.

Gabory, Émile. *La Révolution et la Vendée*. 2 vols. Paris: Perrin et Cⁱᵉ, 1925.

Gachot, Édouard. *Les campagnes de 1799: Jourdan et Allemagne et Brune en Hollande*. Paris: Perrin, 1906.

———. *Les Campagnes de 1799 Souvarow en Italie*. Paris: Perrin, 1903.

Gershoy, Leo. *Bertrand Barere: A Reluctant Terrorist*. Princeton: Princeton University Press, 1962.

Godechot, Jacques. *Les commissaires aux armées sous le Directoire*. 2 vols. Paris: Fustier, 1938.

———. *La contre-révolution doctrine et action 1789–1804*. Paris: Presses Universitaires de France, 1961.

———. *La Grande Nation*. 2 vols. Paris: Éditions Montaigne, 1956.

———. *Histoire de Malta*. Paris: Presses Universitaires de France, 1952.

———. *Les institutions de la France sous la Révolution et l'Empire*. Paris: Presses Universitaires de France, 1951.

Goetz-Bernstein, H. A. *La diplomatie de la Gironde Jacques-Pierre Brissot*. Paris: Hachette, 1912.

Goodwin, Arthur. "Counter-Revolution in Brittany: The Royalist Conspiracy of the Marquis de la Rouerie 1791–1793." *Bulletin of the John Rylands Library* vol. 39 (1957).

Grant Duff, James. *A History of the Mahrattas*. 3 vols. London: 1826.

Greer, Donald. *The Incidence of the Emigration during the French Revolution*. Cambridge: Harvard University Press, 1951.

———. *The Incidence of the Terror during the French Revolution*. Cambridge: Harvard University Press, 1935.

Guillon, Edouard. *La France et l'Irlande pendant la Révolution.* Paris: 1888.

Guitry, P. G. *L'Armée de Bonaparte en Égypte 1798–1799.* Paris: E. Flammarion, 1898.

Guyot, Raymond. *Le Directoire et la paix de l'Europe.* Paris: F. Alcan, 1912).

Hardman, William. *A History of Malta.* London: Longmans, Green and Co., 1909.

Harris, S. E. *The Assignats.* Cambridge: Harvard University Press, 1935.

Hartmann, Louis. *Les officiers de l'armée royale et la Révolution.* Paris: F. Alcan, 1903.

Hawtrey, R. G. *Currency and Credit.* London: Longmans, Green and Co., 1919.

Heidrich, Kurt. *Preussen im Kampfe gegen die franzosiche Revolution bis zur zweiten Teilung Polens.* Berlin: Cotta, 1908.

Hennequin, Louis. *Zurich Masséna en Suisse.* Nancy: Section historique État-major de l'Armée, 1911.

Holborn, Hajo. *A History of Modern Germany 1648–1840.* New York: A. A. Knopf, 1966.

Hueffer, Herman. "Fin de la République napolitaine." *Revue historique,* vols. 73, 74 (1903–4).

Jacob, Rosamond. *The Rise of the United Irishmen 1791–1794.* London: G. G. Harrap and Co., Ltd., 1937.

James, C. L. R. *The Black Jacobins.* New York: Dial Press, 1938.

Jones, E. H. S. *An Invasion that Failed.* Oxford: Blackwell, 1950.

———. *The Last Invasion of Britain.* Cardiff: University of Wales Press, 1950.

Jouan, Louis. *La conquête de la Belgique, mai–juillet 1794.* Paris: L. Fournier, 1914.

Korngold, Ralph. *Citizen Toussaint.* London: V. Gollancz, Ltd., 1945.

Kukiel, General M. "Kosciuszko and the Third Partition." In *Cambridge History of Poland.* Cambridge: Cambridge University Press, 1941.

Kuscinski, Auguste. *Les députiès à l'Assemblée legislative.* Paris: Au Siège de la Société, 1900.

Lacouture, Abbé Joseph. *Le mouvement royaliste dans la sud-ouest (1797–1800).* Paris: 1932.

Lacroix, Désiré. *Bonaparte en Égypte (1798–1799)*. Paris: 1899.

Laprade, W. T. *England and the French Revolution*. Baltimore: Johns Hopkins Press, 1909.

Latreille, Albert. *L'Église catholique et la Révolution française*. Paris: Librairie Hachette, 1946.

Laverma, Matti. *L'artillerie de campagne Française pendant les guerres de la Révolution*. Helsinki: Suomalainen Tiedeakatermia, 1956.

Lavigne, Bertrand. *Histoire de l'insurrection royaliste de l'an VII*. Paris: 1887.

Lebon, André. *L'Angleterre et l'émigration française de 1794 à 1801*. Paris: 1882.

Lechartier, Georges. *Les soldats de la Révolution et de l'Empire*. Paris: H. Charles-Lavauzelle, 1902.

Lecky, William. *A History of England in the Eighteenth Century*. 8 vols. London: 1887–90.

Lefebvre, Georges. *Le Directoire*. Paris: Librairie Armand Colin, 1946.

————. *Études sur la Révolution française*. Paris: Presses Universitaires de France, 1954.

————. *Napoléon*. Paris: Presses Universitaires de France, 1953.

————. *La Révolution française*. Paris: Presses Universitaires de France, 1951.

————. *Les Thermidoriens*. Paris: Librairie Armand Colin, 1946.

Léger, Jacques. *Haiti, Her History and Her Detractors*. New York: Neale Publishing Co., 1907.

Lloyd, Christopher. *St. Vincent and Camperdown*. London: B. T. Batsford Ltd., 1963.

Lobanov-Rostovsky, Andrei. *Russia and Europe 1789–1825*. Durham: Duke University Publications, 1947.

Longworth, Philip. *The Art of Victory the Life and Achievements of Field-Marshal Suvorov 1729–1800*. New York: Holt, Rinehart and Winston, 1966.

Lord, R. H. *The Second Partition of Poland*. Cambridge: Harvard University Press, 1915.

MacDermot, Frank. *Theobold Wolfe Tone, A Biographical Study*. London: Macmillan and Co., 1939.

McDowell, R. B. *Irish Public Opinion 1750–1800*. London: Faber and Faber, 1937.

Madden, Richard. *The United Irishmen, Their Lives and Times.* 4 vols. Dublin: 1857–60.

Mahan, A. T. *The Influence of Sea Power upon the French Revolution and Empire.* 2 vols. London: 1892.

——. *The Life of Nelson.* 2 vols. Boston: 1897.

Mahon, Patrice. *Études sur les armées du Directoire.* Paris: R. Chapelot, 1905.

Majumdar, R. C., Raychaudhuri, H. C., and Datta, Kalinkar. *An Advanced History of India.* London: Macmillan and Co., 1946.

Marshall-Cornwall, James. *Marshal Massena.* London: Oxford University Press, 1965.

——. *Napoleon as Military Commander.* London: B. T. Batsford Ltd., 1967.

Masson, Frédéric. *Les diplomates de la Révolution.* Paris: 1882.

Matheson, Cyril. *The Life of Henry Dundas First Viscount Melville, 1742–1811.* London: Constable and Co., Ltd., 1933.

Mathiez, Albert. *Le Club des Cordeliers pendant la Crise de Varennes.* Paris: H. Champion, 1910.

——. *Le dix août.* Paris: Hachette, 1931.

——. *Études sur Robespierre.* Paris: Éditions Sociales, 1958.

——. *La Révolution et les étrangères.* Paris: La Renaissance du livre, 1918.

——. *Rome et la Constituante.* Paris: A. Colin, 1910.

Maxwell, Constantia. *Country and Town in Ireland under the Georges.* London: George G. Harrap & Co., Ltd., 1940.

Mitchell, Harvey. *The Underground War against Revolutionary France.* Oxford: Clarendon Press, 1965.

Moran, Charles. *Black Triumvirate.* New York: Exposition Press, 1957.

Mowat, R. B. *The Diplomacy of Napoleon.* London: Longmans, Green and Co., 1924.

Muret, Pierre. "L'affaire des princes possessionnes d'Alsace et les origines du conflict entre la Révolution et l'Europe." *Revue d'histoire moderne.* vol. 1 (1899–1900) .

Nussbaum, F. L. *Commercial Policy in the French Revolution.* Washington, D.C.: Seeman Printery, 1923.

Osipov, K. *Alexander Suvorov.* New York: Hutchinson and Co. Ltd., 1941.

Palmer, R. R. *The Age of the Democratic Revolution.* 2 vols. Princeton: Princeton University Press, 1959 and 1964.

―――. "Much in Little: The Dutch Revolution of 1795." *Journal of Modern History* vol. 26 (1954).

―――. "A Revolutionary Republican: M. A. B. Mangourit." *William and Mary Quarterly* vol. 9 (1952).

―――. *Twelve Who Ruled.* Princton: Princeton University Press, 1941.

Pappas, Spyridon. "Un point d'histoire ignoré, l'agence de commerce français d'Ancône (1799)." *Revue d'études historiques* vol. 68 (1902).

Paret, Peter. *Internal War and Pacification, The Vendée 1789–1796.* Princeton: Center of International Studies, Princeton University, 1961.

―――. *Yorck and the Era of Prussian Reform 1807–1815.* Princeton: Princeton University Press, 1966.

Paret, Peter, and Shy, John. *Guerrillas in the 1960's.* New York: Frederick A. Praeger, 1962.

Parkinson, C. Northcote. *War in the Eastern Seas 1793–1815.* London: George Allen & Unwin Ltd., 1954.

Philebert, Général, ed. *Le général Lecourbe d'après ses archives, sa correspondance et d'autres documents.* Limoges: 1895.

Philips, C. H. *The East India Company 1784–1834.* Manchester: Manchester University Press, 1940.

Phipps R. W. *The Armies of the First French Republic.* 5 vols. London: Oxford University Press, 1926–39.

Picard, Ernest. *L'Artillerie française au XVIIIe siècle.* Paris: Berger Levrault, 1906.

Pisani, Paul. "L'expédition russo-turque aux Iles ioniennes en 1798–1799." *Revue d'historie diplomatique* 2 (1888).

Porter, Whitworth. *History of the Corps of Royal Engineers.* London: 1889.

Quimby, Robert. *The Background of Napoleonic Warfare.* New York: Columbia University Press, 1957.

Reinhard, Marcel. *Le Grand Carnot.* 2 vols. Paris: Hachette, 1952.

Richard, Camille. *Le Comité de salut public et les fabrications de guerre.* Paris: F. Rieder et Cie, 1921.

Rivière, Charles de la. *Catherine II et la Révolution française.* Paris: 1895.

Rodger, A. B. *The War of the Second Coalition, 1798–1801*. Oxford: Clarendon Press, 1964.

Rose, J. Holland. *The Life of Napoleon I*. 2 vols. New York: Macmillan Co., 1907.

————. *Napoleonic Studies*. London: G. Bell and Sons, 1904.

————. "The Political Reactions of Bonaparte's Eastern Expedition." *English Historical Review* vol. 44 (1929).

————. *William Pitt and the Great War*. London: G. Bell and Sons, 1912.

Rose, J. Holland, and Broadley, A. M. *Doumouriez and the Defense of England against Napoleon*. London: J. Lane, 1909.

Rose, R. B. "The French Revolution and the Grain Supply." *Bulletin of the John Rylands Library* vol. 39 (1956).

Ross, Steven T. "The Development of the Combat Division in Eighteenth Century French Armies." *French Historical Studies* vol. 4 (1965).

Sagnac, Philippe. *Le Rhin français pendant la Révolution et l'Empire*. Paris: F. Alcan, 1917.

Savary, J. M. *Guerres des Vendéens et des Chouans contre la Républic française*. 2 vols. Paris: 1824–25.

See, Henri. *Histoire économique de la France, les temps modernes (1789–1914)*. Paris: A. Colin, 1942.

Sen, S. P. *The French in India (1763–1816)*. Calcutta: University of Calcutta, 1958.

Sirich, J. B. *The Revolutionary Committees in the Departments of France 1793–1794*. Cambridge: Harvard University Press, 1935.

Six, Georges. *Dictionnaire biographique des généraux et admiraux français de la Révolution et de l'Empire*. 2 vols. Paris: Librairie historique et nobiliaire Georges Saffroy, 1934.

————. *Les généraux de la Révolution et de l'Empire*. Paris: Bordas, 1947.

Sorel, Albert. *L'Europe et la Révolution française*. 8 vols. Paris: Plon-Nourrit et Cⁱᵉ, 1885–1904.

————. *La question d'Orient du XVIIIᵉ siècle*. Paris: 1878.

Stoddard, T. L. *The French Revolution in San Domingo*. New York: Houghton Mifflin Co., 1913.

Stulz, Percy, and Opitz, Alfred. *Volksbewegungen in Kursachsen zur Zeit der französichen Revolution*. Berlin: Rütten and Loening, 1956.

Surtees, John. *Twenty-five Years in the Rifle Brigade.* Edinburgh: 1831.

Sydenham, M. J. *The Girondins.* London: Athlone Press, 1961.

Tassier, Suzanne. *Les démocrats belges de 1789: étude sur le Vonckisme et la Révolution brabançonne.* Brussels: M. Lamertin, 1930.

———. *Histoire de la Belgique sous l'occupation française en 1792 et 1793.* Brussels: Falkfils, C. van Campenhout Succ^r., 1934.

Thompson, J. M. *Napoleon Bonaparte.* Oxford: B. Blackwell, 1952.

———. *Robespierre.* 2 vols. Oxford: B. Blackwell, 1935.

Tilly, Charles. "Some Problems in the History of the Vendée." *American Historical Review* vol. 67 (1961).

———. *The Vendée.* Cambridge: Harvard University Press, 1964.

Tramond, Joannès. *Manuel d'histoire maratime de la France des origines à 1815.* Paris: Société d'éditions géographiques, maritimes et coloniales, 1947.

Vaccarino, Giorgio, ed. *I Patrioti "Anarchistes" E L'Idea dell Unità Italiana (1796–1799).* Milan: G. Einaudi, 1955.

Valjavec, Fritz. *Die Entstehung der politischen strömungen in Deutschland 1770–1815.* Munich: R. Oldenbourg, 1951.

Vandal, Albert. *L'avènement de Bonaparte.* 2 vols. Paris: Plon-Nourrit et Cie, 1903.

Vingtrinier, Emmanuel. *Histoire de la contre-révolution.* 2 vols. Paris: Émile Paul Frères Éditeurs, 1924–25.

Vingvier, J. "La réunion d'Avignon et du Comtat-Venaissin à la France." *La Révolution française* vols. 21, 23, 26 (1891, 1892, 1894).

Wallon, Henri. *Les représentants du peuple en mission et la justice révolutionnaire dans les départments.* 5 vols. Paris: 1889–90.

Ward, A. W., and Gooch, G. P. *The Cambridge History of British Foreign Policy 1783–1919.* 2 vols. New York: Macmillan Co., 1922.

Warner, Oliver. *The Battle of the Nile.* London: Macmillan and Co., 1960.

———. *The Glorious First of June.* New York: Macmillan Co., 1961.

———. *Nelson's Battles.* New York: Macmillan Co., 1965.

Watson, J. S. *The Reign of George III 1760–1815.* London: Oxford University Press, 1960.

Watson, S. J. *Carnot.* London: Bodley Head, 1954.

Wheeler, H. F. B., and Broadley, A. M. *Napoleon and the Invasion of England.* 2 vols. London: J. Lane, 1908.

———. *The War in Wexford.* London: J. Lane, 1910.

Wilkinson, Spencer. *The French Army before Napoleon.* Oxford: Clarendon Press, 1915.

———. *The Rise of General Bonaparte.* Oxford: Clarendon Press, 1930.

Wilson, Arnold. *The Persian Gulf.* Oxford: Clarendon Press, 1928.

Yonge, C. D. *The History of the British Navy.* 2 vols. London: 1886.

Index

309